LIVING LANDMARKS
OF
CHICAGO

Tantalizing Tales and Skyscraper Stories:
Bringing Chicago's Landmarks to Life

Also by Theresa L. Goodrich

Two Lane Gems, Vol. 1: Turkeys are Jerks and Other
Observations from an American Road Trip

Two Lane Gems, Vol. 2: Bison are Giant and Other
Observations from an American Road Trip

Planning Your Perfect Road Trip

As Theresa L. Carter

Peril on the Peninsula

Revenge in the Rockies

Betrayed at the Beach

Publisher

Midwest Road Trip Adventures, 2nd Edition

Midwest State Park Adventures

LIVING LANDMARKS

LANDMARKS

OF

Chicago

Tantalizing tales and skyscraper stories:
bringing Chicago's landmarks to life

THERESA L. GOODRICH

THE
LOCAL
TOURIST

Every effort has been made to ensure the accuracy of the information presented in this book. If you are inspired to visit any of these landmarks, please confirm that they are open before making plans. While the historic information has been thoroughly researched, a worldwide pandemic threw a wrench in the works in 2020 and 2021, so the landmarks' status might have changed since publication.

A summary of resources used in researching this book is in the appendix. For a more complete citation of resources, visit livinglandmarksofchicago.com

Front Cover Image: Currier & Ives. The city of Chicago. New York, Currier & Ives, 1892. Map. www.loc.gov/item/75693210/

Author Photograph: Doug White

Cover: Jim Goodrich & Theresa L. Goodrich

For Jim

who not only inspired this book, but who supported me
during the toughest year of my life.

I love you.

Table of Contents

Foreword, *by Bull Garlington*

I moved to Chicago from the infinite podunkery of Central Florida over 22 years ago and I still get lost. When I'm strolling down the sidewalks downtown looking for a coffee joint or a quiet bar to park my carcass, the only way to find my way is to find the landmarks.

Most Chicagoans give directions like this: *oh, 24th and State? Go two blocks west then eight blocks south.* Like the city is a spreadsheet. Which it is. Kind of. Chicago was laid out on purpose, unlike many of the world's cities, which grew into greatness from old cattle trails and buggy paths. Chicago makes sense. You really can plot your position like it's a giant graph—*if you were born here.* If you weren't, then you'll never wrap your head around the sheer logic of the layout and you'll forever orient yourself like I do, which is to find the lake and count off the historic buildings until you know where you are. By the way, this method does not work.

Not knowing where you are on Chicago's horizontal plane is worse if you can't plot your position on its vertical axis, the soaring skyscraper of its history. You'll not only not know where you are, you won't know why it matters. You could be standing in front of the Blackstone and not know why it's related to the Drake. You could ride the escalator in the Target not realizing you're actually in Sullivan Center, and not even know why that matters, like some kind of blissfully ignorant alien weirdo. Which, if you are a tourist, if you are one of the millions of people who visit Chicago annually (in non-plague years), is completely excusable. You're here to have a good time and see a show and we're awfully glad you stopped by. Please take this book and study up because there'll be a test next time. However, if you live here. If you're a native, or if you're a permanent alien like myself, and you don't know the Blackstone once hosted high-level gangsters with cigars, then you're not really trying (it was Nixon. No wait, it was Al Capone! No wait, it was both!).

Chicago is a city of impossibilities. What, the river is spewing filth into Lake Michigan—which we all *drink*? Whatevs; we'll just reverse its course. What, the city is sinking? Why are you even bothering me!? We'll just raise it up one story—yeah, the whole city. This is Chicago. And the buildings that comprise its storied skeleton are massive jewels of Midwestern architecture; they are the enduring and unforgettable chapters of the great book of America's crossroads. Chicago's buildings are its history. Chicago breathes stone and steel and splendor and opulence through every brownstone window, through every ornamental entrance, through the endless halls of her concrete corpus. In every way, the city is alive.

Which is why Theresa Goodrich's *Living Landmarks of Chicago* matters. It reveals a new voice in Chicago's historic bibliography. Her voice is patient and inviting, like the structures she writes about. But it's more than that. Goodrich's voice is rich. Layered. If you could see her writing style in cross section, you'd see simultaneous strata of municipal ardor fighting for prominence: the gentle maternal voice that only sees the city as good; the quietly furious voice which tells the story of crime and violence that are almost our mortar; the impartial, professorial voice which carefully delineates the history of a structure whose confusing timeline looks like a porcupine in an altercation with a tumbleweed. All these voices speak together to evoke the origin of Chicago's grandeur. What you learn in this book is not so much where the landmarks are or how they were made (you will learn those things) as much as why they matter, why their grandeur persists. Every chapter's story is supported by a journalist's tenacious research to find not merely the first brick in a building, but to track down the very moment the ghost of its form was born.

I said Goodrich writes with several voices—which is a foreword writer's trick to describe another writer's skill of which they are desperately jealous—but it's true, and yet, beneath all of those writers that blend together in Goodrich's style, there is another voice. Hidden in the tone of the serious researcher, and lurking behind the staccato newsroom machine gun typing of the journalist, excitedly raising her hand in the lecture of the historian is a writer in love. In love with a city. In love with its story. In love with Chicago.

Bull Garlington is an award-winning author from Chicago. Learn more at bullgarlington.com

Preface

T his book was supposed to be easy.
It began with a simple concept. My husband and I were hiking in one of our local conservation areas. It was August 2019 and he knew I was feeling a bit out of sorts because I wasn't writing another book. I'd written my first in 2017 and my second in 2018, but we had - wisely - decided that taking another month-long road trip to research my third *Two Lane Gems* travelogue would have been too much. Too much for me, too much for our cat, and too much for us. So, he had an idea: why don't I take the guides I'd already written about Chicago landmarks for my website, TheLocalTourist.com, and combine them into a book?

Brilliant! That's a fantastic idea! And it will be so easy, since they're already done! I'll add a few more. Bada bing, bada boom.

Bada waitaminute - what if I find out how these landmarks came to be in the first place? I can tell their whole stories. I am a storyteller, after all.

The simple idea turned into something much, much more involved. It's also much, much better, and is a work of which I'm truly proud.

It's taken a long time to get here. I was swimming along, researching and writing. This would be a non-traditional guide book. Readers would learn the history of each landmark and then find out everything they needed to know to visit today. The launch party was set. We'd be, appropriately, in the English Room at the Blackstone Hotel on March 26, 2020.

And then...COVID-19. We canceled the launch party. I still had chapters to write, but I couldn't think. I wrote intermittently as I tried to figure out how we were going to survive. I'm a travel writer. My business—my income—disappeared overnight. I was in panic mode. I'd write a chapter here and there, but it was slow. So very slow. I was also contributing the Illinois and parts of the South Dakota sections for *Midwest Road Trip Adventures*, a commitment I'd made pre-pandemic and which involved ten other authors. It wasn't something I could set aside.

And then...cancer. I turned fifty in May 2020 and I knew I was about ten years behind on getting a mammogram. Turns out, I got one at the exact time I needed it. The test came back abnormal. They ordered an ultrasound, which confirmed a mass. The biopsy proved it was cancerous.

Book? What book.

Fortunately, my tumor was tiny. So tiny that it would have to grow five times its size for me to have felt it in a manual exam. (Women - schedule your mammograms!) My treatment has been relatively easy, compared to what I've seen friends of mine who have more advanced cancers experience. Chemo sucks and this is the worst thing I've ever gone through, but I am grateful deep in my soul that we found it when we did.

As we went through the months and months of lockdown, and I went through my additional cancer-dictated isolation, I realized that I wanted to write something that was less of a guidebook, however non-traditional, and more of an exploration into what made Chicago, a city I love, into what it is today. I wanted to bring these landmarks to life.

This book has saved me. Once I got through the first debilitating round of chemo (there's a reason they call it Red Devil), I dove back into researching and writing with everything I have. Sixteen-hour days, six days a week - the seventh reserved for treatment and the ensuing mental fog. Chemo brain is real. Sometimes I wondered if I was doing too much, if I might be hampering my treatment because of sheer exhaustion. And I've realized that it's just the opposite. It kept me focused on something bigger than myself, on creating something that people will love. That I love.

I have poured my heart and soul into this book. It is the best thing I've ever done, and it has made the most difficult time I've experienced in my life, both personally and on a global scale, much more bearable.

These stories illustrate, one after another, intense drive, passion, and vision. These landmarks aren't simple buildings and parks. They're life.

I love this city. I love this book.

I hope you do, too.

Theresa L. Goodrich
April, 2021

What is Living Landmarks?

H istory lines Chicago's sidewalks. Stroll down LaSalle or Dearborn or State and you'll see skyscrapers that have been there for a century or more. It's easy to scurry by, to dismiss the building itself, but a hunt for placards turns up landmarks every few feet, it seems. Here's a Chicago landmark; there's a National Historic landmark. They're everywhere.

Ironically, these skyscrapers keep the city grounded, illustrating a past where visionaries took fanciful, impossible ideas and made them reality. Buildings sinking? Raise them. River polluting the lake and its precious drinking water? Reverse it. Overpopulation and urban sprawl making it challenging to get to work? Build up. From the bare to the ornate, from exposed beams to ornamented facades, the city's architecture is unabashedly various yet provides a cohesive, beautiful skyline that illustrates the creativity of necessity, and the necessity of creativity.

Chicago is the physical manifestation of dreamers, malcontents, philanthropists, and grifters. In 1985, Pat Colander said in the New York Times: "It's a city of contradictions, of private visions haphazardly overlaid and linked together." And it is. Some people love it. Some hate it. Sometimes it's the same people, and sometimes on the same day.

I'm one of the lovers who believes the city is vibrant and willful and beautiful, and while other urban areas have fostered their own breed of characters, Chicago's seem so very...Chicago. It's hard to explain. I'm not going to try.

What I am going to do is tell some of her stories. Not all of them—neither one of us has time for that. Instead, I've chosen

1

fifty significant landmarks built or created between 1836 and 1932. Several of them are hotels because so many historic buildings have been converted to accommodations, preserving the past for years to come. Plus, it's super cool to sleep in a building designed by Daniel Burnham or Benjamin Marshall.

What to expect

Each chapter is a vignette, a short story, if you will, that introduces you to the landmark and brings it to life. After digging into the history, the chapter ends with brief information on the landmark as it is today.

Living Landmarks is organized chronologically. The years associated with the landmarks are when construction was completed, even though the story may have begun many years earlier. The parks are the exception, because while their ultimate size and shape changed over the years, their beginning locations are the same.

After a sound-bite history of the city's origins, you'll meet the oldest house in Chicago—or is it? Kinda. Sorta. Depends on who you ask.

That's Chicago. Nothing's simple, and nothing can be taken for granted. The reason we have a gorgeous skyline and a vibrant culture and a notorious reputation for graft is because of those who built it, envisioned it, manipulated it.

That skyline is also the result of a renewed determination after a devastating loss. One thing you might notice is that few of the landmarks are dated before 1871. That's because the Great Chicago Fire obliterated what had been downtown. The conflagration began October 8, 1871, consumed more than three square miles and killed three hundred people. More than 100,000 were suddenly homeless. The destruction was a defining moment, if not *the* defining moment, in the history of Chicago, and its impact, seared into the city's consciousness, is referenced several times throughout this book.

Maps in the appendices show you where to find each landmark.

There are no footnotes. This isn't an academic paper or a reference book. Because there is a boatload of factual information, I've included a select bibliography. And, if you're so inclined, you can visit livinglandmarksofchicago.com to find additional sources for each individual landmark.

This book isn't about buildings, per se; it's about the people who built Chicago. It's about rich, complex, convoluted passions that shaped a metropolis. Living Landmarks is a bit of humor, a touch of sass, and a whole lot of love for this great American city.

A Note About the Images

Since this book came out in 2021, readers have asked for two things: images and an audiobook. When I originally published this book, I was in the middle of chemotherapy. I didn't have the time nor the energy to source images for buildings dating back to 1836.

Two years later, my husband and I launched a Kickstarter project for the audiobook, and I knew it was the perfect opportunity to find images.

Each chapter now begins with a photo (or map, in the case of the Origin Story). All images are in the Public Domain and citations are listed after Maps and Select Sources. The images were primarily found via loc.gov and hathitrust.org.

Let's meet Chicago, shall we?

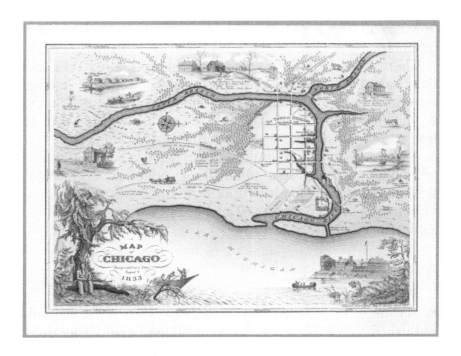

Chicago: The Origin Story

I t's hard to imagine Chicago as less than a destination. She's the kind of city that walks into a room and everybody stops whatever they're doing. She's talented, riotous, at times beautifully serene, and at others, ear-splittingly chaotic. But up until the mid-1800s, she was more often than not a portage to somewhere else.

For centuries, this spot at the southwest corner of a giant inland lake has been a transportation hub. The Odawa, Miami, Ojibwe, Illinois, Potawatomi, and other indigenous tribes could get from one place to another through the network of rivers and streams they called chicagoua. There's a continental divide running through the area, and a short strip of land separates rivers flowing east, to Lake Michigan, and west, to the Mississippi River.

The French explored this stinky, swampy land in the 1600s; Marquette and Jolliet, followed later by La Salle, forded and portaged and mapped. Jolliet suggested that cutting a canal could connect Lake Erie to the Gulf of Mexico, a prescient glimpse of Chicago's future. Gradually, a few European men traded with and occasionally married into the local tribes. Those unions may have been about love, but they were also good business: once you were a member of the family you had the keys to the kingdom. Or, at least, some guidance and a relative safety net.

None of the explorers stayed for any length of time. A few seasonal trading posts popped up over the years, but relations between the original inhabitants and the newcomers had sometimes violent outcomes. By the late 1780s, however, the Revolution had spawned a new country and this land became one of its territories. In 1795, the Treaty of Greenville gave the Americans "one piece of land six miles square at the mouth of Chikago river emptying into the south-west end of Lake Michigan," and it wasn't too much longer before the original inhabitants were kicked out completely.

As you can imagine, that didn't go well.

Chicago's first non-native permanent settler, like his predecessors, was French. Unlike his predecessors, he was black. Jean Baptiste Point de Sable* and Kitihawa, his Potawatomi wife, settled on a plot of land on the north side of the chicagou river. When they arrived isn't exactly known, but according to a journal entry that Hugh Heward, a clerk out of Detroit, made in 1790, the couple was already well established. The de Sables sold their property in 1800 to Jean Baptiste Lalime for the impressive sum of $1200. They could get such a princely amount because, by that time, the property consisted of a home filled with furnishings, as well as a barn and several outbuildings. For a remote trading post in a place that smelled like garlic, this was quite the setup.

In 1803, the U.S. government saw the importance of establishing a presence in Chicago and sent Captain John

Whistler to begin building Fort Dearborn. The next year they completed construction, and with the perceived safety of a military outpost, more settlers arrived. It was more of a trickle than a flood, but their increasing numbers made the Potawatomi none too happy. The locals had already given up so much of their home, and while the French had been transient, these new Americans had no intention of leaving and claimed the land as their own.

At the same time, tensions between Britain and its former colonies escalated, until it became a full-on war in 1812. After General William Hull learned that Fort Mackinac had fallen to the Brits he ordered the evacuation of Fort Dearborn. The order arrived on August 9, and on August 15 Captain Heald led a garrison of 55 regulars, 12 militia, 9 women and 18 children. The small group got about a mile and a half south when around 500 Potawatomi attacked. The tribe took the few survivors prisoner and burned the fort.

In 1816, the United States Army rebuilt Fort Dearborn and the Treaty of St. Louis gave the country the land it needed to create the canal Jolliet had conceived of a century and a half prior. There was no mad rush to take up residence though, and in 1820, there were only about sixty people. Garrisons ping-ponged in and out. In May of 1823, the garrison was ordered to evacuate and left by the fall of that year. On October 3, 1828, Fort Dearborn once again housed a garrison of about sixty. Two and a half years later, they left for Green Bay, but were back at the fort on June 17, 1832. Then, on July 10, the "Sheldon Thompson," a boat bringing soldiers for the Black Hawk War, also brought cholera. Within a week there were 58 fatalities.

Chicago couldn't catch a break.

Except, while all of this do-we-stay-or-do-we-go was happening, Illinois entered the Union in 1818, the wildly successful Erie Canal opened in 1825, and in 1826 Congress gave Illinois the acreage it needed for its very own canal. Three years later the Illinois Legislature appointed a Canal Commission to make this water highway a reality, and in 1830 James Thompson drew the first street grid of Chicago.

6

Prospectors and daring pioneers bought lots and lo and behold, on August 12, 1833, the stinky, swampy land officially became a town.

Was the founder of Chicago's name du Sable or de Sable? If you look around present-day Chicago, Jean Baptiste's name is spelled du—Du Sable Bridge, Du Sable Museum, even the statue of him at Pioneer Court, marking the site of his home. Yet, an earlier tablet at Pine (present-day Michigan Avenue) and Kinzie spelled his name de. An authoritative article by John Swenson in EarlyChicago.com states that de Sable was Jean Baptiste's chosen legal name, and the "du" spelling didn't appear until long after his death.

1836
Clarke House

Picture this: it's 1835. Your family is comfortable. You live in upstate New York, members of the upper-middle class. You've been married for a few years, have a few children (although one, sadly, died), and then your husband trots off to a marshy prairie on the shores of a giant inland lake. He comes back, filled with dreams and visions.

"Caroline! I've found our new home! It'll take three weeks to get there, and it's pretty much a backwater now, but it'll grow. Oh, yes, it'll grow. Shall we?"

9

And you look at your husband, and instead of saying: "Are you off your rocker?" you say, "Sure, honey. Why not?"

In the early 1830s, Henry Brown Clarke was a merchant in Utica, New York. His father was an attorney and judge and his grandfather was a Revolutionary War hero.

Caroline Palmer Clarke was that oh-so-rare early nineteenth-century phenomenon: an educated woman. She attended the first higher education institution for women in the United States. The Troy Female Seminary, founded by and later named for Emma Willard, opened in 1821 with the express purpose of providing women the same educational opportunities as men. What a radical concept.

Henry and Caroline married in 1827, and eight years later Henry's brother-in-law, Charles Walker, returned from a trip to Chicago with tales of potential riches. The two-year-old town's prime location on Lake Michigan along the Chicago River meant it was ripe for expansion. Rumors of the upcoming Illinois and Michigan Canal, which would enable boat passage to the Mississippi River, drove hundreds, and then thousands, to place their bets on this new frontier. Many Easterners had made their fortunes when the Erie Canal opened, and the I & M presented a similar opportunity.

By the time the Clarkes made their westward journey they didn't even have to worry about moving onto Native American land. The Second Treaty of Chicago in 1833 sent the tribe west, and their last dance on their native soil took place in 1835.

Direct descendants of the removed tribes began returning to the Chicago area after World War I. Today, Chicago has the third-largest urban Native American population in the country, representing over one hundred tribal nations.

Once Henry arrived, his merchant background came in handy and he quickly became a partner of Jones, King and Company, a wholesale hardware firm. Instead of settling close to the action, Mr. and Mrs. Clarke purchased twenty acres about a mile and a half south of the nearest neighbor. To get to town they rode a dirt trail that had been worn by the Potawatomi.

Their grand landscape, which stretched from Lake Michigan to what is now State Street and from present-day 16th Street to 17th Street, transitioned from dunes to marshy prairies. The family moved into an existing log cabin which belonged to Dr. Elijah Harmon, the property's previous owner.

Buying that much land that far away from relative civilization might have seemed foolhardy, but it ended up being far-sighted and the reason their house survived. That, and because Caroline wanted a home made of timber.

When the Clarkes moved to Chicago, Caroline wanted a strong house. She didn't want any of that newfangled "balloon" construction, so-called because the buildings went up quickly. Nope. She wanted a sturdy home built of thick-hewn wood. It didn't matter that they'd live in a log cabin with their kids for a year, or that they'd need expensive skilled labor, or that the material would be more costly than boards connected with machine-made nails. She did not pick up and move across the country to live in some flimsy, insubstantial shack.

Caroline wanted timber. Caroline got timber.

The Clarkes moved into their Greek Revival home with its portico and Doric columns in 1836. Although they hadn't finished the interior, they'd get to it. After all, Henry was a mover and shaker: in addition to the hardware store, he'd become a director of Chicago's first bank, volunteered for Fire Engine No. 1, and participated in the canal committee.

And then the bottom fell out. The Panic of 1837, two months after the town of Chicago was incorporated as a city, meant failed banks, including Henry's. The wholesale hardware firm stumbled. Canal talks stopped.

The Panic devastated the Clarkes financially, and in 1838 they ceased all construction. They barely hung onto the home and property itself, and only escaped foreclosure through the largesse of Charles Walker, the brother-in-law who'd enticed them to move in the first place.

Was it time to quit? Turn around and head back to New York?

No way. Henry began dairy farming. He milked cows and farmed and hunted on their vast property. The unfinished south parlor turned into a meat locker. They took in boarders. Alice Barnard, who became Chicago Public School's first female principal, rented a room above the hanging deer, snipe, plover, quail, chickens, and ducks. The smell, to put it mildly, was less than desirable.

The economy began to improve and Henry obtained a position as the city clerk. They had more children. The city continued to grow. By 1840, 4,000 people lived in Chicago. In 1847, Cyrus McCormick brought his harvester manufacturing to the city. The next year both the I & M Canal and the Galena and Chicago Railroad began operations, enticing more and more and more fortune seekers. All of those bodies meant lots of, ahem, waste, which meant disease. In 1849, a cholera epidemic killed nearly three percent of a population that had been quickly climbing to 30,000.

Including Henry B. Clarke.

Caroline, now known as the Widow Clarke, had six children to care for on her own. So, she did what any sensible widow in possession of twenty acres in a city with an exploding population would do. She carved her acreage up into lots and sold them for a hefty sum.

With her newfound financial security, she redesigned her home in the manner with which she wanted to become accustomed. She added gas service and modern lighting. A second portico enhanced the building's symmetry. A cupola provided a view of Lake Michigan and access to its refreshing breezes.

The dreadful, odoriferous meat locker became an ornate double parlor with Italianate fireplaces and colorful medallions on the ceiling. As was the custom, the Widow Clarke entertained calling guests for fifteen minutes apiece while her daughters played brilliantly on the Chickering piano. Only uplifting conversation was allowed during these visits, with no hint of politics, scandal, or impropriety. It was all well and good and proper, and lasted until Caroline died in 1860.

The home stayed in the family for the next several years. Because Henry and Caroline had chosen to build so far south, the Great Chicago Fire of 1871 missed the house entirely. The next year the children sold the home to a successful tailor and his wife, John and Lydia Chrimes.

Even though their new property had escaped the previous year's fire unscathed, the proximity and density of the city's population concerned the Chrimes. They were also fretful of the air pollution because of their ailing son, so they picked up the house and moved it twenty-eight blocks south and one block west.

The house stayed in the Chrimes family for three generations. John and Lydia's granddaughters, Lydia and Laura, knew the significance of the building, but by 1941 they didn't want to live in it anymore. They searched until they could find someone who would appreciate the historical value and preserve the structure for future generations. Ideally, they wanted the city to buy it and turn it into a museum.

The city said no, but Louis Henry Ford said yes.

At the time, Ford was a 27-year-old bishop of the St. Paul Church of God in Christ on the south side of Chicago. He and his congregation built a church next to the house, which they used for offices, a school, events, and Ford's parsonage.

The church didn't just use the house, they also preserved it. According to an article dated August 19, 1962, in the *Chicago Daily Tribune*, the congregation had spent $18,000 restoring and preserving the historic structure.

In 1970, the Commission on Chicago Landmarks officially designated the Clarke House a landmark, and in 1977 the city purchased the home to turn it into a museum.

But first, the house needed to be moved back to its (almost) original location. It had been more than a century since the first move and this one provided a new challenge: the "L" tracks were in the way. On a cold December night, the city stopped the trains and hydraulic lifts raised the Clarke House over the tracks.

And stayed there. It was so cold that the lifts froze. For two weeks train riders would get a glimpse of Chicago's oldest house* as they went on their merry way.

The lifts finally thawed and the house landed in its present location. Since then, it's been faithfully restored to the configuration the Widow Clarke had designed. While none of the displayed furnishings ever belonged to the Clarkes, they are representative of the period, thanks to the National Society of The Colonial Dames of America in the State of Illinois.

Clarke House Today

The Clarke House Museum is a rare look into the time before the Great Chicago Fire cleared the landscape of nearly everything that had been built before 1871. It's also a lesson in fortitude, and the grit required to pick up and move to a marshy prairie on the shores of a giant inland lake.

Technically, a portion of the Noble-Seymour-Crippen House in Norwood Park dates to 1833 and could be considered the oldest house. However, Chicago didn't annex the community until 1893, and the Clarke House became part of the city when Chicago was incorporated, which leads city purists to believe the Clarke House deserves the oldest designation.

1836
Lake Park
Grant Park

G rant Park is one of Chicago's most recognizable and beloved institutions. It hosts the city's biggest festivals. It's got Buckingham Fountain, baseball fields, a skatepark, a bandshell, and gardens and a dog park and the list goes on and on and on. But creating and saving this public space was no easy task. It was such a battle it involved city ordinances and lawsuits all the way to the U.S. Supreme Court. There were also people who essentially said: "Take my money!"

Whodathunk so much drama could play out over a park? So. Much. Drama.

From its beginnings as a strip of sand to its current status as the city's Front Yard, the story of Grant Park is a microcosm of the personalities and interplay of greed and philanthropy that built this city.

It began with a simple notation on a map: "Public Ground— A Common to Remain Forever Open, Clear and Free of any Buildings or Other Obstructions whatever." In 1836, the town of Chicago was only three years old and the city wouldn't be incorporated until the next year. Commissioners for the Illinois and Michigan Canal raised money to build the waterway by selling parcels of land the U.S. Congress had provided for that purpose. The commissioners sold those plots using a map with blocks laid out in a grid, a layout required by the Land Ordinance of 1785 for any new towns and municipalities.

A few of those plots lined Michigan Avenue and faced a strip of land between the street and Lake Michigan. It was prime waterfront real estate, and that meant the same thing in 1836 as it does now: Mo' money mo' money mo' money.

People would pay more for that lakefront property, but only if they knew it would always be lakefront. Or, at least, have an unobstructed view. The canal commissioners promised it would be forever open, and soon houses lined the boulevard.

The strip of sand officially became Lake Park in 1844, seven years after the City of Chicago incorporated. Soon the park's name would be eponymous: erosion meant that during storms the water would come all the way up to Michigan Avenue, and sometimes to the rowhouses' front doors. They needed a breakwater and they needed one fast.

In 1848, Galena and Chicago Union Railroad chugged into Chicago. It didn't take long before Illinois Central Railroad was eyeing that wide-open lakefront. "How's about we build some tracks along the lake to the river?" they said.

Chicagoans, being the savvy bunch they were, said: "How's about you put your tracks over water and build us a breakwater?"

"Done."

Illinois Central secured permission to run trestles over the lake and build a breakwater to stop the erosion of Lake Park, but that was all they could do. They couldn't build any buildings or let trains sit for any length of time. Any structures had to be north of Randolph Street or south of 12th.

That worked for a few years, and residents of Michigan Avenue had a view of Lake Park, followed by a lagoon, then train tracks, and then the breakwater. All Chicagoans could stroll the promenade and take in some fresh air. It was an egalitarian mix of hoi polloi and high society.

The city kept growing and growing, and the harbor became a dumping ground. Rail travel increased exponentially, and in 1869, the Illinois General Assembly decided that Illinois Central could buy the portion of the park north of Monroe Street for $800,000. The railroad would fill the shallow harbor on that side of the park and build a passenger depot. That would be alright, wouldn't it? Especially when that $800k could be used to beautify the park south of Monroe. Right? That would work just fine.

HA! Chicago rebelled, called it the "Lake Front Steal," and the city refused the first installment. Illinois Central probably would have kept fighting, but a scheme to manipulate the price of gold sent the U.S. economy into a downward spiral. This took away Illinois Central's means to pay or even sustain a legal battle. So, they let it drop and in 1873 the Illinois General Assembly repealed the ill-considered act.

Here's a twist for you: the gold scheme depended on the U.S. government putting a stop to its gold sales. The men behind the manipulation included Abel Corbin, chosen to participate specifically because he was married to Ulysses S. Grant's daughter and had access to the President. Grant Park was inadvertently saved by the machinations of Grant's son-in-law.

See? Drama.

17

In between Illinois Central's offer to buy part of the park and the repeal of the act granting the purchase, the Great Chicago Fire of 1871 ripped through the young city. As Chicagoans recovered and rebuilt, they pushed the debris into the lake, filling the lagoon. Businesses needed someplace to go during the clean-up, and many set up transitory structures in Lake Park. Even the city took advantage of the open space and hired William W. Boyington, the architect of the surviving Water Tower, to design the Inter-State Industrial Exposition Building. The supposedly temporary edifice was built to display Chicago goods and prove that the city had recovered. Fairs, art exhibits, a grand opera festival, and conventions filled the giant hall. In 1884, both the Republican and Democrat Parties held their National Presidential Conventions in the Expo.

Other structures popped up. The Chicago White Stockings had built a stadium in Lake Park five months before the fire, so you know what happened to it. They built a new one in 1878. Owner Albert Spalding improved that stadium in 1883, but the next year the team had to leave because the Fed gave the land to Chicago with the stipulation that there could be no commercial enterprises in the park. Baseball wasn't allowed, but apparently other things were okay because there was an armory and the Baltimore and Ohio Railroad passenger depot. The landfill now covered the harbor and extended beyond the tracks; unfortunately, east of the railroad was still a dumping ground.

The park that was supposed to be forever open, clear and free decidedly was not, and by 1890, Michigan Avenue landowners, including Aaron Montgomery Ward, had had enough.

It would be natural to think that Ward had purely selfish interests. He and his partner, George Thorne, purchased two of the lots across from the park in 1887 and a third in 1889. Of course he'd want a better view! Ward and Thorne claimed, however, that they'd purchased those specific lots because they wanted their employees to have sunlight, fresh air, and some relative peace and quiet. That idea isn't disingenuous:

the company provided health insurance at a time when that benefit wasn't typical, as well as other employee perqs like free malted milks.

For twenty-one years Ward consistently fought to not only clean up the park but to also keep it clear. His attorney, George Merrick, filed Ward's first lawsuit to save the park on October 16, 1890. The final suit closed on February 8, 1911. He spent about $50,000 ($1,100,000 in today's money) and incurred the wrath of the city's leaders, the Chicago Tribune, and everyday Chicagoans. He even defied Burnham's Plan of Chicago, which included a civic center, a museum, and a library in the middle of the park. In 1903, Chicago citizens voted for a tax levy to fund the Field Museum and the Crerar Library, and Ward filed specifically to stop those from being built.

If only they knew then what we know now... If Ward had lost, Grant Park would be filled with city hall, a post office, a police station, a power plant, stables, a library, and a museum. There'd be no room for strolls or picnics in a park with no open land.

The only structure that escaped Ward's single-minded pursuit was the Art Institute of Chicago. The planners of the 1893 Columbian Exposition World's Fair needed an impressive place to hold lectures and they wanted a building closer to downtown than Jackson Park, five miles south. The Art Institute needed a permanent home. The solution was to finally raze the "temporary" Expo building and construct a new, permanent structure. After the building was no longer needed for the lectures, the Art Institute of Chicago could move in.

While all of this legal maneuvering was going on things were still happening in the park. In 1893, the South Parks Commission installed a working water fountain because Joseph Rosenberg had left a bequest of $10,000 in his will for a fountain "to provide the thirsty with a drink." He'd worked as a newsboy while growing up in Chicago and nobody would ever give the poor young man a sip of water and he wanted to make sure others didn't have to go thirsty. Another statue was installed in 1897 when the Illinois state legislature honored Civil War General John Logan with a monument on a hill.

One of the biggest changes during this time involved the name. On October 9, 1901, Lake Park officially became Grant Park in honor of the former President and Civil War hero.

In 1907, the Olmsted Brothers published their Versailles-inspired plan for Grant Park. The design was part of the Plan of Chicago and included the centrally located Field Museum. Since Ward's lawsuits put a kibosh on that idea, Edward Bennett, co-author of the Plan, designed the park himself.

Over the next several years the park kept growing, and by 1914 the shoreline extended 2,100 feet beyond Michigan Avenue. Landscaping followed Bennett's Beaux Arts-inspired plan. Ornamental viaducts crossed over the railroad tracks and lengthened roads over what had previously been water. The city wasn't done with landfill yet, and they continued increasing acreage south of 12th Street, now Roosevelt Road. This created the future home of the Field Museum, which opened in 1921; Soldier Field; Shedd Aquarium; and Adler Planetarium; as well as Northerly Island.

In 1927, Kate Buckingham's gift to the city honoring her brother, the Clarence F. Buckingham Memorial Fountain, opened with a performance of "Pomp and Circumstance" conducted by John Philip Sousa himself. The next year the Bowman and the Spearman statues were installed at the park's now elaborate entrance at Congress Plaza. The park was really shaping up.

When the Depression hit, Mayor Anton Cermak and James C. Petrillo, the president of the musicians' union, thought it would be a good idea to offer free concerts to keep spirits up. The city erected a bandshell near the Field Museum; this "temporary" structure stayed up forty years, even longer than the Expo building. The Grant Park Music Festival began its long life with its first concert on July 1, 1935, and every summer performers entertained. There were even events during World War II, and after the war attendance skyrocketed.

In 1978, a new bandshell went up east of the Art Institute. Designed as a semi-permanent structure to satisfy the prohibition of permanent buildings, the Petrillo Band Shell is still going strong.

The rest of the 1900s saw the addition of underground parking garages to remove the unsightly surface-level parking lots. In 1976 Daley Bicentennial Plaza skirted the building restrictions by putting a field house with public restrooms and a fitness facility mostly underground. That section would later become Maggie Daley Park. In 1986, the city removed the "S" curve of Lake Shore Drive and ten years after that the Richard and Annette Bloch Cancer Survivors Garden opened where cars used to turn.

Millennium Park, with its Frank Gehry-designed music pavilion, on-site restaurant, native garden, public art, and Harris Theater, opened in 2004. It pushed the boundaries of what Ward would have found acceptable, but it's become one of Chicago's most popular destinations.

Lake Park Today

Grant Park is a living breathing postcard that illustrates the complexity of this city by the lake. It may have started as a way to increase property values for a few, but for most of its life, it's been Chicago's Front Yard, and everyone can come out to play.

1856
Hull House
Hull-House Museum

In the late 1800s, wealthy Americans toured Europe. It was the cosmopolitan thing to do. For many, it was a shopping trip, and today's museums are filled with their souvenirs. For some, like Potter Palmer, doctors ordered excursions abroad as convalescence. One rather serious young woman from Cedarville, Illinois, whose father had been a Senator and counted Lincoln among his friends, toured the continent twice, but her experiences were a bit different from her contemporaries. While her itineraries included the Vatican and Parisian art galleries and palaces, and she even met Bertha Palmer during one Paris visit, she also saw the underbelly. Her first trip, which lasted nearly two years, introduced her to child beggars in Ireland, the desperate grab of the hungry at the market's close in East London, and the deplorable working conditions of women in the fields and breweries of Germany. During her second, shorter tour, she visited the first settlement house, Toynbee Hall in England, and returned with a plan to change the world.

Or, at least a scheme, as she called it, to improve the lives of a few. Changing the world came later.

Jane Addams and her college friend Ellen Gates Starr moved into a boardinghouse across the street from Chicago's Washington Square in early 1889. They were looking for the perfect place to implement Jane's scheme to "settle" amongst the disadvantaged and downtrodden. They had been so affected by what they'd seen at Toynbee Hall that they wanted to, if not replicate it exactly, create something similar. They wanted to go beyond traditional philanthropy and be actively involved in the daily lives of the people they hoped to help. For these two visionaries, that meant living among them. As they used their connections and gift of persuasion to gather support from the city's wealthy and civic-minded, they searched for the perfect place to call home.

They found it in a run down, dilapidated wreck surrounded by tenements and filth. Jane was on her way to a Bohemian mission and the carriage passed a once-stately Italianate mansion. What others viewed as an eyesore, she saw as possibility. The building "surrounded on three sides by a broad piazza, which was supported by wooden pillars of exceptionally pure Corinthian design and proportion" was the ideal place, so the next day she returned to where she thought she'd seen it. Except it wasn't there. After several days with no luck, she gave up, only to come upon it by accident a couple of weeks later. It must have been meant to be. This was a home where humanitarians had lived.

Charles Jerome Hull built the mansion in 1856 for his family of four. A driven and talented businessman, he and his wife, Melicent A.C. Loomis, moved to Chicago in 1846 shortly after marrying. Although he was broke when they arrived in the young town, he was smart and ambitious and before long had accumulated a small fortune. The couple had two children, Charles in 1847 and Fredrika two years later. In 1852, Louis was born, but he only lived a year and a half. By the time Charles built the mansion at the corner of Polk and Halsted, he'd lost his fortune, regained it, and received his M.D. from Rush Medical College and his J.D. from Harvard Law School. And every Sunday, he'd go to the jail and talk to the prisoners. No sermon, just talk, about things like "Fate and Luck" and "Self-Reliance." He also offered bootblacks and newsboys refuge and a bite to eat in his office and filled a cellar with coal for anyone who needed it. In later years, he helped emancipated slaves buy property and build homes in Savannah, Georgia.

Charles didn't live in the home very long. Melicent died in 1860 and the widower asked his cousin, Helen Culver, to help take care of the children. She did, becoming his business partner as well as a caretaker. Although Charles retained possession, the family moved out of the mansion. As the neighborhood changed, the building housed the Little Sisters of the Poor and a used furniture store, and eventually became storage and offices for a factory that had sprung up behind it.

Helen continued working with Charles, and a story in the University of Chicago Magazine from 1919 stated that: "She had shared, perhaps equally with him, in the success that had been achieved." By the time he passed away on February 12, 1889, his estate had grown to millions, which he left entirely to his steadfast companion, including the home he'd built thirty-three years before.

Despite the condition of the building and its environs when Jane stumbled across it, she saw what could be. She saw its structural integrity, but she also saw the possibilities in the neighborhood in which it resided.

Layers of refuse covered the streets and alleys. In front of each building sat a bin for trash, but in a time before refrigeration and in an area without regular, if any, sanitation services, those bins were boxes of disease. Plus, they reeked. Imagine the odor your kitchen trash emits a day after you've tossed spoiled chicken or rotten cabbage. Now multiply that by the thousands of people living in those tenements and add untreated sewage, livestock and its associated output, and the complete lack of not only bathing facilities but also toilets in general. Childcare didn't exist in this neighborhood. Most of the people were recent immigrants, which meant multiple languages. Many worked for the nearby garment district and in sweatshops, earning pennies per piece, and the worst factories charged them to use the equipment. It was a dangerous, exploitative environment.

Jane and Ellen, who could have lived anywhere, chose to move into the middle of it. While many of Chicago's wealthy were philanthropic, the only way to truly make a difference would be through systemic change. The women weren't quite sure how they were going to improve the lives of their new neighbors, but they knew they'd never figure it out unless they jumped right in.

In May 1889, three months after Charles' death, Helen leased the second floor of the mansion to Jane and Ellen. They furnished it with family mahogany, new furniture, and memorabilia from their European tours. Jane used some of the inheritance she'd received from her father's will to fix the floors and paint the walls. They moved in September 18, and they were so excited they forgot to close and lock a side door which opened to Polk Street. Twenty years later, Jane recounted: "we were much pleased in the morning to find that we possessed a fine illustration of the honesty and kindliness of our new neighbors."

Jane and Ellen immediately invited those neighbors, a mix of German, Greek, Irish, Italian, Polish, and Russian Jewish immigrants, in for readings in their parlor, beginning with a novel by George Eliot. They opened a kindergarten. They hosted art classes and social clubs. By the next spring, Helen was so inspired by what the women were doing that she gave them a free leasehold of the entire house. In an 1874 letter, Charles had written to Helen: "Our idea is to level up from the bottom by giving the poor a fair chance to rise." Jane and Ellen, who'd christened their settlement Hull-House in honor of Helen's generosity, were giving them that chance.

Jane's scheme grew exponentially from a vague idea to a concrete social movement. Residents moved in. These were often women of means and education but no employment. Investors, including Mary Rozet Smith, who would become Jane's lifelong companion, poured money into Hull-House. They built an art gallery. Then a coffeehouse. A gymnasium. Public baths. A kitchen, that would teach the multi-national, multi-cultural immigrants how to cook with the unfamiliar produce of their new home. A music school. They built a playground, and children could be children. Opened May 4, 1894, it was the first playground in the city. Working mothers could leave their babies and toddlers in the nursery. Single women could find a safe place to live in the Jane Club. The textile and labor museum enabled these immigrants of multiple ethnicities to see other traditions, and learn both their similarities as well as their differences. There was even a book bindery, which taught this valuable skill during a time when printing presses were booming. Social clubs, theater, workshops provided life beyond the drudgery. Citizenship classes and a Juvenile Protective Association helped them learn their rights. By 1907 Hull-House had thirteen buildings and serviced thousands of people a week. By 1909, there were forty-five self-supporting residents and two hundred volunteers.

The sheer quantity of achievements, and the steps taken by the residents and supporters to attain them is difficult to grasp.

Hull-House drew and was led by fierce, dedicated, and passionate women. When the 19th Ward Alderman wouldn't do anything about the trash situation, Jane finagled an appointment as the Inspector of Garbage, for which she received an annual salary of $1,000. Julia Lathrop became a resident in 1890. She was a Rockford Female Seminary classmate of Jane and Ellen's, and her father was also a close friend of Lincoln's. Later, she was appointed the director of the United States Children's Bureau, the first woman ever to head a federal bureau in the country. In 1891, Florence Kelley left her abusive husband and she and her three children found refuge at Hull-House. The next year, the Illinois Bureau of Labor Statistics hired Florence, and a survey she conducted revealed the atrocious conditions in Chicago's slums, including children working at the tender age of three. The year after that Governor Altgeld made her the Chief Factory Inspector for the state of Illinois, making her the first woman to hold state-wide office. She fought for 8-hour work days, criminalizing the employment of children under the age of 14, and protecting the rights of workers. In 1895, Florence, Jane, and other residents undertook the massive project of documenting and mapping the income, ethnicities, working conditions, and other group patterns of the 19th Ward. The Hull-House Maps and Papers gave a snapshot of a crowded, underserved section of the city and transformed social science.

Other active and activist residents and supporters included Alice Hamilton, whose research in occupational health and the dangers of toxins in the workplace pioneered the field of industrial toxicology. Sisters Grace and Edith Abbott were Ph.D-level social workers; Grace focused on immigration and child labor and Edith on incorporating social work into education. Both worked with the nascent Social Security Administration. The list of these activists could and does fill several books. Suffice it to say, the whole enterprise was a who's who of people driven to right wrongs and wrest compassion from a society that chose to bury or mock injustices instead of do something about them. The residents of Hull-House did something. The residents of Hull-House did a lot of things.

Jane herself was the biggest activist of all. She was the first woman president of the National Conference of Charities and Corrections, a founding member of the National Child Labor

Committee, a founding member of both the National Association for the Advancement of Colored People and the American Civil Liberties Union. She was vice president of the League for Protection of Immigrants and a committed member of the National American Woman Suffrage Association. All of that kept her in the public eye and in 1908, Ladies' Home Journal christened her "America's foremost living woman."

Not everybody loved Jane and her cohorts at Hull-House. They were excoriated as anarchists and socialists. As hostilities increased in Europe in the early 1910s, Jane, who had always been a pacifist, became increasingly vocal. Her pro-peace, anti-war activities and her status as an unmarried wealthy white woman earned her a thick FBI folder. She was labeled a communist and considered one of the most dangerous women in America. Still, her insistence that war did not solve anything, combined with the rest of her lifelong efforts to make the world a better place, also earned her a Nobel Peace Prize. In 1931, she became the first American woman to receive the award.

Throughout it all, Mary Rozet Smith and Jane maintained their relationship. The connection was so strong that when Jane traveled without Mary she took a portrait of her. This was no small snapshot that fit in a satchel. This was a painting, fit to hang over a mantel, and Jane would pack it along with her gowns and her speeches. Mary died in 1934 and when Jane was near death the following year, she asked her nephew to burn their letters. Unfortunately, he complied.

While the neighborhood, the city, and the world around it changed, Hull-House continued its good work at Polk and Halsted until 1963. That year, the University of Illinois at Chicago decided their extended stay at Navy Pier, where they'd been since 1946, was done and kicked everybody out, along with 8,000 residents and 630 businesses. To accommodate construction of the new campus, all but the original Hull mansion and the dining hall were razed. Still, the work continued, until 2012 when Hull-House Association declared bankruptcy and dissolved.

Hull House Today

The legacy of Jane Addams, Ellen Gates Starr, and the Hull-House residents and supporters continues in many of the social safety nets that still exist. Their work is honored and showcased in the Hull House Museum. One of the most intriguing exhibits is the color-coded maps from the 1895 demographic study, as well as the portrait of Mary hanging in Jane's former bedroom.

1864
Lake Park
Lincoln Park & Lincoln Park Zoo

ake a look at a map of Chicago's north side and you'll notice a huge swath of green along the lake. It stretches seven miles from Ohio Street to Ardmore Avenue, covering 1,214 acres lined with beaches and filled with gardens, sculptures, museums, thousands of trees, and oodles of sporting facilities. That complicated expanse is Lincoln Park, and it was a long time in the making. You don't create a city park of that size by drawing lines on a map and writing: "Insert Park Here." This public space jumped through a lot of hoops and over a bunch of dead bodies to become what it is today.

Wait—dead bodies? Yep. Thousands of them.

Every city needs cemeteries, and in 1837, the year Chicago incorporated, the Illinois legislature gave the municipality the right to use one of the lots sold by the canal commission for a burial ground. Starting at North Avenue, this location seemed remote enough, and for a little while it was.

The city couldn't start using this land until they paid for it, and they finally settled their $8,000 fee in 1842. Once Chicago officially acquired the land they began to sell burial plots, complete with deeds. Some people paid, and some showed up with shovels. The indigent had their own mass grave. The nearly simultaneous opening of the Illinois and Michigan Canal and the introduction of trains in 1848 meant a population boom in a city without health regulations, and cholera invaded. In 1852, the Common Council bought three large tracts of land north of the cemetery to be used for a hospital and a quarantine zone. Fortunately, that particular cholera crisis abated before they needed to use the land for that purpose.

It didn't take long for the city to grow up and around the cemetery. That meant lots of people lived across the street from lots of graves—shallow graves, filled with lots of diseased deceased. East of the cemetery, swales crowded with poison ivy led toward a wide beach of sand that shifted with the meanderings of the persnickety shore. Then there was the Ten-Mile Ditch. Dug to drain water from Evanston, stagnant pools made it more a swamp than a stream.

Altogether, it was a very unpleasant place. Citizens and physicians raised a hue and cry. They wanted the bodies moved elsewhere, and they wanted a park.

The needs of the Civil War temporarily pushed aside those wants. Confederate soldiers who perished at the south side Camp Douglas ended up in the North Chicago cemetery. It's estimated that 3,000–4,000 prisoners of war were buried in the potter's field.

However, civic life didn't come to a complete halt during the Civil War, and in 1864 William C. Goudy prepared an ordinance to appropriate the land located between the cemetery and Webster Street, acreage that had been set aside during the earlier cholera scare, for a public park. On October 21, the city passed that ordinance and declared it would be called Lake Park.

There was only one problem: Chicago already had a Lake Park. Eventually, the first Lake Park would become Grant Park, but until then, one Lake Park was enough for the city. The next year, a few months after President Abraham Lincoln's assassination, the Common Council of Chicago passed the following resolution:

> "WHEREAS, It appears by the records of the City of Chicago, that there are now two public parks designated by the name of Lake Park; therefore
>
> "Resolved, That the park recently set apart from the unoccupied portion of the old cemetery grounds shall be hereafter known and designated as Lincoln Park."

Out of a cemetery, Lincoln Park was born.

Changes happened quickly after that. The city set a budget of $10,000 and the Commission hired Swain Nelson to design the park. His plan turned Ten-Mile Ditch into three lakes, constructed eight temporary bridges, provided landscaping, and developed drives, walks, and sewers. In 1868, O.B. Green donated two pairs of swans from New York's Central Park, the first residents of what would become Lincoln Park Zoo. Musicians performed concerts and Lincoln Park became an escape from the urban chaos.

It was lovely, but there was still that issue of dead bodies. While there had been a few disinterments since the city banned the sale of new burial plots in 1859, thousands, including those Confederate prisoners of war, had been dumped into the potter's field. On February 8, 1869, advocates formed the Lincoln Park Commission, the first of three Chicago park commissions. Owners of cemetery lots were informed that they had to remove the bodies within six months. If they didn't, the commissioners could do it themselves. However, moving bodies was expensive. Then the Great Chicago Fire burned most of the grave markers as well as the plats and surveys telling who was buried where. The only thing that kept them somewhat organized was an old sexton "whose familiarity with the lots and the names of their owners was so great and his memory so accurate that he was able to locate any grave with little difficulty."

According to Pamela Bannos, who did extensive research on the subject for her project "Hidden Truths," about 22,500 bodies were removed out of total estimated burials of 35,628. You do the math. Or don't. It's OK if you don't. Because the truth is, there are still lots of bones in them thar hills, but the only visible remnant is the Couch Tomb, a stone vault that couldn't be budged.

It took until 1894 to secure all the old cemetery lands, but in the meantime, the Commission didn't rest its weary bones. Before the fire, the Commissioners of Lincoln Park had begun directing their attention to increasing the grounds and protecting the shoreline. They were able to secure most of the land, but there was one acquisition that turned out to be quite expensive.

The city *thought* it had purchased the twelve-acre Milliman Tract within the cemetery in 1850, but the sale was determined to be illegal and the Illinois Supreme Court reversed it in 1865. To get the land, the Commissioners had to shell out a total of $138,000. Ouch.

After the fire, there was another big expense. In 1866, John V. Farwell bought a four-acre triangle of land at North Avenue and Lake Michigan for about $8,000. He built a pier, and within six years so much sand had been kicked up by the lake that he'd accumulated nineteen acres. The Commissioners of Lincoln Park wanted that acreage, and President Belden F.

Culver bought it in trust for the whopping sum of $100,000. Not a bad profit, Mr. Farwell.

The park continued to grow. In 1873, the zoo received its second gift of animals, and it was a veritable menagerie. The next year, Lincoln Park bought a bear cub for $10, its first purchase. In the next few years, the park received and bought more and more animals, including more bears. By 1879, park officials thought the wooden bear cage wasn't secure enough, so the following spring they moved them into a new habitat. From which the bears promptly escaped.

According to the Report of the Commissioners, April 1, 1898—March 31, 1899:

"Bears became expert at climbing up the rough, rocky sides of their dens, and in time it was their almost nightly practice to escape and roam around the Park. They were sometimes found in the trees about the Park, and sometimes in winter out on the ice of the lake, headed for the Michigan shore, and they had to be corralled, coaxed, and cajoled by the entire force of Park employés {sic} to return to their official quarters.

"One of them struck out for the business center, and was getting along nicely until, in clambering over a ridge at the south end of the Mall, it fell through the top of an old cemetery vault, and was kept a prisoner there until its recapture. Another, a grizzly, wandered down the Pine Street Drive, and took refuge from pursuers in a tall elm tree near Oak Street. A Park policeman, who had brought up the rear of the chase, was stationed at the foot of the tree to keep the bear from coming down until the next morning, and there is a tradition, though it cannot be verified, that he resigned his position on the spot."

Lincoln Park Commissioners had declared in 1878 that the Zoo would always be free. Guess the bears thought that applied to them, too.

They weren't the only escapees. A decade later, a bunch of sea lions who'd just arrived busted out of their pit. Two waddled straight across Clark Street into a restaurant, a few others roamed around the park, and one took a dive into Lake Michigan. It's said that this last one was heard near Milwaukee.

Then, in 1891, "Duchess" the elephant "took a fancy for a longer excursion, and started on a jaunt westward through and over the channel, across the flower-beds, to the serious damage thereof, and through and over fences, yards, and buildings. A summer-house on North Park Avenue was carried away on her shoulders, the gate of a near-by brewery torn from its hinges, and other expensive pranks committed before the "Duchess" at last allowed herself to be caught with a rope and lassoed to a telegraph pole until her good nature returned."

The other inhabitants of Lincoln Park were less mobile. The Commissioners hired a gardener in 1874 and, before long, Lincoln Park had formal gardens and a greenhouse. The popularity of the latter demanded larger accommodations, and by 1895 Architect Joseph Lyman Silsbee's conservatory housed ferns, palm and rubber trees, exotic fruit trees, and tropical plants. An unused ravine became a lily pond. They imported bulbs from Holland and bought plants from the Smithsonian.

Then there were the sculptures. The first one, installed in 1884, was dedicated to the Ottawa. Mike Ryerson had traded with members of the tribe and, after he made his fortune, commissioned a sculpture from artist John J. Boyle. "The Alarm" depicts a Native American family listening for danger. Ryerson insisted the sculptor portray the man, wife, child, and dog with dignity. Originally placed near the zoo, the family now watches from the lakefront.

Over the next several years, the Commission installed sculptures portraying Schiller, Shakespeare, Hans Christian Andersen, Beethoven, and Benjamin Franklin. Augustus Saint-Gaudens' *The Standing Lincoln* is considered one of the finest sculptures of the President. (Another of the artist's Lincoln sculptures is in Grant Park.)

People had to get to these gardens and animals and sculptures, and what better way than by a boulevard along the shore. Swain Nelson and his partner, Olaf Benson, included a lakefront road between Wisconsin Street and Diversey Avenue in their plan. The act that created Lincoln Park also stipulated that there needed to be a drive from the end of Pine Street (now Michigan Avenue) at Oak Street to North Avenue. The Lincoln Park Commissioners appointed Benson in 1875 to oversee the construction that would connect the park to the wealthy residents at the end of Pine.

As if animals, plants, art, and roads weren't enough, the Commissioners of Lincoln Park also added land. A lot of land. Often, they took a page out of Farwell's and Grant Park's playbooks and made their own. By 1929, they'd added 300 acres of turf extending north to Irving Park Road. Before they were finished, the park had grown by 1,000 acres from landfill alone.

The Chicago Academy of Sciences built the Matthew Laflin Memorial Building, the precursor to the Peggy Notebaert Nature Museum, in 1894. A golf course opened on some of that landfill. The Chicago Historical Society built a museum over the original graveyard. Lincoln Park Zoo added more houses, Marlin Perkins, and a veterinarian. Mayor Richard J. Daley brought the rural to the urban with Farm-in-the-Zoo.

This park was a LOT of work.

Lake Park Today

Grant Park may be Chicago's Front Yard, but Lincoln Park is its playground. The park is multiple destinations in one, and you could spend a week there and still miss a few things.

There's the Chicago History Museum, the Peggy Notebaert Nature Museum, and Lincoln Park Zoo. Boaters dock at three different harbors, and you can catch some sun at one of several beaches.

Families wear the kids out at play lots and the pooches at dog parks. Golfers practice their swing at the driving range and then hit the links at the nine-hole course. There are tennis courts, basketball courts, and football, soccer, and baseball fields. There's a chess pavilion, a skate park, an archery range, and a rowing canal.

Nature lovers soak it in at Lincoln Park Conservatory, Alfred Caldwell Lily Pond, North Pond Nature Sanctuary, and Montrose Point Bird Sanctuary. You can walk, run, or bike miles and miles of trails, many of them on the lakefront path. (Check ahead of time—changing Lake Michigan water levels have caused damage to parts of the path.) Art lovers will appreciate strolling the grounds and discovering the multiple monuments and fountains.

If that activity is making you hungry, there are several restaurants within the zoo, plus seasonal stands along the lake. For fancy-schmancy dining, North Pond offers MICHELIN Guide-worthy cuisine in a pastoral setting. Whew!

All of this is why twenty million people a year visit Lincoln Park. Those early proponents of a park instead of a cemetery had no idea what they started, but it's a good thing they did.

1869
Chicago Water Tower

I n a city of symbols, the one that most emphatically says "Chicago" is the historic Water Tower. One of the few buildings to remain standing after the great Chicago fire, the tower and pumping station are portrayed as representatives of the city's indomitable spirit. Their symbolism goes deeper than surviving the fire, though. Sixty-four feet deeper.

It didn't take long after Chicago incorporated in 1837 for its citizens to realize they had a water problem. With a river flowing around and through the city into an inland sea, you'd think water would be the least of their worries. However, that river, and the fact that it emptied into the lake, was precisely the issue.

When the town began, its riparian location probably seemed perfect. Well, not exactly perfect. It was still a stinky swamp. But easy access to fresh water was certainly a selling point. Not only could they drink it and bathe with it, but they could also dump stuff into it—like trash, offal, and sewage—and watch it flow right into that giant body of water, never to be seen again.

Using the river as a dumpster sounded like a good idea at the time, but the population kept growing. In 1842 there were 4,500 residents. In 1851, 35,000. And by 1860, more than 100,000 people lived in Chicago. All of them needed to drink water, and all of them put things, dirty things, back into the water.

City officials realized early on the need for water works, and in 1842 they hired a private firm to build a pumping station to pull fresh water in from Lake Michigan. This firm installed the station at Michigan Avenue and Lake Street with a pipe that extended 150 feet into the lake.

That wasn't nearly far enough. Not only did trains soon begin bringing people by the carload, they also brought livestock. Industries, like Cyrus McCormick's reaper manufacturing plant, set up shop along the river. There were flour mills, grain elevators, and packing houses. It was a free-for-all of expansion, and all of the residential and industrial waste stagnated in the streets until it went right into the drinking supply.

Sounds lovely, doesn't it?

In 1851, the city built its own water works, moving the pumping house to Chicago Avenue and Pine Street and installing a 600-foot pipe. They thought that their new system would sustain them for another 15 years, which is when they projected the population would reach 100,000.

They hit that number in nine, and even a second pumping station in 1857 couldn't stem the tide of typhoid fever, diarrhea, cholera, and other water-borne diseases.

Ellis Chesbrough, to the rescue.

He'd already convinced Chicagoans to raise their city by ten feet, which would be no easy task now, let alone in the 1850s. His plan was to build the brick sewers above ground level, cover them, and raise the existing buildings to the new street level. Gravity would then work its magic. His system worked to get the sewage out of the street, for the most part, but it still dumped all that excrement and filth into the river, which went into the lake, which was pumped into the city so people could drink it.

They needed a new pumping station, and this time, they were serious. Ellis proposed a two-mile tunnel leading to a water intake crib.

Remember, this was in the 1860s, and his proposal meant digging a tunnel sixty-four feet below the surface of the lake that would connect the crib, itself a massive undertaking, to a brand new pumping station. But hey, if Chicagoans could raise a city by ten feet, they could do this. It took a little less than three years to complete the tunnel and crib.

Next up was the Chicago Avenue Water Tower and Pumping Station. The city tapped prolific architect William W. Boyington to design the complex. Mr. Boyington had a thing for Medieval castles and he decked out his tower with buttresses, battlements, turrets, parapets, and spires. Cloaked in pale yellow Joliet limestone, when the structures were completed they fairly screamed GOTHIC!

One 19th century celebrity hated Boyington's design. At an appearance in Chicago in 1882, Oscar Wilde sputtered: "Your Water Tower is a castellated monstrosity with pepperboxes stuck all over it. I am amazed that any people could so abuse Gothic art and make a structure not like a water tower but like a tower of a medieval castle. It should be torn down."

Most people loved it, though. Lady Duffus Hardy, a British novelist and travel writer who visited two years before Wilde, wrote: "The new water works are the most beautiful illustrations of the vagaries of the architectural brain... Never were so many cupolas and buttresses, pinnacles and towers grouped together on one spot; none but a true artist could have arranged them into so harmonious a whole." After a visit in 1928, when White Castle founders Walt Anderson and Billy Ingram opened their first Chicago store, they designed the franchise to resemble the iconic tower.

The city was ready. In addition to wanting water that wouldn't kill them, they also wanted it to be fish-free. A tongue-in-cheek article in the Chicago Daily Tribune from January 14, 1867 said: "...those who have had small fish brought to their houses several times a day, gratis, will be obliged to patronize fish markets, and pay for all the fish they carry away."

On March 25, 1867, the city celebrated the formal inauguration of the Great Lake Tunnel with a parade and a cornerstone ceremony. In 1869, the water works opened by the shores of Lake Michigan.

Two years later, the Chicago Avenue Water Tower became a symbol of the city's spirit for another reason, the reason Chicagoans think of today: Boyington's Joliet limestone survived the Great Chicago Fire. At 182 and a half feet, the tall tower was a beacon of hope during reconstruction.

Despite all of the expense, effort, and innovation, the water works could only be used for another ten years before another tunnel was needed. Engineers finally realized that reversing the flow of the river would be the only way to fix Chicago's water woes. That happened in 1899, and by 1906, although the pumping station could still be used, the Chicago Avenue Water Tower was obsolete.

The tower may have survived the fire, but it still wasn't safe. Over the years there would be calls to tear the tower down, but each time the public was able to preserve it. There was even talk of moving the tower, but preservationists, including the

Chicago Historical Society, stepped in to stop that nonsense. They convinced the city to reroute Michigan Avenue to keep the cherished landmark right where it is.

There's no need to worry about future threats. In 1969, the Chicago Water Tower became the first water works to be designated as an American Water Landmark. In 1971 it became a Chicago Landmark, and in 1975 both the tower and pumping station were inscribed to the National Register of Historic Places.

Chicago Water Tower and Pumping Station Today

The historic water tower is surrounded by soaring buildings now, but it still stands tall and represents a city that simply will not give up. Inside, the tower contains the City Gallery. This is a free gallery in the wide base of the tower that features the work of local photographers and artists.

Across Michigan Avenue, the pumping station is doing what Chesbrough imagined back in the 1860s, and a little more. In addition to bringing in fresh water (from much further out in Lake Michigan), the nationally recognized Lookingglass Theatre presents plays and musicals inside the historic building.

1872
Page Brothers Building

I n a neighborhood of skyscrapers, the Page Brothers Building is short. It's seven stories tall, but it seems even shorter, since a couple of those floors are hidden by rumbling El tracks. Its neighbor to the south, the glitzy Chicago Theatre, overshadows the relatively stoic structure, but if you take a closer look—and maybe even apply a magnet—you'll discover one of the oldest buildings in the city and one of only two with a cast-iron front. Listed on the National Register of Historic Places and designated a Chicago Landmark, this building at the corner of State and Lake was built in 1872 and is a symbol of recovery after the Great

Chicago Fire and a city reinventing itself. It's also a legacy of Chicago's first architect.

John Mills Van Osdel was born on July 31, 1811, in Baltimore, Maryland, the son of a carpenter, builder, and architect. When John was fourteen, his father moved to New York, but then suffered an injury that prevented him from working, so the teenager became the breadwinner. After his dad got better, the family joined him in the big city. That's when young John, already adept at carpentry, discovered "The Apprentice Library." He dove into this gold mine, learning everything he could about architecture. By the time he was twenty-five, John had moved back to Baltimore, married Caroline Gailer, taught drawing classes, and written a book on carpentry and stair building, and then returned to New York. He wasn't there long before he met William B. Ogden, who was so impressed by the young man that he asked him to move to Chicago and design him a house. John did, and when he arrived in 1837, the town had become a city and his friend had been elected the first mayor.

Before he knew it, John had more work than he could handle. He designed steamboats and the first bridge over the north branch of the Chicago River. He built pumps to lift water out of the early excavations of the Illinois and Michigan Canal. His wife's ailing health prompted a return to New York in 1840, and while there he took a position as associate editor of *American Mechanic* (now *Scientific American*). Back in Chicago a year later, he built the city's first grain elevators. In the mid-1840s, a group of builders convinced him to open an architectural office, and he became the city's first official architect. Within four months, John M. Van Osdel needed bigger offices. It was during this time that Caroline died and he married Martha McClellan.

Over the next couple of decades, one could safely say that John built Chicago. According to *Biographical sketches of the leading men of Chicago*, published in 1868:

"To enumerate all the public buildings, private residences, and extensive mercantile blocks, which

44

were designed by Mr. Van Osdel, and built under his superintendence, would be to give a long list, including many of the best edifices, not only of Chicago, but of Illinois. We will only mention, as specimens, the Cook County Court House, the Chicago City Hall, the Tremont House, all the five-story iron-front buildings in the city, being over eleven hundred lineal feet of such frontage; the residence of Peter Schuttler, corner of Adams and Aberdeen streets, Chicago; the residences of ex-Governors Matteson, of Springfield, and Wood, of Quincy — the three finest residences in the State."

See that? Van Osdel built "ALL the five-story iron-front buildings in the city." And they all burned down.

It's hard to imagine what John must have felt that October of 1871. Panic, surely, and yet he still had the presence of mind to gather his books, papers, and records and race to the Palmer House, where he also grabbed the plans for the under-construction hotel. He scrambled to the basement and buried his life's work two-feet deep, covering it with sand and a thick layer of wet clay. That act would not only save his work, but would also direct future fireproof construction in the city.

After the fire John was immediately in demand and one of his early buildings went up at the corner of State and Lake. He stuck with what he knew and built a five-story iron-front building. Once it was completed, Page Bro & Co. moved in. Headquartered in Boston, the tannery and warehouse sold all manner of leather products. The firm's business had also been destroyed in the fire, but an article in the *Leavenworth Daily Commercial* said: "While their house was burning on Lake Street, Messrs. Page Bro & Co. leased a large building...and took possession of it within forty-eight hours after the destruction of their old building."

Before the fire, Lake Street had been the main drag because of its proximity to the river, so John's new iron-front building faced the east-west street. After the fire, Potter Palmer succeeded, with the help of Marshall Field and Levi Leiter, in making State Street the main thoroughfare. By the turn of the century, the Page brothers were no longer residents and it was time to give the building a face lift. The plan was to turn it into a fine office building, and the first floor was broken up into storefronts, a sixth story was added, and a new State Street facade added large windows. It didn't quite reorient the building, but it did provide a better street presence.

In 1975, the Page Brothers Building was added to the National Register of Historic Places, and in 1983 it became a Chicago Landmark, but that didn't mean it was safe. Both this Van Osdel signature structure and the flashy theater that wrapped around it, also an historic treasure, were threatened with demolition. The theater owners had even filed for a demolition permit in the early 1980s. Since the buildings shared two walls, that would have doomed Page Brothers, too.

The city said no, and in 1985 restoration began on both. The idea was to connect the buildings, but this was a tricky prospect not only because of those shared walls but also because the fifty-year gap between the two landmarks meant construction was drastically different. The Page Brothers building, despite being built right after the fire, had a lot of wood in it, so architect Daniel P. Coffey came up with the ingenious method of using the wood as a concrete cast. Once the concrete was set, the wood was removed. Ba-da-bing, ba-da-boom—problem solved. By the time they were finished, Van Osdel's building had a new penthouse and tons of new office space in place of the five-story light court. It also connected to The Chicago Theatre, and the combined restoration earned the developers a National Trust for Historic Preservation Honor Award.

Page Brothers Building Today

This throwback to Chicago's reconstruction remains a monument to the city's first architect. To see its cast-iron facade is to get a glimpse of what downtown looked like before the Great Chicago Fire. Today, John M. Van Osdel's oldest Chicago building is home to a fast-food restaurant, El Salvador's Consulate General, and Chicago's Sister Cities offices, among other tenants. It also connects to The Chicago Theatre, ensuring that those two landmarks' future stories are forever intertwined.

1873
Palmer House

T he Palmer House is opulence defined. Its chandeliers and sculptures weigh a literal ton. Entering the lobby through the travertine double staircase is like being smacked on one cheek with history and on the other with affluence. To state the obvious, it's gorgeous, and it is the most historic and luxurious hotel lobby in Chicago.

It started with a love story, although it's not as dramatic as one enduring myth would have you believe. There's a consistent narrative about Palmer House's beginnings that usually starts like this: Potter Palmer built his hotel as a wedding gift. The hotel opened on September 26, 1871, but burned down just 13 days later in the Great Chicago Fire.

While that is romantic and tragic, that's not *quite* what happened. Even though the story is repeated over and over and has reached mythic proportions, like the tale that Mrs. O'Leary's much-maligned cow started the Great Chicago Fire, it's not accurate. But, parts of it are true, and it is still a love story, of both a December/May couple and the city they adored.

Potter Palmer, born on May 20, 1826, in Albany County, New York, migrated west in 1852. Although his family owned a thriving farm, he preferred the retail life and had already run his own store before he left New York. With $5,000 in seed money from his father, he moved to the booming town of Chicago and very quickly made his mark. In about five years, his dry goods mercantile on Lake Street grew from a small market to an emporium spread out over four stories. While P. Palmer and Company was not the only dry goods merchant in Chicago, his concept was unique, because his was the first store to offer exchanges, returns and bargain sales. He also had the inspired idea that attractive window displays would entice customers.

Bertha Honoré, born on May 22, 1849, in Louisville, Kentucky, moved to Chicago in 1855 with her parents (naturally, since she was all of six years old). The wealthy Honorés gave their precocious child every advantage, and that included outings at P. Palmer and Company. Potter's fortunes ascended and he and Bertha's parents ran in the same circles. By the time Bertha was a teenager, he'd become a frequent guest at the Honorés' home.

At the ripe young age of thirteen, Bertha must have been fairly formidable because Potter Palmer was smitten, despite being 23 years her senior. Fortunately, he didn't ask her dad for his daughter's hand or act the Lothario. Over the next six years Potter made millions in real estate and cotton speculation, sold his store to young protégé Marshall Field, and took off for Europe at the advice of his doctors.

Bertha grew up. She attended St. Xavier's Academy in Chicago and, after the Civil War, the Convent of the Visitation in Georgetown where she received highest honors. She excelled in botany, logic, philosophy, astronomy, literature, algebra, and chemistry. She also played the harp. Bertha

49

carried herself with elegance, had a waist the width of a thimble, and by all accounts would have been a catch for any man.

Any man with a backbone, that is. Bertha was no wilting flower. Potter returned from his sojourn in 1868, the year after Bertha came back from her studies. Potter bought blocks of real estate on State Street. By the time he proposed and she said yes, he'd succeeded in moving the shopping district from Lake Street to That Great Street.

In 1870, Bertha was 21 years old and her fiancé, more than double her age, was 44. He'd made $40 million by the time he was forty, and the social scene was all a-twitter. The age difference, combined with Potter's enormous wealth, was fodder for the rumor mill. When the couple married on July 29, 1870, it was scandalous enough that the *Chicago Tribune* came to their defense:

> "The engagement has been short—only two months. It is stated that the bridegroom, when going away recently, offered to settle a million dollars on his intended bride but she nobly and persistently refused. This may put an end to the bitter observations of envious or cynical persons inclined to stamp the marriage contract—so momentous to the high contracting parties—as a commercial transaction. No matter who married Mr. Palmer the same cruel and unjust remarks would be made."

While Mr. Palmer couldn't convince his new bride to take a million dollars, he could give her a hotel. Palmer House, Potter's wedding gift to Bertha, opened on September 26, 1870.

September 26, 1870, not 1871. The day after the hotel's inspection, the *Chicago Tribune* reported: "Not less than 5000 of our citizens accompanied by their wives and daughters" attended the Palmer House's opening at State and Quincy. The first Palmer House existed in all its glory for a year and thirteen days before its untimely demise.

50

The confusion regarding the wedding gift timing may have occurred because, in 1871, another Palmer House was underway. The foundation for Palmer House II had been laid at State and Monroe; a boat loaded with iron destined for the new hotel was moored at the docks when the fire tore through the city. Potter was out of town on business and his wedding gift burned. His quick-thinking architect, John M. Van Osdel, took the plans for the new hotel, ran to the basement, and buried them in clay. This not only saved the plans, but it also provided inspiration for future fireproofing.

Potter quickly returned to Chicago and nearly left just as fast, but Bertha told him no way were they going to run."Mr. Palmer," she said, "it is the duty of every Chicagoan to stay here and devote his fortune and energies to rebuilding this stricken city." (According to a 1902 article in the *New York Times*.)

The Palmers stayed. Potter secured a loan for $1.7 million, the largest private individual bank loan in the United States at the time. He never rebuilt his hotel at State and Quincy, but his Monroe Street palace welcomed its first guests within two years. It was grandiose, worthy of a woman who could have gone anywhere in the world but chose to stay. There were electric lights, telephones, and elevators. The lobby resembled a grandly scaled European drawing room, and the barbershop floor was inlaid with silver dollars. The dining room served blue points on the shell, green turtle soup, quail on toast, and smoked beef tongue. Baths could be had if one applied at the office.

Bertha's sister, Ida, married President Ulysses S. Grant's son, and it was only natural that the General would be a guest when visiting Chicago. In 1879, the Palmer House hosted a banquet in Grant's honor after his round-the-world trip; by the end of Mark Twain's 2 a.m. toast, the President might have felt like he'd toured the world again.

In 1874 and 1875 the Palmers had two sons, Honoré and Potter, Jr. respectively. Potter continued his entrepreneurial success and helped beautify the city with his involvement with the South Park Commission. He donated regularly and prolifically. Bertha bought scores of paintings from contemporary artists like Monet and Degas. She invited factory girls into her home to learn about their working conditions—and do something to improve them. She helped millinery workers and shop girls, and when Jane Addams opened Hull-House in 1889, Bertha helped her get what she needed. As President of the Board of Lady Managers for the World's Columbian Exposition of 1893, Bertha insisted that a female architect design The Women's Building, and what Bertha wanted, Bertha got. She also instructed her kitchen to create a dessert that people could carry, and the Palmer House chefs invented the brownie. The woman was a force, and any questions about the age difference between her and Potter must have disappeared quickly.

Potter passed away in 1902, and over the next sixteen years Bertha ran the business, traveled Europe, bought much of Sarasota, Florida, and doubled the estate her husband had left her. After her death in 1918, Honoré and Potter, Jr. realized that Chicago could sustain a much larger hotel. The sons hired Holabird and Roche to design this final iteration of their father's dream. The two inherited their parents' entrepreneurial savvy: instead of shutting down the hotel during construction, they built one half at a time, ensuring continual operation. When the Palmer House was completed in 1925, it was said to be the largest hotel in the world, a distinction it would retain for a short two years.

In keeping with previous standards, the new Palmer House displayed extravagant luxury and innovative features. The lobby's ceiling frescoes were a series of twenty-one allegorical paintings by French artist Louis Pierre Rigal, inspired by Bertha's love of the Sistine Chapel. (In 1996, acclaimed art restorer Lido Lippi, who was one of the lead restorers of the Sistine Chapel paintings, restored those at the Palmer House.) Women had their own floor and each room had a bathtub. Retail stores lined the street level, including C.D. Peacock, a jeweler that began as House of Peacock in 1837 and was the first registered business in Chicago. When the retailer moved into its new Palmer House location, customers entered through bronze hand-forged doors decorated with peacocks. Designed by Louis Comfort Tiffany, they weighed more than a ton. Three restaurants served guests, including the extravagant Empire Dining Room. In 1933, the Empire Room was converted into the hottest supper club in town. For more than forty years, diners heard artists who would become legends, including Ella Fitzgerald, Harry Belafonte, Frank Sinatra, and Louis Armstrong.

Unlike many of its competitors, the Palmer House survived the Depression, but it was soon to leave the Palmer family. Enterprising hotelier Conrad Hilton came to Chicago to buy The Stevens in 1945. When its owner, Stephen A. Healy, kept changing the selling price, Hilton's broker threatened that they'd just buy the Palmer House instead. In the end, Conrad ended up with both.

The hotel changed hands once again in 2005. Its current owners, Thor Equities, completely renovated the hotel from 2007 to 2009 to a tune of $170 million.

Palmer House Today

Entering the Palmer House Hilton is a return to the glitz and glamour of the Roaring Twenties. It begins from the moment you swing through the revolving entry and see those priceless peacock doors. At the landing of the travertine staircase, a sculpture of Romeo and Juliet reminds guests of the inherent romance of the hotel. The real magic happens when you turn left or right and ascend the last few steps into the lobby. The ceiling murals sparkle after another restoration in 2019, as do the massive 1.25-ton, 24-karat gold Tiffany & Co. candelabras. From the moment you enter Palmer House Hilton, you'll feel like you've entered a museum. In a sense, you have.

1873
Bryant Block
Delaware Building

I f you want a taste of what Chicago looked like before the
fire, take a gander at the Delaware Building. Ignoring the
growth of the city around it, this Italianate beauty has

barely been touched and is one of the few structures to retain its 1870s character.

For many years, a McDonald's occupied the first floor. It's now closed, but there's a common reaction, invariably laced with scorn, upon learning that this building is one of the oldest in downtown Chicago: "And there was a *McDonald's* in it!" The general consensus is that a fast-food restaurant wasn't dignified enough for a structure that's been around since 1873. A look at the building's beginnings, however, reveals that there have been decidedly less savory tenants than a purveyor of burgers and fries.

Right after the fire of 1871, James M. Bryant, Esq., hired architectural firm Wheelock and Thomas to rebuild his property at the corner of Randolph and Dearborn. Otis Wheelock was nearly as well known as John M. Van Osdel. Otis arrived in Chicago in 1839, just two years after the city's first architect, but he didn't stay long. He left his hometown of Cambridge, New York, in the spring, hitching a ride on a lumber wagon and then crossing the Great Lakes in the steamer "New England." Chicago wasn't his destination, but his journey took so long that he arrived a day after the last boat of the season departed. Stuck in Chicago over the winter, Otis worked on the old Tremont House and the Clybourne House, which would be the city's first brick building. When he still hadn't been paid for his work in the spring, he left in disgust and headed to Watertown, New York.

He stayed upstate for a bit, then went to New York City and worked with architect Minard Lefevre before heading back to Watertown. Otis was there on May 13, 1849, when a "Great Fire" devastated the town. He stayed and helped rebuild the community, until by the end of 1855 he'd run out of potential commissions.

Otis and his wife, Minerva, arrived in Chicago in January of 1856. He partnered with W. W. Boyington for two years, and during that time they designed the State Penitentiary in Joliet. Otis then went solo, and in 1871, another Great Fire wreaked devastation. Like his time in Watertown, he was overwhelmed with work, and he partnered with Cyrus

Thomas in 1872. Cyrus had come to Chicago from Canada the year before the fire, and the two worked together until December, 1875. During that time, they designed and built Bryant's Block.

In Chicago's early years, multi-unit buildings were often named for the person or company who owned or built them, followed by Block. Bryant Block, on the northeast corner of Dearborn and Randolph, was named for James M. Bryant. Newspaper ads and classified listings would list Bryant Block instead of the actual street address. In *The Stranger's Guide to the City of Chicago* of 1873, Bryant Block was listed among other "Notable Buildings" like Farwell Block, Palmer's Block, Methodist Church Block, and Drake Block—which was burnt and rebuilt for the fourth time.

James didn't actually live in the building, or even manage it. Instead, he hired others to rent the offices and apartments. This didn't turn out so well. In the late 1870s the Chicago Tribune reported multiple stories of arrests, labeling it "notorious." A letter to the editor on June 21, 1879, headlined *The Odorous Bryant Block* and signed by Decency called it one of the very lowest and most degraded dens that infests Chicago. "All day long, all night long," wrote Decency, "in and out go the scores of pimps, thieves, and prostitutes, while before its very entrance stalks back and forth a thing that answers to the name of a policeman, but which evidently cares as little about what is going on under its very nose as does a last year's bird nest." Three days later, More Decency wrote:

> "The janitor (?) of the Bryant Block has not held his office long enough, possibly, to ascertain the character of his tenants. If he has observed nothing disrespectful in their conduct in the daily contact of his official life, he should retire to a distance and take a bird's-eye view of the premises, say from the upper south windows of the Tremont House, where he can see a panorama of vice that is simply 'megatherian' in extent, and for variety surpassing all other establishments."

Not just vice, but *megatherian* vice.

Bryant replied that he had nothing to do with the building and hadn't for years and that it was all Henry P. Isham's fault (whoever he was).

The tenants changed and by 1885, the Bryant Block was filled with "printers, engravers, lawyers, and real-estate men," but somehow the building failed to produce a net income. At least, that's what Bryant's heirs claimed as they fought pesky things like liens and back taxes, and an incredulous court sent the case to a master of chancery to examine the situation. It must not have worked out, because in 1889 Julius H. Huber remodeled the first two floors, added two more to the top, and crowned it with a denticulated cornice and a wrought-iron balustrade. The Real Estate Board moved in, and for the next two decades Bryant's Block was known as the Real Estate Board Building.

The Real Estate Board sold the building in 1910, and at some point, the name changed again, this time to the Delaware Building. Ads for H. R. Enlow, M.D. in 1912 listed a location in the Delaware Building at 36 West Randolph Street. In 1930, investigators discovered a cache of machine guns and forty pints of whisky and gin in one of the building's upper floors.

Delaware Building Today

The Delaware Building, despite its historic status and its prime Loop location, is still struggling. Not only is it in need of a facelift, there was another foreclosure in 2018. There have been talks of turning it into apartments, a shared office space, or a hotel. Hopefully, someone will step in and one of Chicago's oldest landmarks will be around for a long time to come.

1883
Nickerson Mansion
Driehaus Museum

W hen Samuel and Matilda Nickerson decided to
build their new home in 1879 they did *not* mess
around. They chose the hottest neighborhood, the
best architect, and the safest and most expensive materials
they could find. The Nickersons wanted a place that would be
around for a while and they were willing to pay for it. And boy,
did they ever. By the time they moved in four years later,

they'd spent $450,000, or the equivalent of $100,000,000, give or take a few thousand. That's a lot of moolah by any standards, but that's what happens when you build an entirely fireproof structure and hire three decorators.

Samuel grew up in Chatham, Massachusetts, and Matilda in nearby Brewster. It's probably safe to assume they knew each other as kids since they were cousins. Like many young men, especially in the mid-1800s, Samuel wanted to make his mark. His dad gave him boat fare and he headed down the coast when he was seventeen, joining up with his brother, Sparrow, in Florida. After briefly working with his sibling at the general store, a few customers were so impressed with Samuel that they loaned him money to open his own place. That went well, but then a fire burned his store in 1857 and Samuel lost everything. Sadly, that wasn't the last time that would happen.

During his time as a shop owner he had, "through no plunging or speculation, made some obligations," according to an article in the *Chicago Daily Tribune* from March 30, 1890. Samuel made his way to Chicago in 1858 and got into the distilling and wine business. Before the end of the year, he'd returned to Massachusetts to marry Matilda and bring her back west.

Like Potter Palmer, who'd made a chunk of his fortune speculating on cotton during the Civil War, the conflict improved Samuel's finances. In addition to liquor he also dabbled in explosives, two items that were in high demand. This financial success enabled him to pay off his creditors in Florida, even though no one came after him for it. In 1863, mid-war, he left the distilling business entirely. By that time he'd amassed enough money to help start First National Bank of Chicago and was its first Vice President. He invested in the Chicago City railway company. He became President of the bank in 1867, and that same year he helped organize Union Stock-Yard National Bank and held the office of President for that one, too.

Everything looked grand for Samuel and Matilda. They had a fine son named Roland, an active social life, and were rolling

59

in dough. They had a lovely home in a quiet neighborhood at the corner of Cass and Superior.

Until disaster struck again and the Nickersons, like 100,000 other Chicagoans, lost everything. Fortunately, although the First National Bank of Chicago's building burned to the ground in the Great Chicago Fire, the vaults did not. Within three months, on January 1, 1872, First National Bank was back in business.

While the bank rebuilt quickly, Samuel and Matilda chose to rent on the west side of town. It wasn't until 1879 that they hired Edward Burling of Burling and Whitehouse to design a new home. They chose this specific architect because he was known to be passionate about fireproofing. What he came up with would have mollified even the most skittish of fire victims: iron wrapped in brick embedded in mortar, clad in sandstone and limestone, and not a single speck of plaster. There were two fireproof vaults. The home was three stories and 24,000 square feet of extravagance and took four years to complete.

Inside, the Nickersons displayed their wealth with grandiose and nearly ludicrous excess. Each room's parquet floor was laid in a different pattern. At a time when a working man's annual wage averaged $350 a year, Samuel and Matilda paid $3 per tile to line their reception room. Materials used to create this masterpiece mansion included onyx, alabaster, glass mosaics, ebony, walnut, and seventeen kinds of marble. The latter earned it the nickname of "The Marble Palace." It could also have been called a Carved Castle: craftsmen carved the walls of the dining room, the wainscoting, the library's built-in bookcases, the door jams. After settling in, the Nickersons installed electric lighting, and it was one of the first residences to use this cleaner and healthier alternative to gas lamps.

In addition to the reception room, front parlor, smoking room, library, ballroom, and drawing room, Samuel and Matilda's new home had an art gallery where they displayed European paintings and objects from Japan, China, and Korea. By the time they retired to New York in 1900, they'd accumulated over 1,300 works of art. Their collection was so vast that when they donated it all to the Art Institute of Chicago, the museum needed two galleries and a corridor to display it.

"Perhaps the most munificent single gift ever received by the Art Institute as the Institute catalogue states, was the collection of art objects and paintings presented by Mr. and Mrs. Samuel Nickerson. For the housing of these beautiful art treasures the donors bore the expense of fitting up two galleries and an adjacent corridor with marble wainscoting and mosaic floor, besides numerous cabinets." *Musical courier: a weekly journal devoted to music and the music trades, July 1, 1896*

The Nickersons' civic involvement went beyond their arts endowment, and it seems they were truly invested in the culture of the city. Samuel was appointed as a Lincoln Park Commissioner the month after the fire, and he helped fund the Chicago Music Festival, which would become the Chicago Symphony Orchestra. He was already a lifetime member of the Chicago Historical Society and was a founding trustee of the Chicago Academy of Fine Arts, later to be called the Art Institute. Matilda was a north division manager of the Chicago Exchange for Woman's Work, a philanthropic organization that helped indigent women sell things they created for a commission. In 1881, she became its Vice President. For the last four years of their Chicago residency, she was the President of the Society of Colonial Dames.

When Samuel retired, the couple sold their showcase mansion to Lucius Fisher, President of the Union Bag and Paper Company. Mr. Fisher wanted a man cave and hired George Washington Maher to give him one. Maher turned the art gallery into a trophy room lined with animal heads, rare books, and historical weapons. He replaced the former gallery's skylight with a multi-colored stained glass dome and installed a monumental fireplace with an iridescent tile surround.

The Fisher family owned the home until Lucius' death in 1916. For three years, the mansion languished until the threat of demolition loomed. In what may have been the first successful preservation effort in Chicago, more than one hundred men, women, and businesses pooled their money, bought the place, and gave it to the American College of Surgeons. The recipients, although thrilled with the gift, needed more room and they couldn't tear the building down, couldn't make it bigger, and couldn't make any structural changes. Their solution was to build the John B. Murphy Memorial Auditorium next door. The College used the two buildings until they outgrew them in 1965 and rented them out. The first tenant was an advertising firm, followed by R. H. Love Art Gallery. The latter is why the Driehaus Museum exists.

Nickerson Mansion Today

In 2003, Richard Driehaus walked into the R. H. Love Art Gallery with an antique dealer. The wealthy art and history aficionado had his eye on a bust of Abraham Lincoln. Buzz Harper, the antique expert, took one look at the mansion and told Mr. Driehaus: "Forget the bust; buy the building!" And so he did.

After five years of painstaking restoration, including employing an innovative technique using lasers to remove soot that had turned its exterior black, the Driehaus Museum invited the public to marvel at this glorious building. It's decorated with pieces from the late 19th and early 20th centuries, and many of the furnishings and decorations are from Mr. Driehaus's personal collection. There's a vast number of Louis Comfort Tiffany items as well as pieces from the 1893 World's Columbian Exposition and furniture by the

Herter Brothers. Richard Driehaus passed away in 2021, but his legacy continues in this Marble Palace.

1885
Studebaker Brothers' Lake Front Carriage Repository
Fine Arts Building

L   ate 19th century Chicago was a chorus of get things
    done. It was industrial. It was driven. It was
    determined. By the 1880s, Chicago had rebuilt from
the devastation of the fire of 1871 and another in 1874 in
spectacular fashion. The Studebaker Corporation, carriage

makers from South Bend, Indiana, wanted to take full advantage of the excitement. Although they'd had a Chicago presence, it was time to ramp things up. That meant a big, beautiful building in plain sight of their potential customers. They bought a lot on Michigan Avenue and hired Solon Spencer Beman, the architect of Pullman's company town, to make it happen. Beman came up with an eight-story showplace that featured four stories of showrooms topped with four stories for assembly.

When it was completed, the Studebaker Brothers' Lake Front Carriage Repository was a tour de force of rusticated stone, limestone piers, and granite columns. There was an absurd amount of glass because the company needed gigantic windows to show off its wares. While it wasn't the original intention, that glass made the building especially suited for what it would become.

Studebaker outgrew its Romanesque repository in short order and hired Beman to create a new building on Wabash Avenue. Even though the company was moving out, Studebaker also asked the architect to redesign their Michigan Avenue building. At the urging of their friend Charles C. Curtiss, the Studebakers decided to turn the structure into a vertical arts center. To accommodate the building's new mission, Beman took off the top floor and added three. He converted the showrooms, offices, and assembly facilities into studios. He gave the new top floor skylights and 23-foot ceilings, and the first floor gained two auditoriums. On the fourth floor, in the center of the building, Beman turned the lightwell into a Venetian Court featuring a fountain and fresh air.

Would this work? Could a city bent on commerce and industry welcome an artist colony, especially in some of its most valuable real estate?

The answer was a resounding yes. Completed in 1898 and renamed the Fine Arts Building, the location meant tenants had easy access to the Art Institute of Chicago and the Auditorium Building. Architects would be near their clients. Most importantly, the artists would be near each other.

Curtiss, whose father was a former two-term mayor of Chicago, knew that artists gravitated towards one another. He'd been watching the Tree Studios arts colony that Judge Lambert Tree had started north of the river. He himself had built Weber Music Hall, "reputed to be the first building in the city designed exclusively for musicians' and artists' studios," according to the City of Chicago Landmark Designation Report.

Even though he believed in the concept, you have to wonder if Curtiss had any idea of what a hotbed of creativity and controversial characters it would become.

In its early years, the Fine Arts Building was a crucible of talented artists, writers, and publishers, of strong personalities and social justice. L. Frank Baum and William Denslow met in their studios to collaborate on *The Wonderful Wizard of Oz*. Illustrators (and brothers) Frank X. and Joseph C. Leyendecker convinced fellow artists to paint murals on the tenth floor. Jane Addams met with another set of brothers; Allen and Irving Kane Pond designed most of the Hull-House buildings. Irving, who'd worked for Solon Beman on the initial design of Pullman, was a circus fan known for doing backflips, especially after waltzing with Isadora Duncan.

That last bit happened at a meeting of *The Little Room*, a social group that grew out of the habit of gathering in Ralph Clarkson's top floor studio for tea and conversation. On Friday afternoons, Theodore Thomas's Chicago Orchestra performed at the neighboring Auditorium Theatre, and afterward, the artists would cross the bridge that connected the buildings on the tenth floor. This became quite the get-together and continued even after the orchestra moved up the street to its new hall in 1904. The artists and writers would discuss, debate, and put on plays for each other. The afternoon soirees would often last into the wee hours, and one can only imagine the shenanigans these creative types got into. If you were a member of The Little Room, you were definitely one of the cool kids.

This was a place that welcomed all, whether they got along or not. Francis Fisher Brown published the conservative literary journal *The Dial* from its halls. *Poetry*, founded by Harriet Monroe, printed work by Gwendolyn Brooks, Langston Hughes, and Carl Sandburg. When Monroe published Sandburg's "Chicago," editors at *The Dial* mocked the poem and called the magazine a "futile little periodical." Monroe wrote a scathing reply, and the proof is in the *Poetry*: her magazine is still around and *The Dial* died in 1929 (although the current bookshop in the Fine Arts Building is named for the publication.)

The Little Review also pushed boundaries, and so did Margaret Anderson. Her avant-garde publication gave voice to writers who became legends, like Ernest Hemingway, Ezra Pound, and James Joyce. The latter got Margaret and her partner, Jane Heap, arrested. Jane had joined Margaret in 1916 and the couple moved to New York City in 1917. They began posting excerpts from Joyce's *Ulysses* and the people of New York thought that was scandalous—scandalous enough to arrest them. The women were convicted of obscenity and fined $50 each.

Other tenants included Lorado Taft, Frank Lloyd Wright, the Daughters of the American Revolution, and both the Illinois Equal Suffrage Association and the Cook County Woman's Suffrage Party. Those two organizations helped Illinois become the first state east of the Mississippi River to grant women the right to vote. Rose Farwell Chatfield-Taylor, Vice President of the North Side Branch of the Illinois Woman Suffrage League and Western Women's golf champion, opened a book bindery.

The Fine Arts Building was simply a madhouse of people who made things and made things happen.

In 1928, Curtiss died and in 1931 The Little Room disbanded. The party didn't quite end, but things quieted down. The building changed hands multiple times over the next several decades, but surprisingly the only part that went through any sort of upheaval was the theaters. Various owners tried to make them work, even turning them into a movie theater multiplex with four screens. The lowest point was in 1971 when the foreign films were augmented with adult films.

Through it all, though, the Fine Arts Building continued to be a home for creativity and social justice.

Studebaker Brothers' Lake Front Carriage Repository Today

The Fine Arts Building of today is very much, at its core, similar to what it was in the early 1900s. It is a place of art, creativity, and connection. The directory categories are architecture, design, dance, music, visual artist, restorer, piano studio, instructor, therapist, and "other." The on-site bookstore is named *The Dial*, after the literary magazine that was once headquartered in the building. The elevator is still operated by a real person.

1887
Glessner House

T he building on the corner of 18th and Prairie is like a
lava cake rolled in a thick layer of coarsely chopped
nuts. On the outside, it's crunchy and looks like it
could hurt you. But inside, it's all warm and gooey and makes
you feel loved.

In 1880s Chicago, Prairie Avenue was all the rage. During
the previous decade, the comparatively humble Clarke House
had moved out and millionaire mansions moved in. Marshall
Field lived there. So did Philip Armour, of Armour &
Company, and William Kimball, the piano maker. John and
Frances Glessner had a comfortable home on the west side,

but as frequent entertainers who also had two kids, they needed some more space—17,000 square feet of space. So they bought a corner lot in a tony neighborhood and brought in an east coast architect by the name of Henry Hobson Richardson.

Richardson was known for his bold, unique style. It was so distinctive people had a name for it: Richardsonian Romanesque. He was only the second American to attend the famed École des Beaux Arts, a forerunner of what would become a near stampede of American architects in Paris. Upon his return to the states, he eschewed the more traditional, classical designs for his own New World aesthetic. His horizontal lines and innovative use of space inspired Louis Sullivan, Frank Lloyd Wright, and a whole slew of successors.

There was no mistaking a Richardson design, and when the Glessners moved into their new home in 1887, some of the neighbors weren't too happy. Not with the lovely family; it was the house that was the problem. It didn't fit in. It was so close to the lot line it was practically in the street. There were barely any windows—that they could see as they gazed out their own. The heavy front door sat at ground level. What happened to the stairs? Didn't they know a proper home should have stairs to its entrance? The servants had a more impressive entryway, for goodness' sake. George Pullman, the man who'd lifted a city, made train travel luxurious, and built his own company town, was appalled. "I don't know what I have ever done to have that thing staring me in the face every time I go out of my door," he bemoaned.

The exterior may have been imposing, but for the Glessners it was perfect. John and Frances had their own secret garden. Behind the stone walls lay a hidden courtyard. The interior of their home was warm, sunny, and inviting and the Glessners welcomed many into their cozy urban castle. "For all its granite," Mrs. Glessner said, "this home is wonderfully elastic. You can squeeze as many as you want into it."

Even though they entertained, there was no ballroom. The rooms were intimate, with low ceilings and no vast spaces. The massive Parker desk in the library enabled husband and wife to sit across from each other while they worked. Every servant, and the Glessners employed eight, had her own room. To the consternation of their neighbors who had certain ideas of a servant's station, these quarters each had a window that looked upon the courtyard and individual closets. What next, they must have wondered, private bathrooms?

The couple met in 1863 when John boarded with Frances and her mother in Springfield, Ohio. John was a twenty-year-old young man beginning his career in the farm implement industry. Frances was fifteen. Over the next seven years, his career blossomed, and so did their relationship. The two married on December 7, 1870, and moved to Chicago on December 15. Nine years later, John became a full partner in Warder, Bushnell and Glessner. Agricultural machinery was going gangbusters and the Glessner fortunes rose.

John and Frances lived on Washington Street on the west side of town when they hired the boisterous and robust, and boisterously robust, H. H. Richardson. While the architect may not have been for everyone, H. H. understood the Glessners to a tee. After observing an image of Abingdon Abbey on their walls, he quickly sketched out what would become their new home. They loved it, especially how it was uniquely theirs. Sadly, Richardson passed away three weeks after completing their design. Shepley, Rutan and Coolidge carried on his mantle.

The Glessners were not what you might picture when you think of late 19th-century wealthy folk. John, the scion of reapers and mowers, wrote sweet letters to his children when they vacationed at their summer home in New England. The image of a man creating a 36-page leather-bound rebus with pasted pictures and hand-drawn sketches like a lion for "lie on" is not what pops into one's head. Yet, that was John Glessner. He also surprised his wife one year for her birthday by sneaking members of the Chicago Orchestra, led by founding conductor Theodore Thomas, in through the servants' entrance to perform for her special day. Granted, the Glessners were huge supporters, and the early Chicago Symphony Orchestra performed at their house often, but still. Pretty thoughtful, Mr. Glessner.

John, and this should come as no surprise, was also a philanthropist of the highest order. Many of his peers were members of various boards and donated oodles of money. John's memberships seemed to represent an awareness of social responsibility. The Chicago Relief and Aid Society, Chicago Orphan Asylum, Rush Medical College, and the Citizens Association of Chicago all received contributions of his time and money. So did the Art Institute of Chicago, the Union League Club, and the Quadrangle Literature Club. You have to wonder when the man had time to sleep.

Same with Frances. Frances was a doer. She knitted. For herself, for children (not just her own), for her employees, for servicemen. She was a seamstress and a needleworker. She was an accomplished pianist. She was a trained silversmith with a workbench in her basement and her own logo: a G wrapped around a honeybee (beekeeping was another of her passions). Silversmithing was no passing hobby. Frances tutored under Hull-House instructor Annibale Fogliata as well as Madeline Yale Wynne. Wynne was a noted artist and a charter member of the Chicago Arts and Crafts Society, which included Frank Lloyd Wright on its rolls. Wynne also wrote *The Little Room*, the title that artists in the Fine Arts Building used for their social club.

Frances co-founded the Chicago Chamber Music Society. She belonged to The Fortnightly with Jane Addams and Bertha Palmer. She was a member of the Colonial Dames and a founding member of the Chicago chapter of the Daughters of the American Revolution. She attended all rehearsals and performances of the Chicago Orchestra.

And, for thirty-seven years, Frances hosted the Monday Morning Reading Class. Each week from October through May, by invitation only, women arrived at the Glessner House for education, socialization, and lunch. During the first hour, the ladies would sew while they listened to a professional reader. The second hour was devoted to a lighter reading or a lecture. After that, they'd retire to the dining room and parlor for lunch. Women had to be married, with few exceptions, and they had to live on the south side of Chicago. However, if they had been invited and then moved north of the river, they could still attend.

Here's something that won't surprise you in the slightest: the Glessner kids were special, too. George was born six days before the Great Chicago Fire in a home west of the burn zone. Photography fascinated him and he had his very own darkroom in the basement of the Prairie Avenue mansion. George photographed the entire house and kept meticulous records, a hobby that came in handy for preservationists. He installed telegraphs so he could communicate with his friends, and a fire signal repeater so he could keep track of fire engines. After graduating from Harvard, he joined his father in what would become International Harvester. He, his wife Alice, and their four kids moved to the Glessner's New Hampshire summer home in 1916 where he served in the state legislature for four terms.

The Glessners' daughter, Fanny, was precocious and independent; when her marriage proved unhappy, she divorced. Like her brother, she also went east. In 1918, she managed a half-way house in Boston for soldiers and sailors returning from World War I.

What Fanny, or Frances Glessner Lee, is most remembered for is her contribution to forensic science. She'd developed a friendship with Boston's chief medical examiner, George Burgess Magrath. His work so fascinated her that she donated $250,000 to Harvard University in 1931 so they'd create a chair in legal medicine named for him. Not content to merely throw money, she dove right into studying this new field herself. She did that by creating dollhouses. These weren't your standard frilly playthings. These were painstakingly accurate miniature crime scenes, complete with bloating corpses and windows that opened. She called these dioramas the "Nutshell Studies of Unexplained Death," and they changed the course of police investigations. The Maryland Medical Examiner Office still uses them for training.

The Glessners were truly a remarkable family. George passed away in 1929, Frances in 1932, John in 1936, and Fanny in 1962.

Back to the house. John's will decreed that their Prairie Avenue home, which he'd lived in for nearly fifty years, should become "a museum, library, gallery, and educational institution, including a school of design for legitimate architectural assemblages." However, because he died in the midst of the Great Depression, the bequest proved too expensive for the American Institute of Architects. They gave it back to the Glessner estate, who sold it to the Armour Institute of Technology (later Illinois Institute of Technology) in 1938. From 1946 until 1965, the Lithographic Technical Foundation used the building until moving to Pennsylvania. Like the Nickerson Mansion, there was real concern that the historic home would be demolished, so a group of concerned citizens banded together to save it. The newly-formed Chicago School of Architecture Foundation bought the Glessner home in December of 1966. That organization would become the Chicago Architecture Foundation, now the Chicago Architecture Center.

Glessner House Today

Walk into the Glessner House Museum and you'll know how the Glessners lived. You'll see the books they read, the plates they used, and the piano Frances played. Once the Chicago School of Architecture Foundation purchased the home, John's request to use his beloved mansion as a museum and home for architecture could finally be honored. The family began returning belongings and now 90 to 95 percent of the furnishings are original. It's a remarkable collection of late 19th- and early 20th-century decor as well as personal pieces that were important to the Glessners. There's a portrait of H.H. Richardson, for example, as well as a shadow box dedicated to Theodore Thomas containing a palm frond from his funeral and one of the last batons he used to conduct the Chicago Symphony Orchestra. Frances gave John a copper relief portrait by Augustus Saint-Gaudens, the same sculptor who created the monuments of Abraham Lincoln in Grant and Lincoln Parks. On John's side of the Parker Desk is a bronze life mask and hands of President Lincoln, also by Saint-Gaudens. On Frances' side is a diminutive bronze known as "Rolling Bear Cub," the work of New York artist Anna Hyatt Huntington.

Because of George's photography obsession, Frances' diary of forty years, and John's 1923 record *The Story of a House*, preservationists and restorers knew exactly where every item belonged.

1888
The Rookery

O ne of the most celebrated buildings in a city of
celebrated buildings is The Rookery. There are many
reasons for this status. One is because it's one of the
oldest surviving high-rises in downtown Chicago. Another is
its innovative foundation, which has kept it upright despite

being planted on a muddy morass. There's also the beauty of the building itself, with its multicultural influences and fanciful decorations, but perhaps most importantly, it's celebrated because of the gentlemen who designed it.

The Rookery has a powerful presence. As Ira J. Bach said in *Chicago's Famous Buildings*, published in 1965: "It stands there like a stronghearted and cheerful person, forceful yet friendly."

"Forceful yet friendly" could well be used to describe architect Daniel Burnham, and "stronghearted and cheerful" his relationship with his partner, John Root. The pair, although very different, were well suited to each other and left behind one of the most, well, celebrated architectural legacies in Chicago.

Daniel Hudson Burnham, born September 4, 1846 in Henderson, New York, arrived in Chicago with his mother and six siblings in 1855. They were rejoining his father, Mr. Edwin Burnham, who'd headed west earlier. This was not where Edwin wanted to go, and if he'd had any say in the matter, the family would have moved to Rome, New York, but his wife had other plans. Indeed, Elizabeth insisted—with emphasis—that Edwin try Chicago. Edwin's brother was already there and doing well as an attorney, and even from across the country she could see what was happening in the young city. Her children would have a future there, much more than they would in Rome.

When Edwin arrived he tried a venture at a stone quarry in Joliet. According to Charles Moore in his 1921 biography of Daniel, that first business "came to grief because of the dishonesty of the partner, Skelly by name; and quite in despair he contemplated another retreat to Henderson. To forestall this purpose, the determined Mrs. Burnham broke up the home and shipped the furniture to Chicago."

Don't mess with Elizabeth.

Edwin ended up in the wholesale drug business and became quite a successful merchant, successful enough to get his son Daniel out of a few sticky situations. The first was when, at the age of fifteen, Daniel decided to enlist in the

Nineteenth Illinois Infantry so he could fight in the Civil War. His dad extricated him from that predicament, to the young man's disgust. Daniel went back to school, but he wasn't the best student. The only things that kept him from failing were his exceedingly good manners and his "facility in blackboard creations in colored crayons." He was certainly different from his classmates Ferd Peck and Edward Waller, the latter of whom would be his lifelong friend.

When Daniel was seventeen, his father sent him and two of his sisters to Massachusetts so he could attend the New Church School. Two years later, Reverend Tilly Brown Hayward, a Harvard graduate, tutored the young man to prepare him for entrance examinations. Daniel failed to get into either Harvard or Yale, but he did discover architecture. He was nowhere near ready to settle down, though. Back in Chicago, after an unsuccessful gig at a mercantile house, Edwin took him to the young architecture firm of Loring and Jenney, where he apprenticed for an entire year. But Daniel still had a few wild oats to sow and he took off to Nevada. One account said he was hunting for gold. Another that he'd fallen in with a bunch of Frenchmen who had a mad colonization scheme. Both said he ran for state senate, and lost. Either way, he was back in Chicago before the fire. Still at loose ends after the city burned, he tried selling plate glass. He tried being a druggist. Neither of those worked out either, so his dad dropped him at the feet of Peter Wight. You can almost picture him saying "Fix him, please!"

This time, it worked. Daniel worked as a draftsman at the firm of Carter, Drake and Wight, and it was there that he met John Wellborn Root.

While Daniel kind of fell into the field, John was born to be an architect. He was a precocious boy who played the violin when he was two and by the age of seven was drawing family portraits. His father, a frustrated wannabe-architect, decided that John would have the career he didn't. Fortunately, that's what John wanted, too. He was born on January 10, 1850, in Lumpkin, Georgia, and his dad, a blockade runner in the war, sent him to England in 1864 when he was fourteen. Four years later, John attended the College of the City of New York and studied engineering. He dreamed of studying at École des Beaux Arts, where all the best architects studied, but family money had dried up. So, he took an unpaid apprenticeship for a year, then took a paying job with a Mr. Snook. At some point he met Peter Wight and followed him to Chicago.

When Daniel and John met in 1872, it was like two halves had been made whole. They immediately clicked, and the next spring opened their own practice. The early years were lean, filled with long hours. They were young and inexperienced, but with John's design talent and Daniel's charm and newfound persistence, they managed to survive. The big break happened when one of John's friends, George Chambers, convinced Union Stock Yard superintendent John B. Sherman that he should consider hiring the young firm to design his new house. John Root was out of town the day of the scheduled meeting, so Daniel met with him instead. That was a good thing, because where John hated talking business, Daniel was about as charming as they came. In the end, he secured both the commission for the Prairie Avenue house and the hand of Margaret, Mr. Sherman's daughter.

After that, Burnham and Root soared. In 1882, Root unveiled his first attempt at what would be called a floating foundation with the ten-story Montauk Block. This early skyscraper got around the soft clay earth by creating a "raft" of crisscrossed iron bars encased in concrete. Then, in 1885, the Brooks Brothers (yes, those Brooks Brothers) and their agent Owen Aldis hired Daniel and John to build a skyscraper for the Central Safety Deposit Company. The building would immediately be known as The Rookery—whether they liked it or not.

Peter Brooks didn't. He gave Daniel and John a list of at least twenty potential names, but it didn't matter what name was chosen, the building was always going to be called The Rookery. It was the location. That corner had been the site of an iron water tank that survived the Chicago fire and became the first public library. A temporary city hall took shape around it. The water tank and the fire department's stables next door attracted pigeons and rooks. At City Hall, one could expect to get "rooked" by the corrupt politicians. Like it or not, The Rookery it would be.

That same year, William Le Baron Jenney, Daniel's one-time employer, completed the Home Insurance Building. Hailed as the world's first modern skyscraper, it was the first building to use a steel frame instead of pure masonry construction. Daniel and John blended old and new techniques in The Rookery, using steel and iron for the inside frame, masonry for the outer walls, and a floating foundation, called "grillage," to make sure it didn't sink. They even accounted for the inner frame's lighter weight by setting it lower than the masonry.

Outside, John's creativity flowed, reflecting a multitude of influences. The reddish-brown brick and granite decorated with ornate ornamentation exhibited a taste of Queen Anne, Richardsonian Romanesque, Persian, Moorish, Islamic, and Byzantine. John, with his flair for deviltry, as Daniel called it, even included a couple of rooks. Sounds like a mess, but it's harmonious. Inside, Daniel's drafting expertise carved the massive building into six hundred offices with a two-story light court. *Rand McNally's Bird's Eye Views of Chicago, 1893* described walking through the lobby of Carrara marble and mosaic pavement, then entering a "miniature city of shops and booths," including a newsstand, barbershop, telegraph offices, and a café.

Another of the building's distinctive features was the ingenious placement of the fire escape. Instead of stringing up an unsightly zigzag down the side of the building, Burnham and Root put a D-spiral staircase with perforated risers inside the light well. Since it was outside the wall plane, it could technically be considered the fire escape.

Daniel and John moved their offices to the top floor of the eleven-story skyscraper. The choice wasn't just about prestige; it also proved they believed the design to be safe, which was a big concern at a time when such heights were new. The building filled with five thousand tenants, who could take one of ten elevators to get to their offices. As the city began planning the 1893 World's Columbian Exposition, of which Daniel was a driving force, the most influential architects in the country would meet in their sky-high suite.

Daniel's precision, charm, and persistence and John's artistry and creativity combined to create one of the most influential and in-demand architectural firms in the nineteenth century. It helped that they liked each other. When John died, unexpectedly, of pneumonia in 1891, Daniel was heartbroken. Daniel was shaken enough that he wanted to quit the Expo. He said:

> "Our personal relations had been intimate and even fond from the week when first we met. We had lived together for eighteen years without a written agreement — or a quick word — between us. When he died I remained with the Exposition only in deference to the judgment and wishes of my friends among the directors."

By 1905, the light court needed a touch-up, and Daniels' boyhood classmate and long-time friend Edward Waller, who managed The Rookery, knew just the man to do it. Edward had been a long-time patron of Frank Lloyd Wright. Frank updated it by wrapping the iron columns in gilded white marble, replacing John's elaborate ironwork with simpler geometric designs, and adding pendant lighting. This court is the only example of Frank's work in downtown Chicago. In 1931, William Drummond divided the two-story entrance lobby into separate floors and modernized the elevators, replacing the open cages with solid bronze doors that were etched with geometric shapes and, of course, birds.

In the mid-twentieth century the building went through decades of neglect. Somebody even decided it would be "efficient" to paint over and waterproof the light court's glass ceiling. Then in 1988, Baldwin Development Company rescued the landmark and began the restoration process, topping it off with an additional floor. The building reopened in 1992, and before renovations were even done, Brooks

Brothers leased a space of more than twelve thousand square feet.

The Rookery Today

The Rookery stands strong in the heart of the financial district, near the Board of Trade and the Federal Reserve. Tenants have access to a rooftop patio, a bike and runner's room, and the restored Burnham Library. Most of this iconic building is closed to the public, but the light court is open and one of the retail spaces is occupied by the Frank Lloyd Wright Trust.

1889
Auditorium Building

Buildings like the Auditorium don't just spring out of nowhere, especially in a marshy place with sewage problems. Somebody thinks: "You know what we need? We need THIS!" and then figures out how to make it happen.

Ferdinand W. Peck was one of those somebodies. His name doesn't quickly roll off the tongue of Chicago history like Burnham or Palmer or Field, but it should. When his dream of a grand opera theater opened in 1889, he was the fourth richest man in the city, but more than wealth, he made significant cultural and societal contributions whose impact is still felt.

Ferdinand's dad was a Chicagoan before there was a Chicago. His father, Philip Ferdinand Wheeler Peck, arrived in 1831 from New York aboard a schooner named Telegraph. The Captain of the ship was none other than John Naper, the same John Naper that would move west and start his own settlement, which would become known as Naperville. Philip F. W. Peck came prepared for the rugged frontier with supplies, set up shop near Fort Dearborn, and quickly established himself as a successful merchant. He built the first two-story frame structure in the village and took advantage of those early I & M canal lot sales. One of the few to financially survive the panic of 1837, he accumulated real estate until it was said that he was as rich as John Jacob Astor.

In 1835, Philip married Mary K. Wythe from Philadelphia. Of their eight children, only three survived. Ferdinand was the youngest, born on July 15, 1848, in the Peck home on Jackson Boulevard. By the time the young man passed the bar at the age of twenty-one, the family had moved to Michigan Avenue, which meant their home was in the path of the fire. In a cruel twist of fate, P. F. W. Peck, who had been the Second Assistant Engineer of Chicago's first fire department, died from injuries sustained during the blaze.

Ferd, as he was generally known, built on the estate his father had left him, but he did more than just accumulate money. If his legacy is any indication, Ferd had a heightened sense of empathy and devoted much of his energies to philanthropy. He believed in taking care of animals and children and that everyone deserved beautiful music, theater, and dance. He was an officer of the Illinois Humane Society. Founded in 1869 as the Illinois Society for the Prevention of Cruelty to Animals, in 1877 it officially changed its name because of the number of children it protected. He served on Chicago's Board of Education. And, he brought opera to everyone.

Did everyone even *want* opera? After all, opera-goers could afford things like carriages and silk gowns, and were the kind of people whose choice of attire for a performance appeared in the next day's newspaper. What would the workingman or the shop girl care of Verdi or Wagner?

Turns out, quite a lot.

Ferd's proof that his dream of bringing opera to the people would fulfill an actual demand was the Grand Opera Festival of 1885. He hired the young firm of Adler and Sullivan to build a theater within the quasi-temporary Inter-State Industrial Exposition Building. It was a magnificent success, not only because Dankmar Adler had illustrated his acoustic prowess, but also because the place was packed. Thousands filled the auditorium every night, with more waiting to enter. Ferd knew that the city and its people, the real working people and not just his neighbors on Michigan and Prairie Avenues, wanted and needed beautiful, expressive, and theatrical opera.

He began planning. Then, on May 4, 1886, a literal and figurative bomb exploded on the west side. The day before, police had killed strikers protesting for an eight-hour workday at McCormick Reaper Works. Laborers rallied, and when the Mayor showed up he ordered the police to disperse once he noticed the demonstration was peaceful. They didn't. As the last speaker, August Spies, took the stage, two-hundred police swarmed Haymarket Square. A bomb, lobbed by someone unknown, landed in the middle of the police officers. The bomb killed one, but seven more policemen and several protestors died in the ensuing violence. Despite the mystery of who actually threw the bomb and the supposition that most of the police officers died from friendly fire, eight men labeled as anarchists were prosecuted. Four were hung, one committed suicide, and it wasn't until 1894 that Governor John Altgeld pardoned the remaining three.

The injustice of the whole affair kicked Ferd into gear. He was going to build the most magnificent and perfect theater and it would be open to everybody, not just the elite. Ferd used his considerable influence and his most Chicago of pedigrees to secure financing for the grandest grand theater that any city had ever seen. He presented the idea to the Commercial Club. To assuage concerns that the city couldn't sustain the size of theater he wanted, Ferd told them hey, no worries! We're going to include an office building and a hotel. This thing'll pay for itself!

The pitch worked. Investors included Marshall Field, who'd funded the armory for the Chicago police and refused to grant clemency to the alleged anarchists, and George Pullman, who would later lay off thousands of workers but wouldn't reduce their rents. On December 8, seven months after the Haymarket Riot, Ferdinand Peck incorporated the Chicago Auditorium Association.

Ferd hired Adler and Sullivan again. They were a perfect pair: Dankmar Adler would handle the engineering and acoustics, and Louis Sullivan would make it all look good. The new Marshall Field wholesale store inspired their design, which would be ironic except for the fact that the warehouse had been designed by H. H. Richardson, an architect who greatly influenced the up-and-coming Sullivan. Dankmar and Louis drafted an immense ten-story building with a sixteen-story tower constructed of brick and clad in terra cotta with ornate embellishments. After some criticism from other prominent architects, namely Daniel Burnham's partner John Wellborn Root, the lighter material was traded in for load-bearing granite. Heavy, load-bearing granite.

Excavation began January 28, 1887. This building would end up weighing 110,000 tons, and here they were digging into soft blue clay. They'd have to dig down more than a hundred feet to get to solid bedrock. Dankmar worked with fellow engineer Paul Mueller to design a raft, an innovation invented by Root. The engineers crossed railroad ties, topped them with steel beams, and coated the whole thing in pitch, which made it watertight. Ta-da! A floating raft foundation that would sustain the weight of the building and wouldn't rot away even though it was below the water level.

For the most part, the floating raft foundation worked. The building's still there, but if you enter the theater lobby you'll notice there's a tilt to it. That's because after construction began Ferd decided to add another two stories to the tower, which caused the floor to sink up to three feet.

Construction began on June 1, 1887, and President Grover Cleveland laid the cornerstone a few months later. Dankmar and Louis were cutting it close; they'd promised the building would be ready for the Republication National Convention the next summer. In February of 1888 they hired a young draftsman named Frank Lloyd Wright. They scrambled to complete this new Auditorium Building, but they were doing things that had never been done before. It would be the largest theater in the largest building in the world, with the tallest elevator shaft, a hydraulic stage with equipment seven feet below the water level, and air conditioning. The theater would be the first one lit entirely by incandescent bulbs. Drop-down ceiling panels would allow companies to curtain the top balconies for more intimate performances. There were 4,200 seats and only 200 of them box seats, and those were set to the sides as an afterthought. Most impressive of all, Dankmar, without the aid of scientific calculations, designed a theater with perfect acoustics. The bullhorn shape, itself an innovation, transmitted a whisper from the stage to the furthest point in the highest balcony.

There were no bad seats, which is exactly the democratic environment Peck had envisioned.

That all came with a cost, of both time and money. When June of 1888 rolled around, the Republicans nominated Benjamin Harrison in a building that was only five stories tall. By the time President Harrison returned on December 9, 1889, the final tally was more than $3,200,000. But oh, what a theater it was. Decorated by Louis and his young protege, Frank Lloyd Wright, in gold leaf, metal, terra cotta, onyx and stencils, with life-size murals and 55 million pieces of marble tile and lit by 3,500 Edison bulbs, it was transcendent. As the President said on opening night:

"It is my wish, and may it be the wish of all, that this great building may continue to be to all your population that which it should be — an edifice opening its doors from night to night, calling your people here away from the care of business to those enjoyments, and pursuits, and entertainments which develop the souls of men, which will have power to inspire those whose lives are heavy with daily toil, and in its magnificent and enchanting presence lift them for a timeout of these dull things into those higher things where men should live."

Dankmar and Louis moved into offices on the top floor of the tower. The tower became an observation deck, with a 32-foot bilevel turret. The theater was loved by everyone, including the people who'd inspired Ferd in the first place. He sponsored "workingmen's concerts," subsidizing tickets so those who normally wouldn't be able to afford this luxury could attend. The only bah humbug seemed to be Theodore Thomas, founder of the Chicago Symphony Orchestra. According to *Chicago's Left Bank*, by Alson J. Smith, Theodore was not a fan:

"The stage was deep, the acoustics perfect. But to Thomas it was a cavern; the necessary rapport between orchestra and audience could not be established. Moreover, since there were always empty seats, it was difficult to sell season tickets. It cost so much to heat and light it that rehearsals had to be held in other, smaller halls."

In 1893 the World's Columbian Exposition put Chicago center stage, and Ferd showcased his grand opera house to the world. It received universal acclaim. The building also brought recognition to the firm of Adler and Sullivan, as it should. But despite its innovation and beauty and perfection, the Auditorium Building suffered; the projected subsidizing of the theater by the offices and hotel never materialized. The offices were too close to the tracks on Wabash, and hotel guests thought one bathroom for every ten rooms was woefully inadequate. With the exception of Thomas, who'd taken his orchestra up the street to the new Symphony Hall in 1904, performers still loved it. From 1910 to 1929 the Chicago Opera Association, which would reorganize a few times before becoming the Chicago Civic Opera Company, invited tenors and sopranos and altos and baritones to test those pristine, precise acoustics. But when the opera got its own building, too, the end for the Auditorium was in sight. In 1930 and '31, there were even talks of demolition. Talks? They were taking bids. But, tearing it down would be too expensive and the Century of Progress served as the Auditorium's saving grace during the Great Depression. That was a temporary fix. During World War II, the City of Chicago took over the building and turned it into an officer's center. The stage became a bowling alley. Dankmar's perfectly designed acoustical showcase gave new meaning to the sound of pins dropping.

Much later, in its nomination for the National Register of Historic Places, the Auditorium Building would be described as the "most important structure of its time in Chicago and probably in the United States," but in 1946 this treasure was on its last legs. Roosevelt University stepped in and bought it, moving their operations into the former offices and hotel. While they couldn't afford to return the theater to its pre-war elegance, they held onto it until someone could.

A renovation of the magnitude required by Auditorium Theatre would require several someones, and Roosevelt University trustee Beatrice Spachner found them. She rounded up like-minded people and created the Auditorium Theatre Council in 1960. Seven years later, the theater reopened with New York City Ballet's performance of George Balanchine's *A Midsummer Night's Dream*.

Over the next several years the grand theater hosted music legends Aretha Franklin, Jimi Hendrix, Janis Joplin, Pink Floyd, Miles Davis, The Who, and Nina Simone. The Grateful Dead performed at the Auditorium ten times between 1971 and 1977. The building joined the National Register of Historic Places, then became a National Historic Landmark, then a Chicago Landmark. Since that first performance at the reopening, dance troupes including Alvin Ailey and the Bolshoi Ballet have pax de deux'd their way across the legendary stage. In 1998 the Joffrey Ballet began its residency. In 2020, that residency ended.

Auditorium Building Today

Roosevelt University still owns the Auditorium Building. Instead of offices and a hotel, Ferdinand Peck's dream contains classrooms and libraries. The innovative theater continues to present live music, dance, and theatrical performances. It remains one of the most important structures of today in Chicago and in the United States.

1891
Monadnock Block

The Monadnock Block is one of Chicago's architectural darlings. To the casual observer, this block may not seem revolutionary, but it's a two-in-one time capsule of trailblazing construction techniques and evolving aesthetics. From the north it's a tall, narrow building with thin windows, not much ornamentation, and a smooth flare at the top. From the south, it's a tall, narrow building with larger windows, a bit of ornamentation, and a defined, angular cornice. The north building has a thick base, which should put it firmly in the antiquated load-bearing category. The south building, on the other hand, with its narrow piers and larger windows, seems to be built on the more advanced steel frame. Those two assumptions are partially correct, but this block is more complex than that. There's a whole lot going on behind that purple-brown brick.

In the mid-1880s, Peter and Shepherd Brooks, through their Chicago agent Owen Aldis, purchased a thin strip of land south of Jackson at Dearborn Street. They'd been buying up land willy-nilly, and while some thought this particular lot was too far south to be a wise investment, the Brooks brothers and Owen were savvy. That was proven true when the Chicago Board of Trade opened at Jackson and LaSalle Street in 1885, turning what had been the further reaches of the Loop into the city's financial district. By that time Peter, Shepherd, and Owen had already hired Daniel Burnham and John Root to design a building for the north part of their narrow strip, and in 1884 John designed a thirteen-story skyscraper with Egyptian motifs. It wasn't terribly ornate, but Peter and Owen wanted something even simpler. Since the Brooks brothers wanted to hold off construction until after the neighborhood was a little more in-demand, John had the opportunity to rework it. That delay also allowed John to take advantage of the technological improvements in construction. Between the time of his initial design and when they broke ground on the narrow lot, William Le Baron Jenney had erected the Home Insurance Building, changing high-rise construction forever. With the Rookery building, completed for the Brooks brothers and Owen in 1888, Daniel and John blended load bearing walls with a steel and iron internal frame. They'd do something similar with the Monadnock.

The Brooks brothers were, first and foremost, investors. They directed from Boston while Owen handled the details in Chicago. One of the peculiarities of this particular investment is that they wanted to be able to split the revenues between different family trusts, so they instructed Burnham and Root to build two separate buildings. While the structures would share a corridor and exterior walls, they would have their own elevators, heating plants, stairways, and plumbing. If you rented in the Monadnock building, to the north, then your check went to one Brooks family trust. If you rented in the Kearsarge building, to the south, it went to another. And this was before they filled the lot all the way to Van Buren Street with another two buildings.

Peter was adamant about keeping the shared exterior of the Monadnock and Kearsarge buildings, named for New England mountains, simple. If he'd had his druthers, it would be one sheer face from base to summit. To him, projections and decorations meant dirt. Even worse, they would attract pigeons, who would defecate all over his building. Knowing that, Owen was still able to convince him they needed bay windows. Because load-bearing walls required narrow openings, oriels would not only bring more natural light to the interior, but would also increase the rentable space. Now that was a language Peter understood.

Both of those issues—rentable space and natural light—could have been fixed by switching to steel-frame construction, but Peter didn't trust it yet. It wasn't just the concern that it would all come crumbling down in a strong wind; it was also because Brooks wanted a fire-proof building. A *Chicago Tribune* article from April 3, 1890, mentions the contract for a steel core and "walls of brick and terra cotta. The Boston people say that they have seen granite crumble to dust under the influence of fire, and that nothing but material fire-tried and proven by fire shall enter into the construction of the new block."

And, finally, Peter wanted it to look massive. The buildings were named for mountains, after all. They should resemble them in more than name.

John took all those requirements and turned them into a building that's considered a masterpiece. He used his now-proven floating raft foundation to support the massive weight of a building with sixteen stories, a basement, and an attic. The base itself was six-feet thick, and was a definitive statement that you couldn't build any higher with masonry. The Chicago Landmark designation report claimed that this was the highest and heaviest masonry wall-bearing structure in Chicago—and maybe anywhere. From the outside, it looks like it's built entirely of stone and brick. Inside, though, Burnham and Root used cast-iron columns and wrought-iron beams, which enabled more open floor space. Due to its unprecedented height for a masonry structure, they used portal wind bracing, a new technique used simultaneously in the Monadnock and Jenney's Manhattan buildings that supported columns by bracing them with horizontal struts.

In addition to the interior details, John's simple-looking exterior with its smooth slopes at base and summit was the result of special bricks formed in almost a hundred custom-made molds. Those bay windows, gracefully undulating around the building, were supported by cantilevered steel supports, which lessened the weight on the already beleaguered base. The complete lack of ornamentation heralded a future of sheer skyscraper walls that wouldn't come to pass for decades.

John never got to see his "Jumbo," as he called it, completed. He died of pneumonia January 15, 1891, while it was still under construction.

While there had been grumbling that Chicago had too much office space, within three months more than half of the Monadnock was leased. Tenants included two banks, patent lawyer offices, and railroads, including the Chicago and Alton. The building was so successful that the day after all of those leases were touted in the Chicago Tribune, an article announced that another member of the Brooks family, Sarah L., would be erecting an extension. This time, Holabird & Roche designed the plans.

William Holabird and Martin Roche secured permits for those plans, along with four other buildings, on the same day in 1891. They were in a mad rush because the city council would soon be instituting a height restriction of just 130 feet, or about ten stories. William and Martin got their permit for their Monadnock extension in the nick of time. That same evening, an Alderman "introduced an order in the Council directing the Building Commissioner not to issue high-building permits until some definite action is taken by the Council regarding proposed limitations."

The reason for the abrupt switch in architects isn't clear, but it's supposed that much of it had to do with John Root's untimely demise. Plus, Daniel Burnham had his hands full planning the Columbian Exposition. Either way, Owen and the Brooks family hired William Holabird and Martin Roche, who had met while working for Jenney and started their own practice in 1881. Their Tacoma building, completed in 1889, was also encased in bay windows.

The south building of the Monadnock Block was another two-in-one: abutting Kearsarge was Katahdin, followed by Wachusett, also named for New England mountains. Like their counterparts to the north, the exterior of these buildings was uniform, but instead of John's futuristic smooth slate, William and Martin used a more traditional design, with columns capped with round arches on the top floor instead of John's rectangular windows, a cornice instead of a parapet, and touches of terra cotta trim. While Katahdin followed the iron-framed masonry construction of the north two buildings, Wachusett was steel-framed, meaning that only one-quarter of the whole block used the new, lighter method. Owen finally agreed to steel after an engineering exam of older buildings proved it was safe. Despite the different construction methods, the whole southern half features wider spans of glass than its counterpart. To keep a semblance of unity, William and Martin continued both the deep-colored brick and the undulating bay windows.

The interior of all four buildings was luxurious and unified, and every floor except for the very top shared corridors. The lobby was lined with Italian marble, and gorgeous mosaics tiled the floor. The decorative staircase was the first structural use of aluminum in a building—and at that time, aluminum was pricey.

When they completed the south half in 1893, the Monadnock Block was the largest office building in the world.

The roaring twenties brought a building boom. As newer skyrises crowded the Loop, they took the shine off the Monadnock. By the late 1930s, occupancy was down to 55 percent. Owen's nephew Graham Aldis was managing the building, and he launched a modernization project, although he called it "progressive styling." He hired Skidmore and Owings and they restyled and remodeled to the tune of $125,000. New tenants signed on and some existing ones leased more space. Aldis & Co. held onto the building until 1966, when they sold it to Sudler & Co., who added carpets and fluorescent lights. Sudler also had to raise the north wall after construction on the Kluczynski Federal Building across the street caused it to sink nearly two inches.

The 1970s hit, and like so many other buildings in downtown Chicago during that time, the Monadnock struggled. William S. Donnell purchased it for a measly two million dollars. To put it into perspective, the south building by itself cost $800,000 in the early 1890s.

At first, William wanted to gut the block and completely bring it into the twentieth century. When he couldn't secure financing, he decided to renovate it, piece by piece, until it stood in all its 1893 glory. Working with nationally-recognized restorer John Vinci, William spared no expense, even getting marble from the same quarry in Italy that had been used during the original construction. He hired Italian artisans to recreate the mosaic floors. The wood trim needed replaced, so William bought the company that made the original, and still used the same equipment. The entire project took years and cost one million dollars per floor. William even secured tenants for the retail shops that would have been similar to what one would find when the building first opened, like a barbershop and a tobacconist. In 1987, the National Trust for Historic Preservation selected the Monadnock as one of the top historic preservation projects in the country, and it wasn't even done yet. William continued the restoration until it was complete. All-in-all, it took thirteen years.

Monadnock Block Today

At street-level, the Monadnock Block continues to retain its late nineteenth-century character. There's still a barbershop and a tobacconist. There's a hat maker, a custom tailor, and a shoe hospital. Office tenants get the best of both worlds, enjoying modern amenities in a building that straddles architectural history.

1892
Charnley House
Charnley-Persky House

There's an unusual building in Chicago's Gold Coast neighborhood. It's simple compared to its historic neighbors and ornate compared to more recent construction. The building is unique, and its story involves introverts, embezzlement and suicides, towering egos, stolen (or "borrowed") credit, and philanthropy.

James Charnley was more enigmatic than most of Chicago's historical figures. The prosperous lumberman, unlike his wealthy contemporaries, wasn't a member of multiple non-profit boards and didn't appear regularly in the newspapers. Despite being a scion of industry, he pretty much kept to himself. He didn't even help with the 1893 World's Columbian Exposition, which was essentially a requirement for those listed in the Chicago Blue Book. The only social engagement he seemed to keep regularly was the Chicago Literary Society. It's believed his wife, Helen, didn't belong to any organizations at all. Nobody's found a single photo of James, nor are there any interior pictures or drawings of the landmark named for the elusive character from the time he lived within.

James grew up in Philadelphia and arrived in Chicago in 1866 after graduating from college in Connecticut. He immediately launched Bradner, Charnley & Co., a lumber yard and timber mill, with his brother Charles and brother-in-law Lester Bradner. The three Yale graduates were quick successes, but five years later that company dissolved and the two siblings reformed as Charnley Brothers & Co. In 1872, James married Helen Douglas, whose father, John, had been President of Illinois Central Railroad from 1865 to 1871. It was during John Douglas' tenure that the infamous "Lake Front Steal" was attempted, an unsuccessful effort by the railroad to grab a large portion of what would become Grant Park. Apparently John wasn't held responsible, because he returned as Illinois Central's president from 1875 to 1876. After retiring from the railroad, John partnered with his son-in-law, and the company reformed again as James Charnley & Co.

James and Helen seemed to follow their own path. Although Potter and Bertha Palmer were credited with driving the flow of the rich from the south to the north side of the river, the Charnleys were the first to actually live there. By the time the Palmers moved into their castle along Lake Shore Drive in 1885, James and Helen had lived in their Burnham and Root-designed country home on the shores of Lake Michigan for three years. As the Gold Coast took shape around them, the Charnleys left, moving into a townhouse on Erie Street next to Helen's father in 1887.

The reason for their departure from this promising neighborhood is unknown, but it could have been due to grief. They had moved into the spacious home in 1882 with a son and two daughters. The following year, Bettie and Helen, ages four and six, died within weeks of each other from diphtheria.

By 1888, James was pretty much done with the yard trade in Chicago and spent much of his time dealing with lumber interests in Sturgeon Bay, Wisconsin, and Duluth, Minnesota. He also had business down south, and on one trip to the Gulf, he and Helen ran into their friend Louis Sullivan in New Orleans. The year was 1890, and Louis had escaped Chicago to recuperate after the exhaustion of completing the Auditorium Building. The friends, who probably knew each other because Louis' brother Albert had worked with Helen's dad at Illinois Central Railroad, decided to head over to Ocean Springs, Mississippi.

There, they found paradise. As Louis put it in his (third-person) autobiography:

"Louis clasped his hand to his heart in an ecstasy of pain. What he saw was not merely woodland, but a stately forest, of amazing beauty, utterly wild.

Non-commercial, it had remained for years untouched by the hand of man. Louis, breathless, worked his way as best he could through the dense undergrowth. He nearly lost his wits at what he discovered; immense rugged short-leaved pines, sheer eighty feet to their stiff gnarled crowns, graceful swamp pines, very tall, delicately plumed; slender vertical Loblolly pines in dense masses; patriarchal sweet gums and black gums with their younger broods; maples, hickories, myrtles; in the undergrowth, dogwoods, Halesias, sloe plums, buck eyes and azaleas, all in a riot of bloom; a giant magnolia and grandiflora near the front—all grouped and arranged as though by the hand of an unseen poet. Louis saw the strategy. He knew what he could do. He planned for two shacks or bungalows, 300 feet apart, with stables far back; also a system of development requiring years for fulfillment."

James, Helen, and Louis bought their plots of land and the architect began designing their "shacks." Putting the plans in the hands of a local carpenter, the three headed north to Chicago on March 12, 1890. Louis dove headfirst into commercial work. The next year, his friends decided they wanted to move out of the townhouse. The Charnleys bought a plot from Potter Palmer in the Gold Coast district they'd left behind and asked Louis to design their new home.

Louis had distinct ideas about architecture. He wanted to create a new American aesthetic and vehemently believed that classicism was a throw-back that had nothing to do with a modern city. Ornamentation was fine, but it must have purpose, and it must represent the function of the building it decorated. He was a student of Henry Hobson Richardson, whose bold designs influenced a movement. He was a teacher to Frank Lloyd Wright, whose style would consume a culture.

The Charnley home was a revelation. Similar to the Glessners' Prairie Avenue mansion, which had been designed by Richardson, the building was flush with the sidewalk. There was no hidden garden, though; the only outside space was a second-floor balcony, centered over the entrance which was itself centered in the west side of the building. Three steps led from the sidewalk to a narrow entryway, and then the door opened to a three story atrium, the skylight flooding the open space. There was no grand staircase; in effect, the stairs were concealed, like the servants' entrance at the Glessner House and the steps to the second level of the Auditorium Theater. Sullivanesque touches turned what could have been a box into art. Embellishments on the loggia, the mantles, and the banisters proved that this home was designed by a skilled and talented architect.

But was it Sullivan, or was it Wright?

After Sullivan's death, Wright took credit for the Charnley House, and for fifty years this claim endured. Even the Commission of Chicago Architectural Landmarks praised Wright's ingenuity, while at the same time mentioning those "Sullivanesque" features. *A Guide to Chicago Architecture*, published in 1962, lists Adler and Sullivan as the architecture firm, but says that the house was "designed by Frank Lloyd Wright." Because there were no drawings or images from the early years of the home, a man known for his self-aggrandizement could claim that he, and he alone, designed "one of the most artistic and successful of American city houses." Wright even claimed that he'd designed not only the Charnleys' Mississippi "shack," but also Sullivan's.

There's no real consensus on how much of the design can be attributed to each architect. Some believe Sullivan is responsible for most, and others think that Wright was the driving force. Two considerations lean towards Sullivan: one is that he and the Charnleys were such good friends they bought vacation homes next to each other. Would Louis assign the design of their home to a draftsman he employed? The other is that Wright did not claim the house was his until 1932, forty years after it was completed, eight years after Sullivan's death, and during one of the low points of Frank's career.

Either way, the Charnley house significantly departed from the designs of the past and *almost* heralded a new era of American design. But then, the 1893 World's Columbian Exposition, with its Beaux Arts neoclassical buildings, changed the course of architecture in the country. One only has to look at the Field Museum of Natural History, constructed more than twenty years later, to see the fair's influence. After the magic of the White City, commissions for Louis' unique and modern designs dropped precipitously, despite the acclaim for his Transportation Building. That summer, Louis fired Frank for taking independent commissions, a distinct no-no, and the two didn't speak for twelve years.

James and Helen had only lived in their Gold Coast home for a few years when scandal rocked the family. In September

1897, it was discovered that Charles, James' brother and business partner, absconded with $60,000 from Fourth Presbyterian Church. An arrest warrant was issued for the church elder, but he disappeared. Soon after, his wife, who was his second wife and niece of his first, disappeared as well. A couple of months later his son James, Jr., who had been living with his aunt and uncle on Astor Street, checked into the Pfister Hotel in Milwaukee and killed himself with morphine and a revolver. The next year, Charles Jr. committed suicide in Los Angeles, shooting himself with a pistol.

The Charnleys stayed in Chicago for another four years, but finally in 1902 they retired to Camden, South Carolina. James died in 1905 and Helen kept possession of the Gold Coast house, renting it until 1911. Her last renter, Redmond D. Stephens, bought it and lived there for seven years before selling the home to James B. Waller, Jr.

The Wallers were a prominent family, active in society and politics. After Waller, Jr. died in 1920, James III inherited what was still, due to the 1893 fair's influence, a uniquely modern home. In 1927 he added an addition and more bathrooms. He died in 1949 and his widow remained for another twenty years.

For the next decade the Charnley house was a hot potato that was tossed from owner to owner. Finally, Lowell Wohlfeil bought it and lived there with his partner, Larry Duvall. Larry was a docent with the Chicago Architecture Foundation and the two took on restoration projects in the home with architect John Vince. Seven years later, they sold the house to Skidmore, Owings & Merrill (SOM), the architecture firm that had built the Sears Tower. The firm turned the house into the headquarters for their Chicago Institute for Architecture and Urbanism and did large-scale restoration, including removing the 1927 addition.

During this time, the Charnleys' home received National Historic Landmark and Chicago Historic Landmark designations. You'd think that it would be safe from demolition, but after SOM moved out, the house sat vacant for three years and developers threatened to turn it into condos. If they had succeeded, it would have meant the destruction of yet another Sullivan building—there are surprisingly few left in the city.

Fortunately, real estate baron and architecture buff Seymour Persky stepped in. At first he planned to live there, but realizing he'd need an elevator, he hired architect John Eifler to see what would be involved. When Eifler showed him what he'd have to do, Seymour said: "It would be architectural vandalism."

So, he decided to donate it to the Society of Architectural Historians, but only if they moved their headquarters from Philadelphia to Chicago. The move would be fitting, since Charnley grew up in Philly. They said yes, Seymour bought a block of Northern Trust stock for a steal, gave it to the organization, and they used it to buy this historic and architecturally important landmark. They've been there ever since.

Charnley House Today

The Charnley-Persky House remains the headquarters for the Society of Architectural Historians. While their offices are on the second and third floors, docents still lead tours. The tours focus on Sullivan and Wright and the importance of this anti-Classical home in the Pantheon of architecture.

1892
Marshall Field & Company
Macy's on State Street

W
hen Macy's renamed Marshall Field's in 2006,
people protested. They picketed and blocked
sidewalks. The protesters didn't get riled up
because the New York giant had purchased the beloved chain:
the Field family hadn't owned the department store since the
1960s and in those intervening forty years the brand had gone

through multiple owners. No, people protested because Macy's changed the store's name.

What kind of department store engenders that level of loyalty? How did Marshall Field & Company become such a part of the Chicago vernacular that a name change drew ire, protests, and boycotts?

The story begins with Marshall Field himself. He was born on August 18, 1834, on a farm near Conway, Massachusetts. When Marshall was seventeen, he struck out for Pittsfield and he and his brother Joseph lived together and worked at separate dry goods stores. It took some time for Marshall to display his retail charms; he was so timid that the store owner, Deacon Davis, declared he'd never be much of a merchant. But, the ladies liked the handsome and courteous young man, and by the time Marshall left Pittsfield five years later, he was such a success Davis offered him a partnership. Marshall declined; in 1856 he, like many of his fellow New Englanders, was lured west by the prospects of a rapidly growing town named Chicago.

Marshall immediately began working at Cooley, Wadsworth and Company, the largest dry goods store in the city. He could have applied at Potter Palmer and Company, but Cooley was the biggest and Marshall was ambitious. He arranged to live in the store and by the end of his first year had saved half of his $400 salary. In 1857 John Farwell became a partner, changing the dry goods store's name to Cooley, Farwell and Company. Marshall impressed the new partner with his work ethic and his drive to sell and by 1861 he was general manager and a junior partner. Levi Leiter, by all accounts a financial wizard, also impressed Farwell, and in 1864 the firm changed names again, this time to Farwell, Field and Company, Leiter being the Company.

In only eight years, Marshall Field had ascended from a broke clerk living in the shop to a full partner.

The partnership didn't last long. This was partly because Farwell's relaxed personality conflicted with Marshall's taciturn and Levi's brusque ways, but also because the younger merchants received an offer they couldn't refuse.

Potter Palmer's doctor advised him to take a European tour, so he decided to divest himself of his store and offered favorable terms to Marshall and Levi. As Potter jaunted about the continent (gently—he was recuperating, after all), Field, Palmer, and Leiter continued to grow. By 1867, when the two bought out Palmer completely, the dry goods store had twelve million in revenues.

Potter, who'd switched his focus to real estate and hotels, erected a six-story building at the northeast corner of State and Washington. Field, Leiter and Company leased the building and moved in October 12, 1868.

Marshall, all of 34 years old, was quickly becoming one of the richest men in Chicago. He would have been a fine catch, except he was already caught. In a rare impetuous moment, in late 1862 Marshall literally jumped on a moving train to propose to Nannie Douglas Scott, a beautiful young lady from Ohio. The two married a few months later. While the Fields eventually had three children, one of whom died in infancy, the marriage was not exactly blissful. Dinnertime was tempestuous, and Nannie spent increasingly more time in Europe until she finally decided to pack up her bags and move to France.

Marshall's home life wasn't the only thing that was rocky, but despite multiple financial crashes and the devastation of the fire of 1871, the firm fared better than the marriage. Within a few days of the destruction, the company posted signs informing "cash boys and shop girls" that they would be paid in full and where they could collect. Operations resumed almost immediately; Marshall and Levi purchased barns from the Chicago City Railway at 20th and State Streets and moved their wholesale and retail merchandise into the retrofitted buildings. After quickly realizing that location was unsuitable, they moved to Madison and Market Streets. Then, Potter sold the corner at State and Washington to Singer Sewing Company, who built a lovely new five-story building, which Field, Leiter and Company leased for retail.

And then, another crash in 1873. Another fire in 1877. Retail operations moved into the quasi-temporary Inter-State

Industrial Exposition Building until yet another store could be constructed two years later. Through all of this turmoil, revenues climbed. Why did Field, Leiter and Company thrive when so many others failed?

One of the biggest reasons was their limited use of credit. As Marshall said in an interview from 1901:

> "The panic of 1857 swept almost everything away except the house I worked for {Cooley, Farwell and Company}, and I learned that the reason they survived was because they understood the nature of the new country, and did a cash business. That is, they bought for cash, and sold on thirty and sixty days; instead of giving the customers, whose financial condition you could hardly tell anything about, all the time they wanted. When the panic came, they had no debts, and little owing to them, and so they weathered it all right. I learned what I consider my best lesson, and that was to do a cash business."

It also helped that catalog shopping didn't exist and extreme westward expansion meant new towns popped up left and right. These towns needed stores, and in addition to the traveling salesmen employed by Field and Leiter, it was both convenient and cost-effective for the shop owners to travel to Chicago and browse through the thousands of items stocked in the warehouse instead of trying to secure these items on their own.

The wholesale division far outpaced retail in sales, but retail was no slacker. Despite that, Levi wanted to get rid of retail entirely. Marshall did not. Their conflict came to a head in 1881 and Marshall bought out his partner and changed the name to Marshall Field & Company.

Marshall continued many of Potter's innovations when he bought into the business. Fixed prices instead of haggling, guaranteed returns, and attractive displays were all keys to Potter Palmer and Company's success. During a time of buyer beware, Marshall insisted on carrying only quality merchandise. While competitors sold cloth for women to turn into clothing, he offered ready-made attire. He opened buying offices in Europe so he could import the latest fashions and household goods. Marshall's emphasis on customer service was revolutionary. "Give the lady what she wants" is attributed to Field. Ladies were barely shopping at that time, let alone getting what they wanted.

Not only did customers receive this stellar treatment, his attention to staff was also legendary. While the pay wasn't great unless you were a partner, there was a certain status to working at the company and the list of perqs was impressive. Employees could borrow books from their own library branch and be treated by on-site medical staff. They received vacation time, and if they became ill, sick time could be privately arranged. Men had a gym and women had a recreation area. Marshall even secured a guaranteed interest rate of six percent for employee savings accounts, no matter how little was deposited. Marshall promoted from within. He was known for assessing each and every hire and placing employees based on their abilities.

Two of those employees changed the face of Marshall Field & Company and shopping in general. John G. Shedd began working as a stock boy in 1872, and by 1885 he'd been promoted to general merchandise manager for the wholesale division. His scientific method of planning inventories and seasonal purchases fueled such phenomenal growth that they needed a new giant warehouse and hired Henry H. Richardson. The robust architect designed a 500,000 square foot building in his distinct Romanesque style. While it was demolished in 1930, the Auditorium Building will give you an idea of what it looked like: Richardson's design greatly influenced Sullivan's.

The other insightful hire was Harry Selfridge. "Mile-a-minute Harry" was a retailing wunderkind. A mere twenty-one years-old when Marshall hired him as a stock boy in 1879, in four years he moved to retail and in eight years was promoted to General Manager. Marshall implemented Harry's ideas, from installing electric lighting to make the items for sale look better to moving displays out of the glass cabinets and onto tables where people could touch the merchandise. He instituted annual sales and turned the basement into the Budget Floor. During his tenure the departments increased from forty-two in 1884 to more than one hundred by 1902.

One of Harry's biggest innovations was adding in-store dining. In 1890, the elegant Tea Room opened. This brilliant concept meant patrons didn't have to leave when they got hungry and fostered generations of "ladies who lunch." Just two years after the Tea Room opened, twelve hundred people a day dined in the department store. The Walnut Room, which opened in 1905, is still an annual holiday tradition for thousands—thousands who browse, eat, and often, buy.

Harry also began the famous Marshall Field window displays. He'd heard of a store in Iowa that used their windows to draw attention instead of stuff them full of merchandise. Harry grabbed the designer, brought him back to Chicago, and put him to work. Crowds would gather around the windows every day but Sunday. Because Marshall believed in six days of labor and one day of rest, not only was the store closed on Sundays, but he also didn't advertise in the newspaper. He was so serious about this he had curtains drawn on the store displays from Saturday evening until Monday morning.

With all of those contributions, Harry felt his name should be added to the company. That was a non-starter and the innovator left in 1904, eventually opening his own successful chain of department stores in London.

Although Marshall seemed to be all business, all the time, he still found time for love. In 1905 he married his long-time, ahem, friend Delia Spencer Caton. Rumors that they'd been together for years swirled around the couple. Marshall's wife, living in Europe since 1891, died in 1896 of peritonitis. Eight years later, Delia's husband passed away, also from the intestinal disease. The longtime (alleged) lovebirds tied the knot on September 5, 1905, but they didn't get to enjoy wedded bliss for long. In November, Marshall Field II died of a gunshot wound. One story claimed he accidentally shot himself while cleaning his rifle before a hunting trip. Another was a bit more scandalous; he might have been shot while visiting the Everleigh Club, the most luxurious house of ill repute in Chicago, which was only half a mile from the younger Field's mansion.

Then, on January 16, 1906, Marshall Field died of pneumonia in New York City. His death rocked Chicago. His memorial service, held at the Auditorium Theatre, was attended by 5,000 current and former employees; representatives from manufacturing, railroad, banking, and real estate interests; former partners and business associates; and family and intimate friends. The Theodore Thomas Orchestra played. In a monograph presented to his widow, Reverend John Archibald Morison, Ph. D., wrote:

> "The long roll of earth's heroes, whose loyalty to duty has lifted up their statues in the temple of fame, contains no more conspicuous impressive name than that of Marshall Field."

That's some statement.

Before Marshall died, his State Street legacy was well underway. In the early 1890s he'd commissioned Daniel Burnham and Company to erect a series of buildings that would eventually cover the whole block. The first, at the northwest corner of Washington and Wabash, opened near the end of the Columbian Exposition. The store was a tourist destination and the firm employed interpreters to assist the many foreign guests in town for the fair. The second addition, erected in 1902 on the State and Randolph corner, welcomed shoppers through impressive Ionic columns. After Marshall's death, John G. Shedd, who was now president, continued the plans for a new building to replace the 1879 structure at State and Washington. Inside, the 6,000 square foot Tiffany dome, made of sixteen million pieces of favrile, or iridescent glass, still sparkles. The final piece of the Marshall Field puzzle was the corner of Wabash and Randolph. Upon its completion in 1914, the store covered the entire city block.

John, who had worked for and with Marshall for thirty-four years at the time of the merchant's death, continued growing the company, increasing manufacturing concerns until retiring in the early twenties. The next boss expanded to the suburbs of Chicago and purchased Frederick & Nelson, a Seattle store that had the bonus of a very tasty chocolate mint candy called Frango. Then they decided to build the largest commercial building in the world. Construction began on what would become the Merchandise Mart in 1928. The $35 million project wouldn't be completed until 1930.

Then, the Great Depression. Marshall Field & Company struggled. They liquidated the wholesale division and sold the behemoth Mart to Joseph Kennedy in 1945.

During World War II, the company manufactured war goods, thanks to all those factories Shedd had set up. They devoted one thousand square feet in the State Street store to selling war bonds and stamps. The lounges offered stationery and pens so you could handle your correspondence. There was a playroom for children, a beauty salon, a travel service, antiques, tours, and personalized shoppers. You could decorate your entire home, made easier with the assistance of interior designers. The eighth floor presented model homes, complete with roofs and landscaping, as inspiration. The exclusive 28 Shop was a luxury boutique that changed Chicago haute couture and had its own private entrance.

Once you entered Marshall Field's, there was no reason to leave. How could it not capture the imagination of anyone who visited? How could it be anything but a destination?

The glory days began to fade as shopping malls and competing stores popped up throughout the 1950s and '60s. When Marshall Field IV died in 1965, the family sold its last holdings. After a century, there were no more Fields in Marshall Field's.

The company changed hands many times between 1965 and 2005. Some owners expanded with more locations. Others sold some of those off. The amenities that made Marshall Field & Company a destination disappeared, but it's not like any of the owners simply gave up. In 1987, a $115 million, five-year renovation connected the Wabash and State Street buildings with an eleven-story atrium, which included an elaborate indoor fountain. The bargain basement became a nineteenth-century Chicago streetscape with a food court and boutiques. With Dayton Hudson Corporation's acquisition in 1990, eight-hundred and fifty staff lost their jobs and a big part of Marshall Field's identity was lost.

Still, in 2002, the State Street store celebrated its 150th anniversary, and the owners tried once again to infuse some life, this time by leasing space out to independent vendors. By October of the next year, there were thirty unique boutiques.

It wasn't enough. Macy's bought the brand in 2005 and changed the name the next year.

Marshall Field & Company Today

Marshall Field & Company was not just a place for commerce; it was a place for connection and socializing. Shopping became an experience. Marshall Field's no longer exists, except in some branded merchandise and the perpetually popular Frango candy, even though it wasn't a Marshall Field invention. Macy's shoppers can still gaze up at that fantastic Tiffany ceiling, and the Walnut Room tradition continues. Each year the windows feature holiday scenes, but some of them are now used to display merchandise and the scenes tend to repeat from year to year.

1893
Palace of Fine Arts
Museum of Science and Industry

Y ou'd never know it based on its prominence in the folklore of Chicago, but the 1893 World's Columbian Exposition was always meant to be temporary. Creating a permanent White City would have been prohibitively expensive and it *never* would have been done on time. The only building with any durability was the Palace of Fine Arts. Although it was covered with white staff (a mixture of plaster of Paris, glue, and hemp) like the rest of the buildings at the fair, exhibitors wanted this specific building to be made of brick to protect the five million dollars' worth of artwork displayed inside. Lined with columns and topped with copper domes, its beauty prompted the illustrious artist Augustus Saint-Gaudens to declare: "There has been nothing equal to it since the Parthenon." *Conkey's complete guide to the World's Columbian Exposition* was even more hyperbolic:

"Perhaps no building in the world, and certainly no one in the United States, surpasses it in beauty. Connoisseurs have pronounced it perfect in every detail, and have been lavish in the praise of the chief designer, Mr. C. B. Atwood. It is difficult to determine which is the most strikingly handsome and impressive— the exterior or interior."

Such a magnificent structure could not go to waste. Before the fair had even closed, the Columbian Museum of Chicago received a charter from the State of Illinois. Collections and specimens accumulated and the museum, now called the Field Columbian Museum of Chicago in honor of its main benefactor, Marshall Field, opened on June 2, 1894. In 1921, the Field Museum of Natural History, as it was by then called, moved to its own Beaux Arts beauty south of Grant Park.

The Palace of Fine Arts languished. It had been the only remaining building on the grounds since shortly after the fair closed, and during the Field Museum's tenure only patchwork repairs were made. Once the Palace was empty it received so little attention it began to sink into the sandy marsh of Jackson Park and practically disintegrate. While some players wanted to demolish the building, preservationists prevailed. Led by artist Lorado Taft, they raised five million dollars in bonds from Chicago citizens to fix up the place. Potential tenants included a trade school, and Lorado wanted to use it as an extension of the Art Institute of Chicago dedicated to sculpture. However, when Julius Rosenwald offered a cool three mill to use the space as a science museum, and he was backed by the powerful Commercial Club of Chicago, it was kinda hard to say no (although some tried).

Julius Rosenwald, known as JR, was rich. Uber rich. Make-a-difference-in-the-world rich. But he didn't start out that way. He was born August 12, 1862, to Jewish German immigrants. His father, Samuel, arrived in Baltimore in 1854 and survived as a peddler. Samuel and Augusta Hammerslough, JR's mother, married in 1857, and after several moves, the couple ended up in Springfield, Illinois, in a house across from Lincoln's. Samuel worked for his brothers-in-law's clothing house. When JR was old enough, he apprenticed with his uncles in New York City. He eventually opened his own shop with his brother, and after a time the two moved to Chicago to start a clothing manufacturing company. Things were going along fine when after a few years JR got the opportunity of a lifetime and bought a quarter-share of Sears, Roebuck and Co. With JR's business savvy and Richard Sears' copywriting talent, the company went gangbusters, doing fifty million in sales (about 1.4 billion today) by 1907. The next year Sears resigned due to declining health, leaving the company in JR's capable hands.

While he was building wealth, JR was also building a family. In April 1890, he married Augusta "Gussie" Nusbaum, and the two had five children. It was on one family trip to Germany that JR's inspiration for a science museum struck. His son William, who was about eight at the time, became absolutely enamored with the Deutsches Museum in Munich. The museum so enthralled him that he wanted to go every day, and if he went missing, JR and Gussie would find him pushing and pulling levers and marveling at the coal mine. This was a new and wondrous place that celebrated science and industry, and JR knew he needed to create something similar back home.

The idea percolated. In the 1920s he presented the concept to the Commercial Club of Chicago. It took some convincing, but they caught on, especially when Julius offered to contribute a considerable amount of money. With the bond sales and JR's contribution, which ended up being a few million higher than originally planned, the Rosenwald Industrial Museum was a done deal.

Except JR didn't want his name on the museum. You might have noticed that JR didn't add his name to Sears, Roebuck and Co. That was his way. He even refused honorary college degrees because he hadn't earned them. JR told the board that he didn't want his name on the museum, but they voted to add it while he was visiting President Coolidge and wired him the news. Did they think he was joking? Everybody wants their name on a museum. Heck, that's the only reason Marshall gave any money to the Field Columbian Museum.

Not JR. He wired them back immediately and told the board to remove his name. It took three years and several requests, but they finally changed it to the Museum of Science and Industry founded by Julius Rosenwald.

The museum that JR envisioned would be more than an interactive demonstration of science, although that alone would certainly provide a new and different experience to people used to static displays. Context—the context of these advancements within the construct of society, and how they affected society—would be just as important as showing off the latest whizbangitthingamajig, the inner workings of a lightbulb, the rotation of a gyroscope. The first director of the museum, New York Times Science Writer Waldemar Kaempffert, described the approach as "interpretation of the machine." In *From cave-man to engineer; the Museum of Science and Industry founded by Julius Rosenwald, an institution to reveal the technical ascent of man*, Waldemar listed several examples, including the Otis elevator's role in not simply doing away with stairs, but in enabling tall buildings; how the automobile changed the layout of cities and suburbs; and how the typewriter was more than a substitute for the pen—it was a revolution that put women to work.

"As the visitor emerges from the museum he will understand better the spectacle that greets his eyes—the electric lights, the automobiles, the

airplanes overhead, the towering hotels and
apartment houses, the hard roads, Jackson Park
itself. Chicago will seem a part of the museum—the
last great exhibit in the technical progress of man."

Julius Rosenwald's contribution totaled seven million
dollars in cash and stock, but he didn't get to see the
completion of the museum he founded. He died January 6,
1932, and the Museum of Science and Industry opened the
following summer.

Fittingly for a science museum, the opening coincided with
the 1933 Century of Progress World's Fair. They were still
finishing up the restoration and the museum only used ten
percent of the space, renting the rest to University of Chicago
Hospitals for record storage. One of the few exhibits was a
reproduction of an Illinois coal mine. This immersive
experience engaged all of the senses, inviting guests to
descend the shaft in a cage elevator and see exactly what this
subterranean occupation involved, including how it smelled.

During the Depression years, the museum continued to add
exhibits that focused on the past. It lost money. Admission
was free, and remained free until 1991, so the museum
survived on donations. The saving grace came with the hiring
of Major Lenox R. Lohr, who served as director from 1940
until his death in 1968. The former president of the National
Broadcasting Corporation and general manager of the
Century of Progress invited companies to sponsor exhibits.
This move most assuredly would have dismayed Waldemar,
but it worked. GM, International Harvester, and other
companies signed long-term agreements to develop and
sponsor exhibits. By inviting commercial companies to
showcase innovations, the museum thrived.

Ninety percent of the interactive exhibits focused on the
present and the future and only ten percent on the past. The
Santa Fe Model Railroad, installed in 1943, delighted children
and adults. In 1942, the museum hung the flags of Allied
countries, beginning the annual "Christmas Around the
World" tradition. At a dinner in 1949, Major Lenox persuaded

silent film star Colleen Moore to donate her Fairy Castle. Created by a hundred of Ms. Moore's Hollywood friends, she took it around the country between 1935 and 1939 to raise money for children's charities. In 1952 the museum added a walk-through heart, and the next year secured a full-size submarine. Captured by the U.S. Navy during World War II, the German U-boat was installed in the museum as a war memorial on September 25, 1954, and in 1989 became a National Historic Landmark. And it is: it's the only Type IX-C U-boat in the world. Interestingly, Waldemar's 1933 treatise on the museum listed the desire for a full-sized submarine. Major Lenox Lohr, and the city of Chicago, who raised a quarter of a million dollars to move the boat, made it happen.

Palace of Fine Arts Today

If Julian Rosenwald could see his dream now... the Museum of Science and Industry has done more than fill the former Palace of Fine Arts. Its fourteen acres and four hundred thousand square feet are brimming with nearly thirty-five thousand artifacts.

The Coal Mine; U505 Submarine; the Hatchery, where kids have been watching chicks break out of their shells since 1956; and the Fairy Castle continue to be popular, and they're joined by newer exhibits that cover a breadth of disciplines. The museum replaced the walk-in heart with a 3D model. The Santa Fe Railroad became the Great Train Story, a minutely detailed model railroad depicting transportation from Chicago to Seattle. It's located in the Transportation Gallery, which has everything from a model of the Wright Brothers plane to an actual Boeing 727. The Hatchery is now part of Genetics: Decoding Life. Toymaker 3000 is a real working toy assembly line. Yesterday's Mainstreet goes back in time to early 20th Century Chicago, and the Henry Crown Space Center is out of this world. Science Storms showcases the terrific and terrifying power of mother nature: visitors can step *inside* a 40-foot tornado, manipulate avalanches, and make lightning strike.

The Museum of Science and Industry makes science accessible and fun. With more than 190 million visitors since opening in 1933, the museum continues to be the most popular in Chicago.

1893
Art Institute of Chicago

In 1866, Chicago wasn't exactly known for its culture. Culture? Art? In Chicago? Nah—that town was all about making money. It was dirty and consumed with building and the accumulation of wealth. It stunk, with its stockyards and grain elevators and sewage-filled river, and the people that kept coming, thousands of them, hoping to make their own fortune, or at least have a chance.

But even in the mercenary, rapidly expanding city of Chicago, art was necessary, and in 1866, the Chicago Academy of Design began with thirty-five artists. The Dearborn Street studio featured a school and gallery, holding daily classes, regular receptions, and exhibitions. By 1870, they needed more room and moved into a five-story building on Adams Street.

Yes, even in Chicago, art was necessary.

The 1871 fire destroyed the new building and the Academy never recovered. It wasn't for lack of effort, but by 1878 the organization was ten thousand dollars in debt and the artists and patrons didn't see eye to eye on its mission. The Chicago Academy of Design declared bankruptcy and a group of businessmen bought their assets at auction, incorporating as the Chicago Academy of Fine Arts on May 24, 1879.

This new-ish organization enlarged the concept from artist-driven classes, studios, and galleries to an institute with an expansive school and museum. To reflect that mission, they renamed it the Art Institute of Chicago. They hit a home run their first time at bat by making 28-year-old Charles L. Hutchinson, who'd been a founding trustee of the Chicago Academy of Fine Arts, their president. Charles was a wealthy young man; his dad, Benjamin, started the Chicago Packing & Provision Co. and was a trustee with the First National Bank of Chicago at the same time Samuel Nickerson was Vice President. Although Charles worked for his dad as first a clerk and then a junior partner, he was about much more than the holding and accumulating of money. He was about people, and about art, and about art helping people.

The decade after the Great Chicago Fire was a frenetic and meteoric period of building and growth. It was less about recovering from a disaster and more about showing the world, and themselves, that Chicagoans could take anything thrown at them. The first priority was rebuilding. Then, they could attend to things like culture. By the time the 1880s rolled around, the hierarchy of needs, at least as far as the wealthy were concerned, had reached the tip of the pyramid.

The young city's population numbered half a million, most of whom struggled to survive. Many of the wealthiest citizens, like John Glessner, Ferdinand Peck, and Charles Hutchinson, threw their energies towards helping to improve the less fortunates' situations and believed that people should not have to wait for art and creativity, no matter what their status.

Providing cultural access to everyone would raise the city as a whole. The Grand Opera Festival proved there was a need; so did the art hall at the Inter-State Industrial Exposition. The first building Jane Addams and Ellen Gates Star added to Hull-House Settlement was an art gallery.

It didn't take long for the Art Institute to outgrow its space and it did so multiple times in the next several years. Admission was free to the public Wednesdays, Saturdays, Sundays, and holidays, and the demand was so great they went through not one, but two new buildings, both designed by John Wellborn Root. When the city secured the World's Columbian Exposition, which was basically a LOOK AT ME coming out party for the city, the Art Institute of Chicago negotiated a win-win plan for *another* new building. This time, they were in it for keeps. In 1892, the "temporary" Inter-state Industrial Exposition had been holding court at Michigan and Adams for twenty years. Charles was also the fair's Chairman of the Committee for Fine Arts and he proposed replacing the Expo with a building that both the institute and the fair could use. The museum and school would raise most of the money, the park district would provide the land, and the World's Fair would kick in $200,000, but only if the building was completed on time.

It was. From May 1 to October 31, 1893, the World's Congress Auxiliary of the World's Columbian Exposition held lectures, seminars, and the World's Parliament of Religions. After the fair closed, the Art Institute of Chicago moved in, celebrating with an opening reception featuring Theodore Thomas's orchestra on December 8.

The new building, designed by Shepley, Rutan, and Coolidge, who had also completed the Glessner mansion, cost $648,000 to build. It quickly filled with collections and within a year gifts to the museum equaled half the cost of the building. Early holdings included prints donated by Elizabeth H. Stickney, with etchings by Rembrandt and Whistler, and architectural casts sent to the Columbian Exposition by the French government. The entrance hall was filled with reproductions of classical sculptures. The museum also had paintings by Rembrandt as well as Van Dyke, Rubens, and other Dutch masters. In 1890, Charles and his like-minded colleague Martin Ryerson paid $200,000 for the paintings with funds they'd contributed as well as donations raised from Marshall Field, Phillip Armour, and other wealthy Chicagoans. Florence Lathrop Page, widow of Henry Field and Marshall Field's sister-in-law, donated another substantial collection of paintings. She's most famously responsible for the lions at the entrance. Artist Edward Kemeys, a renowned "animalier," or sculptor of animals, had created multiple plaster sculptures for the Columbian Exposition, including a pair of lions that flanked the Palace of Fine Arts. Florence paid to have Kemeys recreate those lions in bronze, and they've guarded the Michigan Avenue entrance since 1894.

For forty-three years, Charles Hutchinson led the Art Institute of Chicago's growth. The school became the largest in the country by the mid-1890s. The building added wings to the north, to the south, and over the railroad tracks. Charles W. Fullerton donated money for a lecture hall in honor of his father. Built in 1897, it was topped with a Tiffany dome. Ryerson donated funds for a library. They needed a sculpture hall, so Isabella Blackstone paid for one. Daniel Burnham thought the museum needed a library focused on architecture, and his 1912 will took care of that. McKinlock Court honored a soldier who'd fallen in World War I.

And, the collections grew, as people like the Nickersons donated the acquisitions made during their travels. Bertha Palmer, who'd made collecting Impressionist paintings an art form, stipulated not one but two bequests in her will for a grand total of half a million dollars. Her sons then donated an additional thirty-two paintings and pastels from her holdings. Clarence Buckingham, whose sister would later have a grand fountain built in his honor, bequeathed significant works of art as well.

The museum also purchased art, including its first major acquisition in 1906, El Greco's *The Assumption of the Virgin*. Some of the funds to increase the Art Institute's holdings were

124

raised by door fees and memberships, but the majority came from donations and bequests.

When Charles died in 1924, the museum and school—the Institute—he'd shepherded had become world renowned. It helped to establish Chicago as a place of both commerce and culture, and it's a reputation the city has held ever since.

In 1925, the museum acquired the Helen Birch Bartlett Memorial Collection. This remarkable bequest included pieces by Gauguin, Modigliani, and Van Gogh, including his *The Bedroom*. Picasso's *The Old Guitarist* and Georges Seurat's *A Sunday Afternoon on the Island of La Grande Jatte* were also part of the donation.

That same year, The Goodman Theatre opened where the Modern Wing now stands. A few years later, one and a half million people would visit the museum's "A Century of Progress" exhibition in just five months.

Over the next several decades, the Art Institute of Chicago continued to increase the breadth and depth of its holdings. In 1930, Grant Wood won a $300 prize in a contest held by the museum for his *American Gothic*. Georgia O'Keeffe, a former student, donated her husband Alfred Stieglitz's collection in 1949. In 1956, the museum installed Narcissa Niblack Thorne's exquisitely detailed miniature rooms. The museum acquired decorative art. Armor and weaponry. Religious art. Native American art. Art from Africa. Asia. Ancient Greece, Rome, and Egypt. Etruscan art. Byzantine art. Art from everywhere and every time.

They needed room for all that art. The Morton Wing provided some on the south side of the original building in 1962 and they moved Lorado Taft's *Fountain of the Great Lakes* to make space for the addition. The allegorical fountain, installed in 1913, now faced Michigan Avenue. The Rubloff Building expanded the school and the museum in the 1970s, and in 1988 the Daniel F. and Ada L. Rice Building provided yet more space. Finally, in 2009, Renzo Piano's Modern Wing added another 65,000 square feet, making the Art Institute of Chicago the second-largest art museum in the United States.

Art Institute of Chicago Today

With nearly 300,000 works of art from every part of the world and spanning 5,000 years, the Art Institute of Chicago is truly a global museum. It goes beyond the celebration of art to provide an encyclopedic look at humanity. The names of the people whose generosity made, and make, the museum possible can be found in the names of the collections, the names of the halls, and the names of the buildings. Each piece is accompanied by a descriptive plaque that includes, where applicable, who donated it.

If you can't visit the museum, more than 50,000 works of art are available to view online and download. These are public domain, which means that all rights are waived and you can basically do anything you want with them. It's a continuation of the belief that art is for everyone.

1893
Newberry Library

Walter Loomis Newberry was the kind of man who prepared. Before moving to Chicago in 1833 he'd already invested in real estate. The town was barely a town, but Walter went ahead and plunked down some cash for a piece of swamp. As the town became a city, canal fever inspired speculation and quick riches, but Walter took the steady route, which protected him when the panic of 1837 destroyed less methodical men. Who would've thought he'd end up in a rum barrel?

It didn't take long for the Newberry name to gain prominence. Oliver Newberry, Walter's brother, owned a shipping company out of Detroit and he hired an agent named George Dole to handle his Chicago interests. George opened a slaughterhouse and made the first shipment of beef aboard one of Oliver's ships. In 1839, Newberry and Dole loaded their brig Osceola with 1,678 bushels of wheat, beginning Chicago's status as the biggest grain exporter in the country. Walter came at it from the other direction, serving as Galena and Chicago Union Railroad's first president. He also kept buying and selling land and got into banking, too.

When Walter wasn't busy making money, he was giving away his time. The man was a reader, and in 1841 he helped found the Young Men's Association and became its first president. Not to be confused with the Young Men's Christian Association, the YM (no C) A was dedicated "to establish and maintain a Reading Room and Library, and to procure Literary and Scientific Lectures, and to promote the intellectual improvement of its members." Subscription fees and taxes were low, because even though membership wasn't free, the founders wanted to bring in all classes of citizens. The association procured newspapers and periodicals and Walter provided the first books. The group would eventually become the Chicago Library Association.

In addition to the YMA, Walter presided over the Chicago School Board, twice. He helped found and was a president of the Chicago Historical Society, and for a time, their collections were stored in his home. At one point, he was an Alderman, city comptroller, and acting mayor.

On November 22, 1842, Walter, age 38, married Ms. Julia Butler Clapp, age 24. They had a son, Walter, who died. They had another son, another Walter, who also died. Mary Louise was born in 1845 and eight years later Julia gave birth to Julia Rose. Because Walter prepared, he drafted a will with the help of his Chicago Historical Society co-founder Judge Mark Skinner. The document was set to be your standard divvy-up-the-goods amongst children and relatives. But Mark, recognizing both Walter's passion for books and the Newberry family's history of ill health, suggested a contingency clause: if Mary Louise and Julia Rose died without issue, then why not bequeath the money to start a public library? Walter really wanted the Newberry name to continue, and this would make sure that it would.

Walter had never been very healthy. He'd been accepted to West Point, but he couldn't attend because of his constitution. He would often travel to Europe, as the rich did in those days, and even married Julia in Paris. But his final trip across the Atlantic ended on November 6, 1868, when Walter died of tuberculosis at sea. The captain couldn't exactly throw him overboard, so the shipmates put him in a rum barrel. (Whether there was rum in it or not is up for debate.)

His daughters didn't live much longer. Mary Louise died in 1874, and Julia Rose in 1876. Neither of them married, and their mother, Julia, died in 1885. The contingency clause kicked in: Walter's nieces and nephews got half of the estate, and the balance of $2,149,201 could be used to start a public library.

Enough time had passed since the will had been drafted that Chicago already had a free public library, established in 1872 in an old water tank. The executors of the Newberry estate, William H. Bradley and the delightfully named Eliphalet W. Blatchford, proposed a non-circulating research institution that would be open to everyone. Eliphalet, another early member of the Chicago Historical Society and co-founder of the Chicago Academy of Sciences, was installed as the library's first president, a role he held until his death in 1914.

William Frederick Poole became their first librarian, leaving his post at the Chicago Public Library, which he'd directed since 1873. Poole was pretty much *the* man for the job. He was president of the American Library Association and an accomplished bibliographer and library administrator who wrote the book on indexing.

Poole's early focus was on building the nascent Newberry Library's collections. Walter's books had gone up in flames in 1871. The first book the library possessed was a Caxton memorial Bible, the 98th out of 100 copies that had been printed ten years before. The library was in the unusual situation of having few books, but lots of money. Eliphalet donated a few, but most of the acquisitions were purchased. In the first six months, the Newberry acquired 6,457 volumes and 4,907 pamphlets, and only 359 volumes and 742 pamphlets were donated. By the end of 1888, Poole had bought 25,000 books.

While Poole envisioned a library with broad holdings, the Newberry quickly focused on the humanities. One of the first big purchases, in 1889, was the entire musical library of Count Pio Resse of Florence, Italy. This treasure trove included the first opera ever publicly performed in 1600, Jacopo Peri's "Euridice." Maria de Medici signed it herself. The next year Poole secured the Henry Probasco collection. Poole was intimately familiar with the catalog; since he helped advise the Cincinnati collector twenty years before, he knew the $52,294 price tag was worth it. This collection, which included Shakespeare folios, rare bibles, and early editions of Homer, Dante, and Horace, immediately established the Newberry Library as a destination for scholars.

This valuable and quickly growing cache of knowledge needed a suitable home. Henry Ives Cobb had already been hired to design the Chicago Historical Society's new building at Dearborn and Ontario. Eliphalet and his colleagues liked the young architect's style, so in 1888 they hired him to design the library as well. At first, the plan was to build on the site of the former Newberry homestead at Pine and Ontario, but they changed their minds when they realized that the block between Clark and Dearborn on Walton Place would give them 3,000 more square feet. Additionally, the lot fronted Washington Park and it was also on the Clark electric car line. It may have helped that the location was charmed: it had been the site of the former home of Mahlon Ogden, brother to Chicago's first mayor, and the house miraculously escaped the 1871 fire unscathed. Bonus: Walter used to own it. He'd sold it to Arthur Cowles in 1861 for $130,000. Eliphalet et al used the funds from Walter's estate to buy it back for only $45,000 more.

In November 1893, the Newberry Library moved in. Poole died the next year, leaving a collection of more than 160,000 items. That same year the library created an in-house bindery. Another rich Chicagoan left a bequest for a library in his will, so in 1896, the John Crerar Library, Chicago Public Library, and Newberry Library entered into an agreement to make sure there wouldn't be much overlap. Crerar would focus on the sciences, Chicago Public Library would provide general literature and Chicagoana, and the Newberry would concentrate on the humanities. Between the time of the agreement and 1913, the Newberry would donate a quarter of its books to Crerar, including John Audubon's *Birds of America*.

The Newberry would also continue to aggressively expand its own collection. In 1901, they acquired Prince Louis Lucien Bonaparte's 17,000-item linguistics collection. Other significant acquisitions included founding trustee Edward E. Ayer's donation of approximately 50,000 books and original manuscripts focused on North American Indians. John Mansir Wing gave the library his personal collection of the history of printing and money. Over the years the Newberry amassed an encyclopedic stockpile of items related to maps and travel, genealogy, local history, American history, religion, Medieval and Renaissance studies, and Midwest journalism, business, and organizational history.

In the 1940s, librarian Stanley Pargellis instituted public programming, and in the '60s, Lawrence Towner further developed conservation and research. Incredibly, the first fundraising efforts didn't happen until 1964.

Newberry Library Today

This world renowned research library is like a candy store for scholars, students, and anyone interested in the human condition. If you're fourteen or older, you can obtain a free reader card. While you can't check items out of the library, you can get comfortable in one of the reading rooms, and they offer copying services for a fee.

In addition to exhibitions, the Newberry Library has hosted an annual book sale; it's the one time you could take books out of the library. The Saturday of the four-day sale, they hosted the Bughouse Square Debates in Washington Square, the park across the street.

From the 1910s through the 1960s, Washington Square was given the ignominious moniker Bughouse Square. Why? Because it attracted a bunch of bohemians, socialists, atheists, and other free-thinkers. Their raucous debates seemed a little crazy to conservative society, so the masses nicknamed the place after the slang word for mental health facility. While the lively discussions ended during the red scare days, Newberry revived them as a one-day annual event in 1986. Each July, speakers would get up on literal soapboxes and try to persuade you to their line of thinking. Heckling was frequent and encouraged. The best "soapboxer" would win the Dill Pickle, an award named for a club/theater/speakeasy that had been located near Washington Square down Tooker Alley. A guest at the Dill Pickle might have heard Carl Sandburg read a poem, seen a play by Theodore Dreiser, or had an illicit cocktail with Ben Hecht.

1894
New York Life Building
Kimpton Gray Hotel

O ne of Chicago's oddities is that its passion for
celebrating and preserving its past is often surpassed
by its desire to build something new. Since the city's

beginnings there's been a cycle of construction, destruction, and construction again. Some of that destruction was unintentional, but even structures that survived the Great Chicago Fire didn't escape the wrecking ball: Mahlon Ogden's home was razed for the Newberry Library, and the Nixon Building, one of the few buildings in the Loop to survive the conflagration, was replaced by the New York Life Insurance Building. Built in 1894, this seminal structure is now the Kimpton Gray Hotel.

The Kimpton Group is known for renovating and preserving historic buildings, and it's a good thing they took an interest in this particular one at the corner of LaSalle and Monroe. Preservation Chicago fought for years to protect the gray lady, but even though the building had received preliminary Chicago Landmark status in 2002, it was still in danger. In 2006, the group declared the New York Life Insurance Building one of the city's most threatened. That same year there was a proposal to tear down half of the skyscraper to erect a fifty-one story high rise.

Fortunately, the hoteliers stepped in and averted this blasphemy. The building at the corner of LaSalle and Monroe wasn't just old; it was one of the last remaining examples of William Le Baron Jenney's steel frame construction, and the closest link to the first skyscraper in the world.

At a time before planes and automobiles and when trains were just gaining steam, William Le Baron Jenney had serious wanderlust. Like Samuel Nickerson and Marshall Field, William was born in Massachusetts and left home when he was seventeen years old. William didn't head into the western frontier right away, though. Luckily for the adventurous young man, his dad owned a successful whaling fleet. When gold rush fever struck William, he hitched a ride around Cape Horn to California in 1849. Gold may not have struck William back, but San Francisco provided inspiration through tragedy: the gateway city burned in May 1850 and the future architect observed a city using brick to rebuild from the ashes.

Wanderlust pulled the young man's strings again and he was soon sailing the South Seas. While in the Philippines, the eighteen-year-old noticed bamboo huts whose light frames swayed but didn't break. Intrigued, he continued his trip around the world and enrolled in the Lawrence Scientific School at Harvard. Harvard wasn't challenging enough, so he sailed again—this time to Europe. (There were definitely benefits to being the son of a man who owned boats.) William studied engineering and architecture at École Centrale des Arts et Manufactures in Paris, graduating in 1856, a year after his classmate Gustave Eiffel—you know, *that* Eiffel. The young man's next adventure took him to Mexico, where he worked as an engineer on the Tehuantepec Railroad Company. After that he returned to France for a few years, then landed in Cincinnati before joining the Union Army in 1861.

Serious wanderlust indeed.

During the Civil War, William's engineering skills made him invaluable. The Union put him to good use, as it did another New England man, Frederick Law Olmsted. William met the landscaping genius at Vicksburg and they must have hit it off, because they worked together many times in the following decades. After the war, William headed to St. Louis with General Sherman. William was discharged from the army with the rank of Major in 1866 and the next year married Elizabeth "Lizzie" Hannah Cobb in Cleveland, Ohio, and the two moved to Chicago.

And there they stayed. William opened an architectural office, and for a short time partnered with Sanford E. Loring, with whom he wrote "Principles and Practice of Architecture" in 1869. That same year, the newly-formed West Parks Commission hired William to transform the city's west side. His vision for the marshy prairie included three lush parks filled with lagoons, swaths of velvety green lawn, and native and exotic plants. He connected these pastoral settings, now known as Douglas, Garfield, and Humboldt Parks, with broad boulevards. While he designed the western parks, his wartime colleague Olmsted designed the southern. Olmsted and his partner Calvert Vaux were also commissioned to design the town of Riverside. The landscape artists laid out the streets and William engineered and built an innovative steam-powered water tower for the village. After Olmsted and Vaux resigned from the project in 1870, William took over. He liked the town so much he built his own home in the community.

Before the fire of 1871, William's work included many residential commissions, and his designs had a flow similar to his boulevards and parks system. This open plan would later be celebrated by one of his protégé's protégés, Frank Lloyd Wright. After the fire, the city was in sore need of builders and William was both an architect and an engineer. His firm became a training center for up-and-coming architects and the list of people who worked for him was an embarrassment of creative riches: Louis Sullivan, Irving Pond, Martin Roche, and William Holabird were a sample of those who whet their design whistles with Jenney.

At first, Chicago's resurrection was awash with blocky, load-bearing buildings that had a tendency to sink into the marshy terrain. William and his contemporaries searched for more viable construction techniques. Ever the engineer, in 1879 Jenney built the First Leiter Building (the Second Leiter Building would be built in 1891), the first building that used cast-iron columns.

A few years later, William Le Baron Jenney changed skylines forever. The birth of the skyscraper happened almost by accident. Construction had started on the Home Insurance Building when the bricklayers strike of 1883 brought it to a halt. Stone masons had already laid the foundation and it was time for the bricklayers to take over. Instead, they went on strike and William went home in the middle of the day. William's contractor Henry Ericsson recounted the story in his autobiography:

"So unusual was this that Mrs. Jenney could only surmise that {William} must be ill, and as she rose to greet him she found no immediately convenient place to lay the heavy book she was reading. Inadvertently she laid it down on top of a bird cage which stood on a table. At that an inspiration struck Jenney: if so frail a frame of wire would sustain so great a weight without yielding, would not a cage of iron or steel serve as a frame for a building?"

136

Aha! William created a framework of columns, piers, girders, and floor beams. Since the load was now distributed, bricks became mere curtains. Without the need for thick supporting walls, bigger windows allowed more light. At only ten stories, the Home Insurance Building may not have been the tallest building in Chicago when it was completed in 1885, but it was the most innovative.

Over the next several years, William honed his design. In 1893, the New York Life Insurance Company commissioned an office building at the corner of LaSalle and Monroe. The skeleton frame allowed for more and bigger windows as well as more internal space, making buildings more efficient. Not only did this novel construction mean the usable square footage could be maximized, it also minimized the length of time it would take to finish the project. They erected the steel frame in only ten weeks and completed the whole building in just nine months. It happened that quickly, in part, because crews could build the facade on different levels at different times; they didn't have to finish one floor before moving to the next. Never before had anyone seen a building's exterior constructed on multiple levels at the same time. This feat made the New York Life Insurance building an attraction during the World's Columbian Exposition. Colleagues clamored to know how they did it and more than fifty architects requested drawings. Before the final terra cotta cladding was added, William and his partner, William Mundie, published detailed explanations of their method in both *The American Architect* and *Building News*.

New York Life Insurance moved into their twelve story building in April of 1894. Four years later, Jenney and Mundie added a thirteen story building adjacent to the original, and topped the first building with another floor. In 1903, another floor was added, bringing it to its current height of fourteen stories.

New York Life Insurance Building Today

When the Kimpton Hotel Group purchased the historic building in 2014 it had a neglected infrastructure and, although it had been used as an office building, the interior was built for a late-nineteenth / early-twentieth century workforce. According to "the Gray," published by The Kimpton Gray Hotel, the granite and terra cotta facade were "comprehensively restored in surgical fashion," down to preserving the original double hung windows. The LaSalle Street entrance showcases the grand double staircase of Georgia gray marble, which gave the hotel its name, and the coffered ceiling. The first floor elevators sport ornate bronze doors that date back to the 1930s, and the stairs lead to a second story with "triumphal-arch" door surrounds with Classical-style ornamentation and Ionic columns. Boleo, on the 15th floor, serves South American street food and beverages, but the main attraction for any architecture fan is the exposed steel framework that makes this property unique and one of the most important buildings in Chicago.

1894
Tree Studios

Smack dab in the middle of the River North and Magnificent Mile neighborhoods sits what had been one of the oldest artists' colonies in the country. Lined up on State Street between Ontario and Ohio, Tree Studios rented space at reduced rates to artists. It began when the Trees, world-travelers and dedicated supporters of the arts, decided to build an Art Palace in their backyard.

The year was 1894 and the economy was shattered. The Panic of 1893 had started a nationwide depression that would continue for years. Banks closed, businesses failed, including even seemingly infallible railroads, and laborers went on strike. In Chicago, the glow from the World's Columbian Exposition, which opened about the time the panic began, had quickly worn off as the White City disappeared. Workers who'd found temporary jobs during the fair were suddenly unemployed and Chicago was overrun with the destitute and homeless.

In the midst of this despair, Lambert and Anna Tree decided to open, of all things, an artists colony. The wealthy couple lived on an entire city block bounded by Ontario, Ohio, State, and Cass (now Wabash) Streets. His Chicago pedigree stretched back to 1856. Hers, all the way to 1832. Subscribers to society rags *Elite* and *Figaro* could follow the Trees' comings and goings, whether it was a jaunt to the Northwest for a holiday, a reception at the Palmers' for Baron and Baroness Hengelmüller, or a European visit with their son and his wife Ethel, Marshall Field's daughter. They were philanthropists and supporters of the arts, which meant the usual memberships on various boards and lots of donations. There were signs, however, that maybe this couple was a bit more dedicated than their wealthy peers. In a letter to the Commissioners of Lincoln Park dated July 8, 1889, Lambert said:

"Recently, while residing abroad in an official capacity, I caused to be executed in bronze a statue of Robert Cavelier de La Salle, and my purpose in doing so was that I might on my return home offer it as a gift to Lincoln Park."

Lambert, who was Ambassador to Belgium from 1885 to 1888, decided to commission Count Jacques de Lalaing, "Belgian sculptor of distinction," to sculpt a monument without even knowing if his city would take it. He donated another sculpture five years later. Lambert had seen "A Signal of Peace," by Cyrus Edwin Dallin, at the World's Fair, bought it, and gave it to Lincoln Park in 1894. While Lalaing's sculpture was a monument to the country's European settlers, Dallin's statue celebrated the original inhabitants. According to the Chicago Park District, Lambert "wrote that Indians had been 'oppressed and robbed by government agents, deprived of their lands... shot down by soldiery in wars fomented for the purpose of plundering and destroying their race, and finally drowned by the ever-westward tide of population.'"

Obviously the arts, and their role in the community, were a big thing for the Trees, but starting an arts colony was a whole different level of patronage. Especially when they built it in their backyard.

Haines H. Magie, Anna Josephine's father, moved to Chicago in 1832 from New Jersey. It wasn't officially Chicago yet; there were only about two hundred people hanging around Fort Dearborn and the town wouldn't be incorporated until the next year. Haines opened a dry goods store on Lake Street, and he was said to have been the Marshall Field of his time. He was certainly successful enough to buy a whole city block, which he did around 1840. There's little mention of Anna's early years; she was a woman at a time when most were referred to by their husbands' names, not their own.

Conversely, Lambert's biography is well documented. He grew up in Washington, D.C., the son of a lifetime postal clerk, and moved to Chicago in 1856. After graduating from the University of Virginia and being accepted to the bar in the nation's capital, Senator Stephen Douglas recommended that Lambert head west. He did, and his law practice thrived. He married Anna three years later and they had a son, Arthur, in 1869. The following year Lambert was elected a Cook County Circuit Court judge, quickly building a reputation as a stickler against corruption in city government. So quick, that as soon as he donned the robe, he instructed a grand jury to investigate members of the city council for charges of malfeasance. The result was a round of indictments and a city on notice: there was a new judge in town, and he meant business.

After retiring from the judgeship in 1875, Lambert and Anna spent a few years in Europe. When they returned, he unsuccessfully ran for both the U.S. Congress and Senate. During this time, Haines died, leaving his son-in-law Lambert an estate worth four million dollars, including his homestead north of the Chicago River, making him the richest man in Chicago.

In 1885, President Grover Cleveland appointed Lambert as the Ambassador to Belgium. He held that post for three years before serving a short stint as the Russian Ambassador. That lasted less than a month because he resigned when President Harrison took office.

Already inclined to support the arts, their many years in Europe and the influx of painters and sculptors during the Columbian Exposition influenced the Trees to develop an environment where artists could be free to create. The couple split their block in half and hired New York architects Parfitt Brothers and Chicago-based Hill and Woltersdorf to design a studio. Studio Building, or the "Arts Palace," as the *Inter Ocean* dubbed the project, would line State Street with retail shops on the first floor and studios on the second, "all with the northern light that is indispensable to a correct studio," as Judge Tree said. Those retail shops would enable the Trees to charge artists rates that they could afford.

Studio Building was popular from the start. The studios had connecting doors so that artists could mix and mingle. Without private bathrooms, the studios weren't originally designed to be apartments, but that didn't stop the artists from moving in. This became a place where they both worked and lived. Signs warned models to put on some clothes before trotting to the facilities. Artists were advised not to cook stinky food, like cabbage, as it would offend their neighbors. Those were halcyon days of creativity and community. The artists were so close that, when a baby in a basket was abandoned on their doorstep in July 1903, five of them stepped up to be guardians for the poor waif. They named him James Vincent Whistler, after James Whistler, the artist, and St. Vincent's orphan asylum, who was taking care of the baby. Sadly, shortly after Mr. and Mrs. T. G. Hoges fostered young James in August, he died of pneumonia.

Later that year, Anna also died while the Trees were returning from what would be her final trip to Europe. Lambert lived for another seven. With both of them gone, the Studio Building could have been in danger, but Lambert and Anna had set up a trust for the building that was effective through 1959, stipulating that only artists could live and work in the studios and that rents would remain affordable.

The Tree estate sold the residence to the Medinah Temple Association, a.k.a. Shriners, who razed the house and built an Ottoman-themed shrine with a convention hall that would seat six thousand people. The artist studios were in such demand that in 1912, Hill and Woltersdorf built an extension on Ohio Street, and in 1913 another on Ontario Street. These two additions and the Medinah Temple to their east created a courtyard. When the Shriners added onto the back of their building, it slashed the courtyard almost in half.

During the trust's lifetime the arts colony thrived. Resident artists included J. Allen St. John, the illustrator who brought Tarzan to life; Louis Grell, muralist of the Chicago Theatre; and John Storrs, whose sculpture of Ceres still oversees the Financial District from atop the Board of Trade. Actors Burgess Meredith and Peter Falk lived there for a time. Even after the protective trust ended and the Shriners bought Tree Studios, artists continued to try to keep the arts colony going. It's estimated that, in spite of low turnover and a small number of spaces, more than six hundred artists have lived and worked in those studios. But, with no more rent restrictions, the people for whom those studios were built couldn't afford them anymore.

With its prime location between River North and the Magnificent Mile, Tree Studios was in constant danger of demolition. The original building didn't get Chicago Landmark designation until 1997, and it took another four years for the annexes and courtyard to be protected. But, protected they were, and in 2001 Albert Friedman purchased the property and began restoration.

Tree Studios Today

Tree Studios is no longer an arts colony, but it does continue to provide opportunities for artists and arts-related businesses. The first floor spaces are a mix of retail shops and

restaurants. And if you step inside one of those studios, you'll
see that northern light still shining.

1895
Chicago Varnish Company
Harry Caray's Italian Steakhouse

T he first time you see the building at the southeast corner of Kinzie and Dearborn, you'll do a double take. Then a triple. You'll realize you're staring. "There's a whole lot going on," you'll think, what with those red bricks and white accents, an exuberant number of dormers and stepped gables and a steeply pitched roof. There are quoins and voussoirs and all sorts of other architectural elements that combine to create a distinctive and complex exterior. The Chicago Landmarks Designation Report states there's a "nearly hedonistic pleasure in decoration," yet the architect displayed a "controlled sense of craft." You agree with that assessment.

If you think there's a lot happening on the outside, just wait until you find out what happened inside, underneath, and before the building even existed. Bootleggers, tee-totalers, insects frozen in amber and vaults encased in walls, hidden tunnels, future presidents, and egg-throwing apes all played a part in the history of what is now Harry Caray's Italian Steakhouse.

The story of this corner starts with a man in a canoe. Dr. Alexander Wolcott Jr. landed at Fort Dearborn at the end of August 1820. He was the new "Indian Agent," assigned to interact with and pay annuities to the area's original inhabitants. He was also the settlement's first doctor. He moved into a cabin north of the river and west of the Kinzie residence. Three years after arriving, Alexander married Ellen Kinzie, the not-quite-eighteen-year-old daughter of John, in the first non-native wedding. The newlyweds moved into the fort, possibly because Alexander's housekeeping was so bad his neighbors called his cabin the Cobweb Castle. In 1830, the US government divided the land around the river into blocks and sold them to raise money for a future canal. Dr. Wolcott bought Block Number 1 for $685 (or $692, depending on the source).

Twenty-eight days later, he died, and his will went into probate, another first.

During the growing pains of Chicago's early years, Block Number 1 changed hands a few times. William B. Ogden, the city's first Mayor, owned it for a bit. Grant Goodrich, with his partner Alexander N. Fullerton, had law offices on the property. Mr. Goodrich (a relation by marriage to the author of this book) was an attorney, a judge, and a good friend of Abraham Lincoln's. Grant was such a good friend he invited the future president to become his law partner. Abe declined, but the two remained close.

Mr. Goodrich was a tee-totaler of the driest order. He co-founded Northwestern University in Evanston and was partly responsible for that northern Chicago suburb's lack of liquor. With his dedication to abstention, he probably wouldn't have been too thrilled with the future shenanigans that would take place on Block Number 1.

By mid-century, railroad tracks lined the northern side of the river. With the ability to ship via both train and boat, this area was the perfect location for industry. It was a district of warehouses, filled with smoke, grime, and noise—an unlikely place to build one of the most magnificent buildings in the city.

The Chicago Varnish Company began as a small family affair in 1865. Their product was a resin preparation that protects wood, furniture, coaches, and carriages and gives them a glossy finish. It was also used for maritime purposes and painting restoration. It doesn't sound very glamorous, unless you're the author of *Commerce, manufactures, banking and transportation facilities, 1884*. Then you'll wax—or varnish—rhapsodic:

> "When the wondering attention of the first traveler was directed to a smooth, rounded, translucent, yellowish mass, now known as the Gum Copal of commerce, the quantities in which it was found may have led him to speculate on its possible utility, but it is entirely improbable that he ever entertained the remotest conjecture as to its value in the arts, or the immense traffic to which it was eventually destined to give rise... Where I sit writing, this, the desk on which I lean, the chair in which I sit, and indeed the most of the furniture which meets the eye, owes its lustrous beauty to a cloudy mass of gum which years ago exuded from

giant trees in the heart of Madagascar. The luxurious carriages which roll so noiselessly along our streets bearing perhaps the representatives of millions, the magnificent pianos of modern manufacture, from whose mirrored surfaces the face of the beholder is thrown back as from the depths of a lonely well, owe their exquisite perfection of gloss to the same pale, tasteless Copal gum."

By the early 1890s, the Chicago Varnish Company wanted a building suitable for this wondrous lacquer. They bought the northwest corner of Block Number 1 and hired one of the city's architectural sweethearts. Henry Ives Cobb was in his early thirties when he was given the commission for the new showroom. He may have been young, but he already had the Union Club and the Palmer Castle (both demolished) under his belt, and in 1893 he added the Chicago Athletic Association and the Newberry Library to his credits. Instead of being associated with a distinctive style, like H. H. Richardson or Louis Sullivan, Cobb was known for his adaptation of different genres. For example, Newberry was Richardsonian Romanesque and the Chicago Athletic Association was Venetian Gothic.

For the Chicago Varnish Company Building, completed in 1895, Cobb chose Dutch Renaissance Revival. Its spirited exterior stood out among the factories, warehouses, railroads and shipyards like the petals of a bright red tulip above a late April snow. (Which happens in Chicago frequently.)

The location may not have been the best place for a showroom, but the company used it as such for fifteen years, even installing a resin museum. Customers and clients could get a close-up look at insects that were thousands of years old, frozen in the same material that would be glossed over carriage doors and fireplace mantels. The Chicago Varnish Company moved out of their Dutch masterpiece in 1910, and a few years later they donated their collection of hardened resin and encased bugs to the Field Museum.

The company leased out the building to various interests until 1925, when Thomas Alexander Somerville purchased it. His company, Hunter, Walton & Co, sold wholesale butter, eggs, and cheese. He was serious enough he put his company name in giant letters on top of Cobb's masterpiece. Fourteen years later, another food-based company purchased the building. Louis Caravetta wanted the space for his Ehrat Cheese Company and its Italian specialty foods.

Sounds innocent enough, doesn't it? Only if you forget this is Chicago, where there is always a suspicion of impropriety and corruption, especially in the 1920s.

In addition to the legitimate sale of foodstuffs, there was also quite a bit of mischief occurring at Kinzie and Dearborn. Gustav Muller, an Al Capone confederate, was rumored to have run a speakeasy in the building during Prohibition. In 1926, a raid netted dozens of illegal slot machines. On January 4, 1934, Chicago patrolman John Moore called the police station. According to an article picked up by the *Gettysburg* (Tennessee) *Times* from January 5:

> "I want help," he reported emphatically. "I am being egged by a brace of apes and my horse has been snapped at by a bear and I want a transfer to the motorcycle detail."

Apparently, two chimpanzees and a bear were on their way to a photo shoot. Their trainer told them to wait in the car while he met with the photographer. Being wild animals, they didn't, especially when a kind passerby helped them out by opening the rear gate of the vehicle. The bear headed for the nearest saloon and the chimpanzees found a truck full of eggs, most likely idling in front of Hunter, Walton & Co. The apes entered the warehouse and then the elevator, each biting a leg of the operator. Finally the trainer emerged from his meeting, rounded up the wayward animals, and the truck driver cleaned "raw omelet out of an ear."

Louis Caravetta bought the building in 1939 and his future son-in-law Frank Nitti, nee Nitto, had an apartment on the fourth floor. According to most accounts, Frank had taken over the Chicago Outfit while his buddy Al Capone languished in prison. In 1942, Frank married Louis' daughter Annette, giving her $75,000 for the privilege. The hush-hush is that the money was a thank-you present for flushing out her boss, Ed O'Hare, which put him directly into the path of a speeding bullet. Ed, Capone's former attorney, allegedly gave up the goods that put Al away.

Frank killed himself the year after he and Annette married. It wasn't because the marriage was that bad: he was about to go to prison himself for his part in a Hollywood film industry extortion plot. Rather than be locked up, he got drunk and shot himself in the head. Frank may not have been in the building for very long, but a later tenant would discover that he'd gotten quite a bit of use out of it.

The Caravettas kept the building for the next few decades. In 1971, Kinzie Street Steak and Chop House opened the first restaurant. Nine years later, different restaurateurs opened Miller's on Kinzie, also a steakhouse. Finally, in 1987, Harry Caray's Italian Steakhouse opened on the northwest corner of Block Number 1, and it's been hitting home runs ever since.

Chicago Varnish Company Today

Harry Caray's Italian Steakhouse is, of course, a restaurant, and a fine one at that. Any place that's survived the tumultuous River North dining scene for more than thirty years does so for good reason. It's more than just a celebrity name on a gorgeous building. It's Holy Cow-worthy good food and good service.

This is a place that's also very much rooted in the past. CEO Grant DePorter may be even more obsessed with the building's history than he is with the Chicago Cubs, and he wrote a book on the team. The first floor of the Chicago Varnish Company Building is decorated with sports memorabilia, celebrity photos, and a bust of Harry Caray, the famed baseball announcer, himself. Head towards the stairs to the basement, though, and you'll be stepping back in time.

The walls of the staircase are lined with photos and newspaper clippings telling the stories of the building's past inhabitants. Annette, Frank, Al, Ed O'Hare the scoundrel and Butch O'Hare the hero—their stories are told through these windows to the past. At the bottom of the stairs, there's an actual window cut into the brick wall. Inside is Frank's address book, filled with names and numbers of prominent people who would make the Outfit's activities go a little smoother. There's also a vault, within a vault, within a vault. This belts-and-suspenders safe shows signs of multiple attempts to crack it.

Elsewhere in the basement, DePorter discovered secret rooms, another vault, bricked-over doors, and a passageway that led to the underground tunnels favored by bootleggers and gangsters. He's documented, and publicized, all of it, and one media appearance garnered the attention of Nitti's descendants. They've kept in touch and provided DePorter with a priceless collection of the property's titles, going all the way back to Dr. Alexander Wolcott.

1897
Chicago Public Library
Chicago Cultural Center

T he Chicago Cultural Center is big, bold, and beautiful. It's a solid institution in a solid building anchoring the intersection of Randolph and Michigan. Filling an entire block, the stone structure stands as an impressive monument to culture; it seems like it was always meant to be. The short story is that the People's Palace, as it was quickly nicknamed, began as Chicago's first central public library and then became the first free cultural center in the country.

But this is Chicago, and there are no short stories. This is a town of tantalizing tales with twists, turns, and convoluted machinations.

Prior to 1872, Chicago didn't have a free public library. However, it did have private libraries, and it had books. Lots of libraries, and lots of books. It's estimated that the Great Chicago Fire burned between two to three million volumes. Two to three million irreplaceable tomes of knowledge and information. If you need to cry, go ahead. It's understandable.

The Chicago Library Association, a fee-based organization formerly known as the Young Men's Association, lost 30,000 volumes. The Chicago Historical Society lost another 50,000. The YMCA, not to be confused with the YMA, lost 10,000. The Academy of Sciences and Union Catholic Library Association, 5,000 each. Plus dozens of smaller society, church, school, and private libraries lost their own collections.

It was devastating. Incalculable. After the fire, John Robson, a Brit and Chicago Library Association's librarian, attempted to rebuild, but after a few weeks he went home to England. He didn't give up, though. He applied to British authorities for a new set of English Patent Reports and attempted to gather individual donations. Another Englishman, A. H. Burgess, had a more efficient idea. He used the media to appeal to the British public. England could provide Chicago with a free library, as both a sympathetic gesture and a keepsake for future goodwill. This idea sounded grand to Thomas Hughes, a prominent member of Parliament and author of *Tom Brown's School Days* who had visited Chicago in 1870 and been impressed. In short order, thousands of volumes made their way across the Atlantic and the eastern United States all the way to Chicago. Even Queen Victoria, Prime Minister Benjamin Disraeli, and Charles Darwin, among other British luminaries, sent books.

Now Chicago had to figure out what to do with them. It didn't seem right to put these gifts into private collections when they'd been given to re-create an ostensibly free library. So, Chicago fixed it. On March 7, 1872, a mere five months after the fire, the state legislature passed the Illinois Local

Library Act, giving municipalities the power to use tax dollars to fund public libraries. On April 3, a city ordinance established the Chicago Public Library and five days later the members of the first Board of Directors were appointed.

The next step was to find a place to store all of those books, and the library board found one in an old iron water tank, which was a perfectly logical location. The books from England and elsewhere began arriving shortly after the fire and the library formed within six months, so protecting those volumes was of the utmost concern. Encased in walls of solid brick and stone masonry, the iron tank had already proven it was fireproof. It also had a hollow center fifty-eight feet in diameter. Library board president Thomas Hoyne christened it a new "reservoir" of knowledge. On January 1, 1873, this unique repository opened its doors, and while the books weren't quite ready to be checked out, there were current periodicals and newspapers, and more than 50,000 people visited the library in its first five months.

The quirky tank location was a short-term fix, and on May 1, 1874, the Chicago Public Library, with famed librarian William F. Poole at the helm, opened at the corner of Wabash and Madison. Thomas Hoyne checked out the first book: *Tom Brown's School Days*, by library benefactor Thomas Hughes.

Chicagoans lapped up this free and easy access to knowledge. By the end of the first year, Poole had increased the collections to 40,000 books with a circulation of 399,156 volumes, surpassing the circulation of all other single libraries in the country save Boston. Despite the demand, funding was lacking, and it got to the point where purchasing new books was suspended for half a year. In 1875, the library had to move to cheaper digs at Lake and Dearborn. This time, the library stayed put for more than a decade before moving to the fourth floor of City Hall, where it stayed for another eleven years.

The Chicago Public Library needed a permanent home, one that would be worthy of its mission—and fireproof. On October 23, 1880, the board created the Future Library Building committee. In March of the following year, the board solicited private subscriptions to build the library as a memorial to the world's generosity. This Memorial Association of Chicago gained in popularity and the Academy of Design and Academy of Sciences, two private schools, latched on. However, the conflict of conflating public and private enterprises killed that idea.

The library board rebounded. It set its sights on Dearborn Park: at 62,500 square feet, the square was big enough and the location in the central business district was ideal. Getting it, however, was another matter.

The problem came from a pesky little notation on an old map. After the U.S. Government no longer needed Fort Dearborn, it sold lots at an average rate of $5,000 per acre. The block between Randolph and Washington to the north and south, and Michigan and what is now Garland Court to the east and west, was marked as "Public ground, forever to remain vacant of buildings." At the time the lots were sold, this plot, known as Dearborn Park, provided a square of green and a lovely view of the lake, which meant people would pay more for the surrounding lots.

Over the years, railroads moved in and the view disappeared. Down the street Lake Park grew and the square seemed superfluous. Still, it remained mostly free and clear, although temporary buildings popped up here and there. The Committee on Future Library Building took a bill to the U.S. Congress multiple times to try to obtain the park, but never got on the legislative calendar. The Academy of Design tried, again, to be part of the new building. After the library's earlier experience with the private organization, it said no, so the Academy did an end-run and joined forces with the Soldiers' Home. These Union Army veterans had connections, including Senator John A. Logan, and in January of 1886, Congress passed a bill that granted Dearborn Park to the Chicago Public Library, the Academy of Design, and the Chicago Soldiers' Home—without the library's knowledge. The bill stated that all three were public institutions. That was obviously false. Eventually the Soldiers abandoned the Academy of Design and agreed to work solo with the library.

What a mess. And it wasn't over for several years. After the effort required to take this all the way to Washington, an Illinois ruling in 1888 declared that deciding the fate of Dearborn Park was actually a local matter. The state legislature then passed an act stating the Soldiers' Home in Chicago could build their memorial hall on the north quarter of Dearborn Park. Once again, this was done without the knowledge of the library. Before any construction could begin, owners of the abutting lots had to provide permission. Finally, after more negotiations, on February 12, 1891, a Chicago ordinance stated that the Chicago Public Library could build on Dearborn Park as long as it incorporated a Grand Army of the Republic Memorial Hall for the soldiers. In fifty years, the space would revert to the library.

After that rigamarole, you better believe the Chicago Library Board wanted something magnificent. A call went out for designs, and in January 1892, thirteen firms submitted drawings. The Fine Arts Building's Solon Beman and Jenney and Mundie, the inventors of the skyscraper, were two of the firms that sent submissions. Shepley, Rutan and Coolidge, H. H. Richardson's successors, submitted the winning design. That same year, the firm also secured the contract for the Art Institute of Chicago, a landmark whose construction would begin in 1892 and finish at breakneck speed, opening in time for the 1893 World's Columbian Exposition.

Construction of the library took a bit longer. To ensure the building wouldn't sink, Chief Engineer William Sooy Smith directed workers to drive 2,357 wooden piles 75 feet into the hardpan clay. This seemingly extreme effort meant there's been no noticeable settlement in more than a century.

When the building opened on October 11, 1897, it was immediately dubbed The People's Palace, due to both its grandeur and the fact that the people had paid for it through a tax levy. Although the exterior design is unified, two entrances illustrate the building's original dual purpose. The Randolph Street approach features Doric columns, chosen because the Doric order was associated with the military, and that entrance led to the Grand Army of the Republic section of the building. A grand marble staircase ascends to a rotunda topped by plaster carvings of swords, shields, helmets, and flags and a stained glass dome created by local company Healy and Millet. Beyond the rotunda, for several years the Memorial Hall held Civil War artifacts, including Ulysses S. Grant's saddle and Custer's hat. Above walls lined with dark green Vermont marble march the names of thirty Civil War battles.

Library patrons entered from Washington Avenue past Ionic columns into a palatial vestibule. Overhead, an arch glittered with the names of great thinkers. The whole entry glittered: the grand staircase was made of Carrara marble, the same marble used by Michelangelo, and dark green Connemara marble from Ireland, and everywhere you looked the surfaces were embedded with mosaics from Tiffany.

In the General Delivery Room, light filtered through a massive dome, also by Tiffany. It's still the largest stained glass Tiffany dome in the world. Those 1890s artists decorated it with Zodiac signs and favrile glass shaped like fish scales. Quotations in multiple languages, to reflect Chicago's many cultures, line the walls. On the east side of the room, there are quotes in Chinese, Egyptian, Arabic, Greek, and Hebrew. On the west, they're in German, French, Spanish, Italian, and Latin. Author names decorate the arches dividing the center from the wings.

And this is just where John and Jane Q. Public would pick up their books. To read their selections, they'd head to the reading room, a cavernous space stretching the length of the building. Massive windows provided light in the rich room colored with Pompeian reds and modeled after the Venetian Doge's Palace.

The building was, and is, a resplendent kaleidoscope. When the board declared with "inspired recklessness" that it wanted a building that would suit the needs of a city of three million inhabitants, it didn't suspect Chicago would reach that number by 1930. By the 1960s, the building was at its breaking point, and demolition threatened. Destroying The People's Palace might seem extreme, but this was a time when historic treasures were being blasted away left and right. Not even Sullivan's grand Old Stock Exchange escaped the jackhammer, but that loss kicked already serious preservationists into even higher gear. They weren't about to lose the Chicago Public Library, too.

A high rise was slated to replace the building, but the legend goes that a well-placed "I don't think that would be nice," in the *Chicago Tribune* by Eleanor "Sis" Daley prompted her husband, Mayor Richard J. Daley, to rethink that plan. There were other forces at play, most notably preservation activist Charles Staples. He tirelessly campaigned to save the Chicago Public Library and, with Senator Adlai Stevenson, was instrumental in securing its listing on the National Register of Historic Places.

Now that it was safe, it was time to get spruced up. From 1974 to 1977, Holabird and Root expertly and sensitively updated the building while keeping its historic beauty. Before the renovation was even complete, it was designated a Chicago Landmark.

In 1977, the central library building became known as the Chicago Public Library Cultural Center. When Mayor Richard M. Daley, Sis' son, dedicated the Harold Washington Library Center in 1991, the People's Palace became the Chicago Cultural Center, making it the first free municipal cultural center in the world.

Chicago Public Library Today

The evolution from free public library to free cultural center was an inspired transition that illustrates the importance of the arts in Chicago. The Chicago Cultural Center has multiple gallery spaces and has hosted thousands of arts performances. Preston Bradley Hall, formerly the General Delivery Room, is open to the public when it's not being used for concerts, conferences, weddings, and private events. The Main Reading Room, originally considered too bold for a library, is now the

Sidney R. Yates Gallery. The Grand Army of the Republic Rotunda and Memorial Hall are also in demand for private events. Located next to the hall and rotunda, the Claudia Cassidy Theater, named for an influential theater critic, has frequently accommodated concerts, lectures, and other programs.

This free treasure truly is the People's Palace.

1899
Schlesinger and Mayer
Sullivan Center

F orm follows function is an architectural mantra that has been repeated so often that it's become white noise. It's something someone says when they're talking about architecture, especially when they're talking about architecture in Chicago in the late 19th and early 20th centuries. But for one architect, *form ever follows function* was a plea for the belief that each structure should be designed for its specific use. One building should not be interchangeable with another, especially when what happens within a building differs based on its occupants.

To Louis Sullivan, a building was not a building was not a building.

Louis Sullivan was by all accounts a genius and by most an arrogant misanthrope with an ego to rival that of his protegé, Frank Lloyd Wright. He suffered no fools, and to him, fools were those who relied on the tired influence of Greek and Roman classicism. Just because you slapped neo on the front didn't make it new. What Louis wanted, what he felt architecture needed, was an entirely new design language that was utilitarian without being boring, and artistic without being frivolous. He wanted a distinct, and democratic, American architecture—and he created it.

What is now known as Sullivan Center is considered the most significant example of Louis' design ethos. In 1973, Hugh C. Miller, in a study prepared by the Office of Archeology and Historic Preservation for the National Park Service wrote:

> "Sullivan's superior sense of scale, proportion, rhythm, and organization, coupled with his unparalleled imagination as an ornamentalist, is a declaration not of his style alone, but of his architectural principles. The Carson Store building {Sullivan Center} is both an exploitation of the aesthetic possibilities of the steel frame and a statement of the system of construction epitomized in the Chicago School movement."

Louis' genius came at a price. Many people didn't want to work with him, and even the center now named for him was completed by one of his biggest rivals. Built in stages between 1899 and 1906, the complex was his last major commercial commission, even though he lived until 1924. That's a long dry spell for someone as influential, creative, and immodest as he was. A testament to the brilliance of this particular structure is that it's still, partially, being used for its original purpose, more than 125 years after its conception.

The building was originally commissioned as the home of Schlesinger & Mayer. The dry goods store began when two friends joined forces in 1872, taking advantage of the hubbub of rebuilding after the fire. Leopold Schlesinger and David Mayer both emigrated from Germany. In 1862, Leopold came directly to Chicago as a twenty-year-old seeker of fortune. David's parents brought him to America in 1852, when he was just an infant. The two met while working at a dry goods store in Chicago, and after the fire decided they needed to open their own mercantile. In 1873, Schlesinger & Mayer became a family affair when Leopold married David's sister, Henrietta.

The brothers-in-law's first location was a small store at Madison and Desplaines. After quick success, they opened a second location further west on Madison at Peoria. By 1881, however, they knew that State Street was the place to be, so they leased space in the W.W. Boyington-designed Bowen Block, also at Madison. This Parisian-esque building welcomed customers through a corner entrance and was grandly situated to take advantage of traffic from the new cable cars that ran up and down the city's shopping district.

All that traffic, and the friendly competition with Marshall Field & Co. to the north and with Carson, Pirie, Scott to the west, meant booming business. Leopold and David rented more space until they realized they needed a building of their own. In the early 1890s, the two men hired the innovative firm of Adler & Sullivan, which was fresh off its success with the Auditorium Building. The architects didn't get very far before the economy crashed in 1893. Work stopped, and soon, so did Adler & Sullivan's partnership. While most of their clients went with the more genial Adler, David was a fan of Louis' unique, modern designs and insisted on staying with the irascible genius. By 1899, construction began.

This was to be a building unlike any other in a city known for its ingenuity. The first floor featured enormous windows, and above, slightly smaller central panes flanked by narrower strips of glass provided a maximum amount of natural light, a layout known as the Chicago Window. While the rounded corner entrance at State and Madison replicated the footprint of Boyington's Bowen Block, that's where the similarities ended. This new skyscraper stretched twelve stories, and the exposed structure celebrated its altitude. In *The Tall Office Building Artistically Considered*, Sullivan's treatise from 1896—which was about the time he began designing the new Schlesinger & Mayer building—he described the perfect skyscraper. It would have a base that expressed the function within and allowed as much natural light as possible, followed by however many floors were necessary. These would be identically designed because their functions were identical. The top should have a cornice that essentially capped the structure, a signal to the observer that this is where the building ended and the sky began. Instead of hiding a building's height, Louis emphasized it.

The design he created for Schlesinger & Mayer followed this tripartite prescription, and strong horizontal lines highlighted the store's sheer mass. Louis also saluted the building's geographical location: his famed ornamentation was inspired by the Midwestern plains. It's about as Sullivanesque as you can get, although Louis can't take all the credit. His chief draftsman and ornament designer, George Elmslie, worked side-by-side with Louis to create the riotous cacophony of decoration that makes this building unique from all others in downtown Chicago. Instead of terra cotta, stone, or marble, the flourishes were displayed in cast iron that had been painted red and overlaid with green to imitate oxidized bronze. Formed into leaves, berries, flowers, vines, and geometric forms, it embellished the first floor and tempted passersby to stop, stare, and ultimately, enter. According to the Chicago Landmark Report, the base had to "delight the casual pedestrian, but it also had to entice the shopper." The design, like most of Louis' signature ornamentation, stemmed from a love of nature that had been fostered during his childhood on his grandparents' Massachusetts farm.

As the building took shape, the business began to fall apart.

Louis had drafted a three-part plan, designed to help minimize revenue losses during construction, a step-by-step approach that predated the Palmer House's celebrated expansion by twenty-six years. Although Schlesinger & Mayer tried to mitigate any losses, debt continued to mount and the process took a toll on Leopold. After thirty years, he was done. He sold his portion of the business to Henry Siegel of New York on June 14, 1902.

David wasn't too far behind. The next year, after his new partner, Henry Siegel, declined to provide additional investment, David approached John Pirie and proposed a merger with Carson, Pirie, Scott & Co. Their lease was due to expire and David thought it would be a perfect solution. This was a big deal, though, and the competitors needed time to mull it over.

Around the same time, "Mile-a-minute" Harry Selfridge was feeling the need to spread his wings and in 1904 approached his boss and partner, Marshall Field. Marshall declined to give him his own store, so Harry decided to strike out on his own, and he took his $1.5-million settlement, added another $3.5-million, and bought David out on May 15. On June 13, Schlesinger & Mayer officially became H. G. Selfridge & Co.

That lasted all of two months. Almost immediately, Harry realized that he didn't want to take over someone else's business; he wanted to start his own. In one of the quickest turn-arounds ever, he sold the building and leaseholds to Otto Young, who leased the land from Marshall Field, and sold the store itself to Carson, Pirie, Scott & Co., thereby completing David's proposal from the year before.

During all of this, the building still wasn't done. The first nine-story section, located east of State Street on Madison, opened in December of 1899. Construction had lagged as Leopold and David struggled with their mounting debt and entrepreneurial exhaustion, and the twelve-story corner

Living Landmarks of Chicago

section wasn't completed until after Carson, Pirie, Scott & Co. took over in 1904. With Louis' advocate, David, out of the picture, so was Louis, and the new owners hired Daniel Burnham in 1906 to construct the final section.

Carson, Pirie, Scott & Co had more success in the new building than their predecessors. The store had already been around for decades before purchasing H. G. Selfridge & Co. It began similarly to Schlesinger & Mayer, with a couple of immigrants.

Born in Scotland in 1827, John Pirie moved to Ireland when he was fifteen to work at his uncle's dry goods store in Newry. There he met Samuel Carson, and the two moved to Belfast before making their way to America. In 1855, the pair opened a store in LaSalle, about a hundred miles southwest of Chicago. They moved to Amboy and opened additional locations in other towns, inviting brothers George and Robert Scott, whom they'd met in Newry, to join them. John married Samuel's sister, Sarah, and Samuel married John's sister Elizabeth, making their partnership even more of a family affair than Leopold's and David's would be. In the 1860s Carson-Pirie made the leap to Chicago, opening a wholesale store during the Civil War. They brought George and Robert up from downstate to manage their successful business and ventured into retail, hiring another Scotsman, Andrew MacLeish.

Things looked rosy, and then Samuel Carson died in 1869. John insisted on keeping Samuel's name in the business. Then two years later the Great Chicago Fire wiped them out, but Carson, Pirie & Co (Andrew MacLeish was the "Co.") recovered quickly. By 1873, Carson, Pirie & Co had become Carson, Pirie, Scott & Co.

For over a century, the retail giants occupied their Sullivan-designed masterpiece at the corner of State and Madison. A few changes happened over the years: in 1955 the cast iron was gilded for Carson's centennial; the next year, it was painted black, and in 1962, gray. The mosaic floor in the entrance disappeared, as did the cast iron S & M script on the first floor piers. In 1948, the cornice, one of the pieces that

Louis considered essential for a perfect skyscraper, had deteriorated to the point that it had to be removed.

The losses, especially in comparison with the complete demolition of most of Sullivan's architecture, were minimal. In 1960, Carson's hired Holabird & Roche to add three more bays to the south end of the building. In the late 1970s, they hired the Office of John Vinci to restore the facade and the main entrance, including repainting the ornate cast iron ornamentations their original colors. In 2002, they even went so far as to have the cornice rebuilt, and by 2006 the building more closely resembled its structure of a century before.

The building survived, but Carson, Pirie, Scott & Co. did not and the department store moved out. With their exit, this piece of architectural history became known as the Sullivan Center, named for the irascible genius who changed architecture forever.

Schlesinger and Mayer Today

Joseph Freed & Associates bought the Sullivan Center in 2007. The firm converted the upper floors into offices, and some of those are now occupied by the architecture program of the School of the Art Institute of Chicago. Freed & Associates continued to bring the building back to its former glory, including the restoration of the cast iron decorations. During this painstaking work, the lower floors remained empty. Finally, in 2012, Target Corporation moved in, bringing retail back to this prime location.

1904
Orchestra Hall
Symphony Center

T he renowned Chicago Symphony Orchestra is one of
the most respected orchestral organizations around
the world. It's known for its distinctive sound, its

powerful brass section, and its many recordings, which have garnered more than sixty Grammy Awards. But its beginnings were fraught with uncertainty and chaos. The creation and early survival of Chicago's orchestra, and its permanent home on what is now Michigan Avenue, came down to a few dedicated philanthropists, a public that needed the arts, and one man in particular who insisted on creative freedom and excellence.

Up until the end of the 19th century, Chicago was not known for its cultural aspirations. That doesn't mean they didn't exist, but in comparison to New York, Boston, and other cities that had been around a lot longer, Chicago was the wild wild west. It was perceived as a town of merchants and industrialists who cared more about making money than enjoying the finer things in life. Who had time for frivolous things like concerts when there were hogs to be butchered and railroads to build?

Chicago did. Its first orchestral organization dates back to 1850, a mere thirteen years after the town officially became a city. Chicago didn't even have its own public water works when Julius Dyhrenfurth formed the Philharmonic Society. After that first season of eight concerts, the society continued intermittently under multiple leaders, none of whom could make a go of it. Then in 1860, Hans Balatka breathed new life into the Philharmonic, and through the Civil War Chicagoans flocked to hear them. After six successful years, interest waned and attendance dropped. Hans discontinued the Philharmonic Society and in 1868 reorganized it, but attendance was discouraging. Still, he continued, and on November 26, 1869, Hans conducted the First Grand Symphony Concert at Farwell Hall.

Hans was "a good musician and an able Conductor," according to Philo Adams Otis in *The Chicago Symphony Orchestra*. That November, however, good and able was overshadowed by the arrival of a touring orchestra from the east led by a former child prodigy. Immediately following Hans' concerts, on November 27, 29 and 30, Theodore Thomas' Grand Concert Organization performed in the same venue. For weeks local critics denounced Hans and lauded Theodore, to the point that Hans accused one pundit in particular, the *Tribune's* George Upton (a.k.a. "Peregrine Pickle"), of attempting to break up his orchestra. The reality was that Theodore Thomas had set a higher standard, and from that point on, Chicago demanded it.

Born in Germany in 1835, Theodore took up the violin and before he was ten years old, the boy was paying the bills with performances at weddings, balls, and taverns. His family immigrated to New York City in 1845 and the prodigy quickly became a regular member of several pit orchestras.

Theodore was ten years old. Ten!

At the ripe old age of fifteen, he set off on his own, touring the country on horseback and setting up concerts which he arranged completely, from venue to publicity to ticket sales to performance. He realized he needed an education and returned to New York, where he studied conducting. At nineteen he joined the first violin section of the New York Philharmonic Society.

Theodore visited Chicago three times as a violinist before 1869: in 1851 as a solo violinist with Jenny Lind, and then in 1854 and 1858 with a small orchestra. He began touring the country with his own orchestra in 1862, making his first appearance in Chicago as a conductor seven years later.

Chicago wanted more of the Theodore Thomas Orchestra. In 1870, they returned for a seven concert series. The next year, a line of ticket buyers stretched down Washington Street hoping to secure seats at the Crosby Opera House. It was Saturday, October 7. On Sunday, the city would go up in flames. In *The Chicago Symphony Orchestra*, Mr. Otis recalled leaving his home on South Michigan on October 9th:

> "...there I observed a line of men walking north, carrying violins, 'cellos, trombones and other instruments. I learned, on inquiry, that they were members of the Thomas Orchestra, who had just arrived at the Twenty-second Street Station of the

Lake Shore road. 'We are going to the Opera House for rehearsal,' replied one of the men."

Theodore gathered his musicians and they moved onto St. Louis for their next engagement. He'd lost so much money, though, that he wouldn't return to Chicago for several years.

That return would cement Theodore's place in Chicago music history. From 1877 until 1891, Theodore led Summer Garden Concerts in the Inter-State Industrial Exposition Building in Lake Park. The location, with its cool breezes, enticed men and women of all ages to come downtown, enjoy ice cream and lemonade, and pay twenty-five or even fifty cents for a dose of Bach, Beethoven, and Brahms. Charles Norman Fay took in a performance during that first season. When Charles and Theodore met in person four years later, they became friends. In 1889, Charles met up with his friend in New York. By this time, Theodore was fifty-three years old and he was tired. He was tired of traveling. He was tired of playing in scratch orchestras. His wife, Minna, was dying. He complained that New York City couldn't support his orchestra so he had to disband it, and he couldn't find any patrons. New York treated him as a "music merchant, a commercial proposition, subject to the laws of supply and demand."

Charles asked him to come to Chicago. "I would go to hell if they gave me a permanent orchestra," Theodore said.

Hell, with caveats. Theodore listed his requirements, and the successful Chicago businessman agreed to every one. The conductor would have absolute control over his orchestra and would have the freedom to create programs without regard to box office receipts. An association would provide all necessary operational funds and guarantee against any loss. Charles acquiesced, but Theodore wasn't done yet. There were to be "no entangling associations of any kind with piano houses, musical colleges, or newspapers." Orchestra members would receive contracts for twenty-eight weeks a year, with a series of symphonic concerts on Fridays and Saturdays for twenty of those weeks. These weren't the demands of a prima donna:

they would ensure artistic freedom as well as financial support for his musicians.

Minna died in 1889, leaving behind Theodore and five children. The next year, Theodore married Charles' sister, Rose. Rose was a force in her own right. Not only did she form the music clubs at the World's Columbian Exposition, out of which grew the National Federation of Music Clubs, she also founded the Anti-Cruelty Society in 1899, an organization that to this day works to prevent cruelty to animals.

When Charles returned to Chicago and presented the proposal to his colleagues, he found immediate support. On December 17, 1890, he and fellow businessmen met at the Chicago Club and held the first meeting for incorporation of The Orchestral Association. Charles went to work securing funds. The proposed guarantee was $50,000 a year for the first three years, and he figured he could get ten men each to guarantee $5,000 per year. Marshall Field was the first to sign on. Then Nathaniel K. Fairbank, followed by George Pullman. When Charles approached Ferdinand Peck, who'd completed his Auditorium Building the year before, Ferd suggested a more reasonable sum of $1,000 a year. That would require a lot more investors, but they made it happen. The rolls of those initial investors include the Armours, Blackstone, Fullerton, Hutchinson, Wacker, Leiter, Gage, and McCormick, a veritable checklist of Chicago's wealthiest.

The first concerts performed by the new Chicago Orchestra took place October 16 and 17, 1891. They filled the acoustically perfect, though cavernous, theater in the Auditorium building with the sounds of Wagner, Beethoven, Tchaikovsky, and Dvorak. They also filled the seats, but it would be one of the few times that would happen. The theater was simply too large, and that first season was rough. They had to share space with other performers, and there was no way they could sell season tickets when there were open seats every night. One concert brought in an abysmal $598. The season ended with a loss of $53,613.41. The second season didn't fare much better, with another loss over $50,000.

Those losses were bad, but what happened with the 1893 World's Columbian Exposition was worse. Exposition authorities hired Theodore as the Director of the Bureau of Music, which seemed logical considering his preeminence. However, his steadfast belief in artistic freedom may have precipitated accusations of a scandal. Piano firms exhibiting at the fair insisted that no musicians could use instruments from companies that did not have a presence, which meant, for one, no Steinway & Sons. If a Steinway piano was found to be in use, teams would be dispatched to dump it outside the gates.

This restriction was unheard of, and Theodore flat out told them that his musicians would use the best instruments, period. The exhibiting firms asked for Theodore's removal, newspapers accused him of accepting bribes, and on May 17, Director-General George Davis asked for his resignation.

Theodore ignored the request. According to Otis in *The Chicago Symphony Orchestra*, the conductor would have resigned, but it would have put his one-hundred and fourteen orchestra members out of work and they had families to feed. The musicians performed every announced concert and Theodore led all but the last, on August 12, when he finally resigned. During this time the fair had been struggling and the loss of an official music program didn't seem like a big deal, but suddenly the crowd came en masse and the officials realized they still needed a Music Director. They came crawling back to Theodore.

He said no.

After two seasons of heavy losses followed by a summer of vitriol, Theodore considered skipping a third season with the Chicago Orchestra, especially when he was offered the conductorship of the Boston Symphony Orchestra. What a coup that would be! He wouldn't have to train the audience, he wouldn't have to deal with Chicago's acrimonious press, and he definitely wouldn't miss those piercing winters which were beginning to damage his health. New York wanted him back, too. But, he thought of Charles and all of his other Chicago friends who had fought for the creation of this orchestra, put in the work, and guaranteed it with their own money. Until the orchestra was either permanently established or abandoned altogether, he'd see it through.

The struggles continued. The orchestra could not fill the theater in the Auditorium building, and because they shared use of the theater with other performers, sometimes they'd have to find other venues. They had no permanent rehearsal space. By 1896, Theodore was repeating a consistent refrain: the Chicago Orchestra needed a smaller, permanent hall. Without it, he'd have to quit. But, the rent they paid for the Auditorium was keeping it afloat, and Ferd wrote him a letter telling him that it was the massive building's salvation.

Theodore, a man of integrity who felt his obligations keenly, stayed.

None of this happened in a vacuum, and The Orchestral Association in 1898 appointed longtime orchestra supporter Daniel Burnham as Chairman of a Committee on Organization with the goal of getting that permanent hall. But the next year, the weather, attacks in the media, and stress had gotten to be too much, and on November 14, 1899, Theodore attempted to resign one more time. No one responded to his letter and he appeared at a meeting of the trustees. He complained of the continued attacks by the press. According to *The Chicago Symphony Orchestra*:

> "Thereupon one of the Trustees, President of a steel corporation, and one of the 'misguided lot of wealthy citizens' of Chicago, said quietly: 'We do not wish to think of your resignation, Mr. Thomas. You are engaged to play only the great works of ancient and modern times, and nothing else. If there are any deficits in giving the concerts, we will take care of them.'

Mr. Thomas never again suggested his resignation."

The Trustees were determined to get Theodore his hall. They found a perfect spot, occupied by livery stables, on Michigan Boulevard between the Pullman Building and the Railway Exchange. In 1902, Bryan Lathrop purchased the land for $450,000, and then later shared the title with Daniel Burnham and John Glessner before they transferred it to The Orchestral Association. In February of 1903, Charles wrote an article with the desperate prediction that the orchestra might be abandoned at the end of the season if people didn't step up. Money came in, but slowly. On March 24, Charles made a second appeal, and within three weeks they'd raised $375,000, half of what they needed. Burnham, who was donating his services, printed the architectural designs in the papers to generate excitement. Season ticket sales opened in June, and although they were $6,000 higher than the previous year, the season still suffered a loss. The Trustees kept at it, and an insert in the March 4 and 5, 1904, program announced that $625,000 had been subscribed, and in the book of the final concert of the season on April 29 and 30, they announced that the next season would be in their brand new hall.

The first few concerts of the Chicago Orchestra's fourteenth season took place in the Auditorium, but finally, on December 6, Theodore and his musicians held their first rehearsal in their new home. It wasn't quite done yet, with floors covered with detritus and the stink of drying plaster permeating the air, but Theodore was pleased, sending a cablegram to Burnham, who was in Manila, that the hall's "Quality exceeds all expectations."

On December 14, 1904, Theodore Thomas conducted his first concert in the new permanent home of the orchestra he'd built. He would conduct only four more concerts before succumbing to pneumonia on January 4, 1905. The next day, pianist and frequent collaborator Ignace Paderewski sent the following in a telegram to Rose Fay Thomas, the conductor's widow:

> "Scarcely any man in any land has done so much for the musical education of the people as did Theodore Thomas in this country. The nobility of his ideals, with the magnitude of his achievement, will assure him everlasting glory."

Theodore's death, although not quite unexpected considering his declining health, still came as a shock and was an unreserved tragedy, but the orchestra he'd poured his life into was now on solid footing. Frederick Stock, a fellow child prodigy and German immigrant whom Theodore had recruited when he formed the orchestra, was appointed temporary conductor while the Trustees searched for a permanent replacement. After everyone else they approached declined, they unanimously voted to give the job to Frederick.

In 1905, the Chicago Orchestra was renamed the Theodore Thomas Orchestra. While a respectful honorific, the name hampered fundraising efforts, and eight years later, the Trustees renamed it the Chicago Symphony Orchestra, founded by Theodore Thomas.

Frederick held the position of Music Director until 1942. During his tenure he oversaw the first summer concerts at Ravinia, began youth concerts, and created the Civic Orchestra of Chicago, which to this day trains musicians for positions in the top orchestras in the country. On May 1, 1916, Frederick began the orchestra's long history of recording with Felix Mendelssohn's "Wedding March" from Incidental Music to *A Midsummer Night's Dream* for Columbia Records.

Frederick and Theodore are credited with building the foundation of the Chicago Symphony Orchestra. Since Frederick's death in 1942, that standard of excellence has continued and been enhanced by conductors including Fritz Reiner (1953—1962), who established the Chicago Symphony Chorus in 1957; Sir Georg Solti (1969—1991), who took the orchestra on its first overseas tour and led them in more than one hundred recordings, and Daniel Barenboim (1991—2006). Barenboim led the orchestra in its first appearance in his native Argentina, and oversaw the development of the new Symphony Center. When he left the CSO, he cited frustration with fundraising activities as one of his reasons. Theodore Thomas would have agreed.

For the next four years, Bernard Haitink was the orchestra's Principal Conductor, but he declined the position of Music Director due to his age. Riccardo Muti filled that role and has been continuing the Chicago Symphony Orchestra's standard of excellence ever since.

The building itself underwent a few changes over the years. In 1907, the Cliff Dwellers Club moved into the top floor in a space specifically designed for them. Chicago novelist Hamlin Garland and sculptor Lorado Taft founded the arts club, originally called the Attic Club and renamed in 1909. It stayed on the ninth floor until moving next door—and thirteen stories higher—in 1996.

In 1950, Daniel Burnham, Jr., gave the interior a $75,000 polish. By 1966, the building needed an overhaul, and Harry Weese and Associates added a new HVAC system and modern elevators. Fifteen years later, the original Lyon and Healy pipe organ was replaced, and Skidmore, Owings & Merrill enlarged the stage and added new lighting, among other improvements. Then in the 1990s, the firm oversaw a $110 million project, taking on the much-needed job of adjusting the acoustics, which had been a major complaint over the years, as well as creating the Symphony Center music complex.

Orchestra Hall Today

Today Orchestra Hall resides inside the larger complex of Symphony Center. It remains the home of the Chicago Symphony Orchestra, the Chicago Symphony Chorus, and Civic Orchestra of Chicago. Buntrock Hall is a rehearsal and performance space, and event organizers can rent the Grainger Ballroom, which overlooks the Art Institute of Chicago. The Chicago Symphony Orchestra continues its long history of excellence established and insisted on by Theodore Thomas.

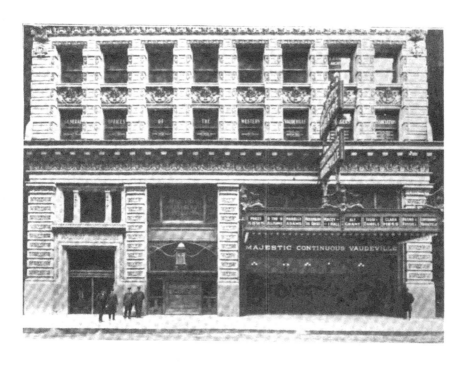

1906
Majestic Building and Theater
CIBC Theatre

B
y the early 1900s, Chicago's cultural options were impressive. The Auditorium Theatre presented opera in an acoustically perfect setting. Orchestra Hall showcased, well, the Chicago Orchestra. The Fine Arts Building fostered a vertical village of creativity. The Art Institute's collections were growing at an astounding rate, and

the Newberry, Crerar, and Chicago Public Libraries educated a city.

Theater was thriving, too, but then again, Chicago had always had a soft spot for the stage. Touring troupes performed before the town was even incorporated, and the first legitimate company took over the empty dining room of the Sauganash Hotel in 1837. It didn't stay long—a mere six weeks—before the company went on its own tour. The company came back the next spring, but only lasted through 1839. In 1847, the Rice Theater opened, and although it burned down three years later, the wooden structure was replaced with a more permanent brick one within six months. McVicker's Theater opened in 1857; fire destroyed it twice, but it kept coming back for more. Smaller immigrant companies popped up in the city's neighborhoods. Theaters, like everything else in Chicago, rebuilt after the Great Chicago Fire and flourished like never before. Even Hull-House got into the act, establishing an amateur theater in 1899.

On New Year's Day in 1906, Chicago's newest theater opened to a sold-out crowd. The Majestic Building and Theater was an elaborate affair with a French Renaissance-style façade and terra cotta formed into leaves, lions, and shells. At twenty stories, consisting of a five-story theater topped by offices, this Grande Dame was reported to be the tallest building in Chicago and she towered above her neighbors. To ensure there would be no unsightly view of the skyscraper from any vantage, architect Edmund R. Krause clad all four walls in white enameled brick. Inside, a two-story lobby contained an art collection said to be second only to the Art Institute's. The theater itself offered more than two thousand seats, fifty-four of them perched in exclusive boxes that flanked the stage.

All of this grandeur might seem befitting of a venue devoted to serious plays and elaborate musicals, but it didn't begin that way. This theater was dedicated to vaudeville. "Elegant" vaudeville, but vaudeville nonetheless.

In the late 1800s, Charles E. Kohl was the vaudeville king. His entree began when he opened Chicago's first Dime

Museum with partner George Middleton in 1882. These "museums" were essentially storefront circus sideshows and were named for the admission they charged. Kohl and Middleton eventually opened three of these museums in Chicago. Considered low brow, the vaudeville venues were popular, especially because they featured future sensations like Harry Houdini. By the mid-1890s, Charles and George were able to bring this entertainment to an even bigger audience by leasing both the Olympic Theater and Chicago Opera Theater, the latter managed by George Castle. In 1900, Charles bought out the first George and partnered with the second to build a theater that would elevate vaudeville, yet keep it affordable.

They only needed a million dollars.

Charles and George found an investor in Augusta Lehmann. A Grande Dame herself, Augusta was a German immigrant who grew up on a Minnesota farm and married Ernst J. Lehmann, also a German immigrant, in 1871. Ernst's claim to fame was the founding of The Fair, a department store that competed successfully with the likes of Marshall Field and Schlesinger & Mayer and by 1882 filled the north side of Adams Street from State to Dearborn. Ernst accumulated money and real estate until wild horses dragged him through Hyde Park. According to an April 7, 1890, article in the *Chicago Tribune*:

> "Mr. Lehmann was driving a pair of spirited horses attached to a phaeton. South of Grand Crossing the vehicle sank deep in the mud. While the team was being urged to extricate the phaeton one of the horses became unmanageable, and after dragging Mr. Lehmann out of the vehicle, broke loose, and started off through the marsh, Mr. Lehmann in pursuit."

Police were still searching for Ernst at two in the morning. They found him, and even though he almost immediately headed to recuperate in Hot Spring, Arkansas, he would never be the same. Upon his return to Chicago, he began throwing money around, buying horses off the street and carrying loose diamonds in his pocket. Augusta filed a petition asking for an inquiry into his mental condition. The court decreed that Augusta should commit him to the Bloomingdale asylum for the insane in White Plains, New York. On May 22, a jury declared Mr. Lehmann "distracted and incapable of managing and controlling his estate" and turned it over to Augusta.

Ernst died a decade later, never leaving the asylum. During his commitment Augusta wasn't content to live on her allowance from the estate. Instead, she continued to expand her holdings, and by 1905 she was one of the largest players in Chicago's real estate market. That year she bought out her partner Otto Young, gave her sons control of The Fair, and secured a loan for one million dollars to build a new theater.

Construction of the Majestic would make it the most expensive theater in Chicago, but once it opened, getting inside didn't require a commensurate expenditure, despite the venue's elegance. Acts performed from early afternoon until 10:30 at night six days a week, and patrons could come and go as they pleased at the pittance of only fifteen to seventy-five cents for the entire day.

But the Majestic Building and Theater wasn't quite the egalitarian entertainment house those affordable rates might suggest. Despite the Illinois Civil Rights Act of 1885, which prohibited segregation, the separation of blacks from whites was common. At the Majestic, it was built-in to the theater itself. Whites could enter the two-story lobby underneath the impressive marquee. They could cross the ornate mosaic floor, browse the impeccable art collection, and relax in the nautically themed men's smoking lounge or the "veritable gem" that was the women's resting room.

Black patrons, however, had to duck into the alley and climb a set of steep stairs to a concrete landing and then ascend five flights up an isolated staircase to the separate-but-not-equal balcony. Because that segregation violated the law, it's difficult to discover when it ended, and while that entrance and staircase still exist, at some point before 2004 the stairs were closed off at the second level.

Kohl and Castle managed the building and Augusta secured both the loan and the architect: forty-one percent of the buildings designed by Edmund R. Krause were commissioned by the Lehmanns. For this project, Edmund employed George Rapp as an assistant designer. It's believed that George designed those distinctive bathrooms, especially since he and his brother Cornelius, who founded Rapp & Rapp in 1906, became known for their themed interiors. The brothers would go on to design many of the city's deluxe movie houses, including The Chicago Theatre.

Charles Kohl passed away from heart disease in 1910, and the next year his widow, Caroline, bought out the entire interest in not only the Majestic but also the Olympic, the Chicago Opera House, the Academy of Music, and the Bijou, making her the largest holder of theatrical property in Chicago. The year after that, in 1912, Caroline is credited with saving vaudeville in the city by preventing an attempted takeover by outside—read New York—interests. The *Inter Ocean* headline from April 29 screamed "Chicago Woman Triumphs in Big Vaudeville War." Despite this triumph, not once in the article is she called Caroline, only Mrs. Charles E.

Caroline, with the help of George Castle, brought entertainers like Eddie Foy, Jack Benny, W.C. Fields, Fanny Brice, and Harry Houdini to the Majestic's stage. They began presenting musical comedies and melodramas, and in 1929 the American Opera Company performed six operas. But in 1932, the Depression claimed another victim. The Majestic Theater went dark and stayed dark until the Shubert Organization, out of New York, purchased the building, renovating and reopening in September 1946.

Formed by three brothers in the late nineteenth century, the Shubert Organization was a theatrical powerhouse. When the brothers purchased the Majestic, Lee and Jacob renamed it after Sam S., who had died in 1905 in a train accident. The '40s and '50s were a heyday of musical productions, including *South Pacific, Oklahoma, Kiss Me Kate, Guys and Dolls*, and so many more. By the 1960s, though, audiences preferred movies, and during the '70s and '80s, the Shubert Theater was the only live theater in the Loop. It survived by continuing with musicals. *Jesus Christ Superstar. Annie. TheWiz. Evita. Cats.* The Shubert held on as long as it could, but in 1989 the old Majestic went dark once again.

In 1991, another New York group saved this historic Chicago theater. The Nederlander Organization purchased the Majestic Building and Theater and presented musicals, concerts, and pre-Broadway openings. In 2004, the building was designated a Chicago Landmark, and the following year it was closed once again for a major renovation to the tune of $25 million.

They installed elevators so balcony patrons didn't have to exit the theater to get down to the lobby. They doubled the restrooms. They reduced the number of seats to give audiences more leg room. They analyzed the paint chips so they could repaint the theater in its original color scheme. They refurbished the original fixtures and buffed the mosaic floor. Sometime in the several previous decades, someone had decided it was a good idea to wall over a hidden archway and install drop ceilings. Nederlander decided it wasn't and revealed the original vintage decor in the two-story lobby.

The office building above became a Hampton Inn, providing convenient accommodations for theatergoers. Another change of Nederlander's was the decision to sell naming rights. When the theater reopened in 2006, gone was the Shubert name. Since then, the theater's been variously called LaSalle Bank Theater (2006), Bank of America Theater (2008), PrivateBank Theater (2015), and since 2017, the CIBC Theatre.

Majestic Building and Theatre Today

CIBC Theatre is one of five theaters managed by Broadway In Chicago, which is also a Nederlander Company. Other theaters include the Auditorium Theatre, James M. Nederlander Theatre, Cadillac Palace Theatre, and the Broadway Playhouse at Water Tower Place. Despite its renovation, the number of restrooms as well as obstructed sightlines are an issue, but the Majestic still shines with long-running shows like Jersey Boys, The Book of Mormon, and the biggest hit of them all, Hamilton.

1910
The Blackstone Hotel

T he Blackstone Hotel is woven into the mythology of Chicago. It's hosted politicians, gangsters, movie stars, jazz greats, and royalty. It's the Hotel of Presidents and claims the original smoke-filled room. The day after it opened, the *Chicago Tribune* declared: "The

Blackstone is to be, in fact it already is, one of the landmarks of Chicago." The April 17, 1910 article praised the design, the amenities, and the location, and while its anticipatory statement proved true, it's doubtful the reporter had any idea just how important this hotel would become.

Or maybe he did, because The Blackstone was the dream of Tracy and John Drake, sons of John Burroughs Drake, whose Grand Pacific Hotel had been a political hub in a city that hosted more national political conventions than any other. It also didn't hurt that the hotel was named for one of the biggest movers and shakers of 19th century Chicago.

Timothy Beach Blackstone was a railroad man. Descended from one of the first European settlers in New England and the sixth son of a Massachusetts state senator, his occupation came about by accident. Forced by health issues to drop out of school in 1847, he began working for the New York & New Haven Railroad. Being outside suited him, and within a year he was an assistant engineer for the Stockbridge & Pittsfield Railroad. His boss, Roswell Mason, who would become the Mayor of Chicago from 1869 to 1871, thought Timothy would be the perfect man to supervise the construction of the Illinois Central Railroad between Bloomington and Dixon. Off the young man went to La Salle, Illinois. Three years later, the town elected Timothy its mayor.

Ironically, considering the hotel that would be named for him, politics weren't his thing. He served one term, said thank you, and spent the rest of his life working on the railroads. By 1861, the Joliet & Chicago Railroad appointed him its president, and when that company reorganized to become the Chicago & Alton Railway Company, he became its president, too. He served in that position from 1864 until 1899, never once taking a salary (although he did own stock). At one point the Board of Directors, which included John B. Drake, tried to force him to take $10,000 a year, but he refused.

Apparently that's the kind of guy Timothy was. In a biography written by Ida Hinman in 1917, she quotes a tribute from his friend and fellow Chicago & Alton man Col. J. H. Wood:

"During his presidency, he personally assumed and paid all requests for charitable and political purposes or public spirited enterprises for which contributions from the Alton were solicited. At one time his personal check was given to wipe out an obligation incurred by a director of the Alton and which he did not think should be paid by the stockholders of the company, although the directors were anxious that the company should assume it."

After the Great Chicago Fire, Timothy invited his now homeless friend John Crerar to live with him, and he did so for twelve years. (John was another philanthropic soul who would bequeath two million dollars to the city of Chicago so they'd build a library, which opened in 1897.) Timothy also gave money to help others. According to Ms. Hinman, the "money he spent lavishly usually went to charities and philanthropies. He gave liberally to widows and orphans of employees, and is said never to have turned away a worthy applicant. No one will ever know how much he gave away."

Timothy and his wife, Isabella, lived on the northwest corner of Michigan Avenue and what was then Hubbard Place in a three-story mansion. The location offered cool breezes off of Lake Michigan and a view of the park. After Timothy's death from pneumonia in 1900, Isabella didn't want to leave her home of several decades. She stayed for another six years, but Otto Young finally convinced her to sell. She agreed, reluctantly, stipulating that the only way Otto could buy it was if he promised to tear down the mansion. If she couldn't live in it, no one could. Otto died a few months later, and his estate leased the lot to the Drake brothers in 1908 so they could build their hotel.

And what a hotel it would be. Tracy and John hired architects Marshall and Fox to design the building. The firm would become known for its luxurious apartment buildings, and that's precisely the feel that the brothers wanted for their future guests. As Tracy wrote in an article for *The*

Architectural Review in 1913: "The nearer a hotel can approach to the home itself, the more it appeals to the better class of discriminating American travelers." The hoteliers insisted on providing bathrooms in each room, to be located on an exterior wall with a window and direct ventilation. Contrary to their competitors' condemnation that moving away from centralized bathrooms would be a waste of space, the Blackstone gained "nearly three floors of rooms that otherwise would be lost."

Within those bathrooms, mirrors equipped with side lights provided ample brightness for shaving. Women could plug in curling irons. And perhaps most impressively: "If as the guest leaves his room he turns the key in his door all the lights in the room will be extinguished automatically." The Blackstone also had air conditioning, filtered water, and an ice machine. It was truly ahead of its time.

The common areas and meeting rooms were equally luxurious. The English Room was a real English room, disassembled from an unspecified 18th-century manor, moved to Chicago, and reassembled. Timothy had been an avid art collector and supporter, and the Drakes honored that passion with a dedicated Art Hall. Diners had a choice of a French restaurant on the second floor or a cafe and orangerie in the lobby. There were street level retail shops, which included Fannie Mae Candy when they began producing their chocolates in 1920. The Crystal Ballroom hosted elegant soirées. The year the Blackstone opened, the Illinois chapter of the American Institute of Architecture awarded the hotel its Gold Medal.

All this innovation and luxury made The Blackstone *the* place to be. According to the National Register of Historic Places nomination form, The Blackstone was the first hotel to become a place for prominent Chicagoans to congregate.

Designed for transient guests, its comforts enticed Mrs. Robert S. McCormick, Mayor William "Big Bill" Thompson, and Alderman "Hinky Dink" Kenna, among others, to make it their home-away-from-home. Governor Lowden used it as his de facto headquarters during the race riots of 1919. Al Capone got his hair cut in the subterranean (and windowless) barber shop. In 1936, Richard J. Daley, Chicago's mayor from 1955 to 1976, celebrated his wedding reception in the Crystal Ballroom. But it wasn't just Chicagoans who congregated at the Blackstone. Every U. S. President from Theodore Roosevelt to Richard Nixon stayed in the hotel. Warren G. Harding was chosen by a few Senators as the Republican nominee in the now-infamous "smoke-filled room." And talk about nefarious characters puffing on cigars: in 1931, Lucky Luciano held the first ever crime convention in the Crystal Ballroom.

Despite its auspicious beginnings, the Blackstone would have a tumultuous life. Ten years after opening their first hotel, Tracy and John opened their namesake Drake Hotel on the opposite end of Michigan Avenue. In 1927, they used the Blackstone as collateral for a loan. Five years later, they defaulted and Metropolitan Life held the Blackstone's mortgage. The company leased the hotel to Arnold Kirkeby in 1936, who bought it outright five years later. Sheraton Hotels purchased it in 1954, and they changed the name to Sheraton-Blackstone Hotel. After years of neighborhood decline, Sheraton sold the property in 1973 to Mark Friedman.

In 1995, in a sale that almost did the place in, Heaven on Earth Inns purchased the historic building. Maharishi Mahesh Yogi, founder of Transcendental Meditation and former guru to the Beatles, bought it with the intention of turning The Blackstone into a meditation center. After four years, an electrical outage that shut down the elevators prompted a safety inspection, which shut down the hotel. It wouldn't reopen for nine years.

Between 1932 and 1999, despite the changes in ownership and its many troubles, The Blackstone continued to draw celebrities, presidents, and royalty. Marilyn Monroe visited in the '50s, and the Duke and Duchess of Windsor in 1959. JFK heard about the Cuban Missile Crisis while in the Suite of Presidents and rushed to D.C.—after a bowl of Boston Clam Chowder. Jazz Showcase invited greats to perform in the former Café and Orangerie. During their tenure, the Sheraton blocked the windows in the second-floor restaurant facing the lake and turned it into the Mayfair Theatre. For seventeen years and 7,114 consecutive performances, audiences flocked to see the hit *Shear Madness*, but when the hotel closed, so did the show.

For years the Blackstone sat vacant. Sage Hospitality, a division of Marriott International, finally purchased the hotel in 2005. After ninety-five years, the last six of those neglected and empty, this beautiful building was in sore need of some attention. She finally got it. After an extensive renovation that took more than two years and over a hundred million dollars, the Renaissance Blackstone opened in 2008.

The renovation focused on historic preservation, and according to developer Sage Hospitality Resources, the Chicago Landmarks Division was stricter than its peers in other cities. Thousands of decorative terra cotta pieces were restored and recast. The tenth floor Presidential Suite and the ninth-floor smoke-filled room, or the Vice Presidential Suite, were preserved. The Art Hall, English Room, Barbershop, and Crystal Ballroom were buffed and shined, and the boarded-up windows let in light again as the Mayfair Theatre became popular restaurant Mercat a la Planxa.

Much of the time and expense of the renovation was dedicated to the rooms. Marshall and Fox's exterior bathrooms were moved to interior walls, which meant reconfiguring the whole plumbing stack. They also enlarged the rooms, and when the hotel reopened there were 335 rooms and suites as opposed to the original 400, and more than 13,000 square feet of meeting space.

In 2017, Marriott transferred the hotel to its Autograph Collection, gave it a quick revitalization, and this storied building became The Blackstone once again.

The Blackstone Today

With its distinctive green mansard roof and red brick exterior, The Blackstone is an elegant fixture on Michigan

Avenue. There's an emphasis on the building's history, but the hotel provides modern amenities, just like it did when it first opened in 1910.

The Blackstone's art collection includes more than 1,600 pieces, most of which are created by local artists. Displayed on each floor and in every guest room, the hotel itself is a veritable gallery. Contemporary pieces by locals are exhibited in the fifth floor Art Hall, counterbalanced by the classic architecture.

1911
Federal Life Building
Arlo Chicago

In 1916, Rand McNally & Company published a panoramic photo of Michigan Avenue. The image stretched across two pages of their annual compendium, *One Hundred and Twenty-Five Photographic Views of Chicago*, and captured a row of buildings that overlooked Grant Park. The scene was a man-made cliff with beginnings in 1885, and if you compare it to the view you see today, it's not all that different. Nearly all the buildings are still there, including Burnham's Railway Exchange and Orchestra Hall; Adler and Sullivan's Auditorium; Beman's Fine Arts Building; Cobb's Chicago Athletic Club; and Shepley, Rutan, and Coolidge's Chicago Public Library. That streetwall of historic structures, which became the Historic Michigan Boulevard District in 2002, is one of the defining images of Chicago. It's a three-dimensional display of the city's past, representing its architectural, commercial, and cultural development.

The official Chicago Landmark District extends from 11th Street north to Randolph Street. The 1916 photo's boundaries are a little different, beginning at the Blackstone Hotel at what was once 7th Street and ending with the Federal Life Building half a block north of Randolph. Those seemingly disparate bookends have something in common: they were both designed by Benjamin Marshall. The Federal Life Building, unlike the gloriously restored and well-documented hotel, nearly disappeared.

Benjamin Marshall's architectural career began after visiting the World's Columbian Exposition. Born in 1874 to a wealthy miller, he had money and connections, like his prep school classmates John and Tracy Drake, but not much direction. The White City changed that. He'd been designing clothes for a wholesaler, but after finding a love for architecture at the fair he apprenticed with the firm of Marble and Wilson. When Marble passed away in 1895, Wilson made Benjamin a junior partner. He dove into his chosen field, designing residences for Chicago's wealthy, and when Wilson retired in 1902 Benjamin opened his own practice. Things were going great, until disaster struck. He designed the Iroquois Theater, which opened November 23, 1903. It was gorgeous, and advertised as "Absolutely Fireproof," but on December 30, a raging inferno consumed the packed theater and killed more than six hundred people.

Somehow, Benjamin escaped the fallout relatively unscathed. In 1905, he partnered with Charles E. Fox, who'd gone the more traditional career route with an education at Boston Tech (MIT) and a job as a draftsman with Holabird and Roche. Charles became the construction specialist and project manager, and Benjamin was the charming bon vivant who secured commissions and brought clients' visions to life. Marshall & Fox established their reputation with commissions like the Blackstone, and in 1911, Federal Life Insurance hired them to design their Michigan Avenue highrise.

The insurance company occupied the building until 1957, when Maremont Automotive Products purchased it. In the '60s the auto parts firm installed sculptures in the lobby, including a new Calder. The next decade, the National Bank of Greece moved in, and the building became known as the Atlantic Bank Building. In between its temporary home on North Franklin and its permanent location in Greektown, the Hellenic Museum and Cultural Center exhibited Greek heritage and culture in one of the upper floors. In 2002, another company took over with the intention of turning it into luxury condos. Even if the building wasn't in the best shape, the location was worth it, but two years later, they foreclosed. Finally, a developer purchased the abandoned building in 2012 and the Fire Life Building would be restored. Scaffolding appeared, hiding the first couple of floors as rehabilitation plans began. The exterior would be rejuvenated and the interior made habitable again. Like many other historic buildings in downtown Chicago, it would be converted to a hotel. Renovators sent out pieces of the century-old terra cotta for repair and the facade took on a pockmarked appearance. But then the work stalled over issues with permits and an air rights dispute with a neighbor. Without those air rights, they couldn't add additional floors to the top of the building, floors that were required to make the hotel profitable. It seemed like this former Benjamin Marshall beauty might be destined for life as an eyesore or as an eventual pile of rubble.

Fortunately, Oxford Capital Group, helmed by architecture fan John Rutledge, took over the property and began its transformation. He'd already done this with the London Guarantee & Accident Building, opening it as LondonHouse Hotel in 2016. In an illustration of how small Chicago really is, Oxford had purchased the London Guarantee & Accident Building from Crain Communications, the same company that now owns the building next to 168 North Michigan and that caused the previous developer so many problems.

Oxford secured the permits and the air rights, adding five floors to the original twelve. In doing so, they fulfilled Benjamin Marshall's original plan for sixteen floors and added a bonus. Because cranes weren't allowed on Michigan Avenue or Garland Court, they had to install equipment on the twelfth floor and use pulleys to ferry the materials up the side of the building. Then they'd move the equipment up a floor until they completed all five, using an old-school technique to add modern glass-walled construction.

Because the exterior ornamentation had been damaged and the interior was essentially gutted, the building was not eligible for landmark designation. That meant Oxford had carte blanche. They could have razed it and started from scratch. Instead, they found the original Marshall and Fox designs for the terra cotta at the University of Texas and commissioned Boston Valley Terra Cotta to recreate the missing pieces—a whole third of the original. They kept the century-plus brick and mortar and within those solid bones, built Hotel Julian, named for the patron saint of travelers.

The hotel honors the architect of the building with a mural of Mr. Marshall himself. By all accounts a dashing, charismatic man, he was not only a talented architect, but he also threw quite the shindig. Think Gatsby, but for real. The mural depicts Benjamin's handsome visage flanked by his signature white Packard to the right and to the left, his studio. "Studio" is, well, underplaying it a bit. This extravagant North Shore villa, built in 1921, was the height of jazz age decadence. It welcomed movie stars, dancing girls, a President, and a future King. Forget guest books; Marshall had them sign a coffee table. Callers might meander through the Tropical Garden, with its palm trees, orchids, banana trees, and swimming pool. They could mingle in the Pompeian Room, or recline in the Egyptian Room while boats sailed in Wilmette Harbor. When it was time to work, there was space for forty-five draftsmen.

This was a man with panache, an architect whose extravagance extended beyond the designs he and his partner, Charles Fox, created, to his life.

Marshall and Fox parted ways in the mid-1920s. Benjamin continued as a solo act until the Great Depression, followed by World War II, destroyed his lifelong financial security. He sold the Studio and he and his wife moved into another building he designed, the Drake Hotel, where he lived until he died in 1944. Despite the visibility of his buildings, including the South Shore Cultural Center, innovative high rises on Lake Shore Drive, and his hotels, he didn't achieve celebrity status until fairly recently. For years, the architect languished in relative obscurity compared to Burnham, Adler, Cobb, and Sullivan, but in 2002 a group of dedicated fans formed the Benjamin Marshall Society. This non-profit group celebrates the complex and influential architect who so greatly impacted Chicago's skyline.

Federal Life Building Today

In April 2023, Hotel Julian became Arlo Chicago. The hotel is a primely located boutique property that illustrates how adaptive reuse can save an endangered building. While it's not technically part of the Historic Michigan Boulevard District, one look at its ornate white terra cotta front topped with a glass-curtain addition, and there's no doubt that this skyscraper bridges past and present.

1912
D. B. Fisk & Company
Hotel Monaco

I t's not obvious the structure at Wabash Avenue and East
Wacker Place has been there for more than a hundred
years. Hotel Monaco looks like a mid-century creation,

with a sheer, modern face that doesn't have any of those flourishes and frills one expects from something built in the early 1900s. But two things give it away. One, it's a mere mite of a high rise by Chicago standards. The second indication is almost hidden: around the corner on the east side of the building, way up at the top of the exposed brick, is a ghost sign: D. B. Fisk & Co.

Founded by David Brainerd Fisk shortly after he moved to Chicago, D. B. Fisk & Co. would quickly become the milliner for the west. That's because it was the *only* milliner for the west. David, who was a ripe old thirty-five years, brought his wife, Lydia, and their three children from Upton, Massachusetts to start fresh in 1853. He'd worked in his father's general store and as the town postmaster before deciding to take his chances in the exploding town. He would become one of the city's wealthy, but he didn't follow the route of many of his fellow entrepreneurs: instead of opening a dry goods store, joining the railroad boom, or investing in real estate, David opened a wholesale millinery. Ladies, even in rough-and-tumble mercenary Chicago, needed hats. This was especially important during a time when hair-washing was a monthly activity. David filled that need, and within two years he'd added a partner and moved from Wells Street to the center of commerce on Lake Street. When that partner retired four years later, David added his son, Daniel M., and John E. L. Frasher and they became D. B. Fisk & Co. Competitors popped up, including Gage Brothers, Webster Brothers, and Keith Brothers, but David's company set the standard. The March 27, 1871, issue of *Harper's Bazar* (as it was spelled in 1871) praised the firm with an absolutely gushing article. A small portion of it said:

> "Their great success has been achieved by their enterprise, sagacity, integrity, industry, good taste in the selection of their stock, promptness in procuring the latest and best styles, ample means and rare facilities for making the manufactures of their goods, both in the Old World and in the New,

tributary to their wishes; thorough acquaintance with the wants of the trade, and constant attention to the interests of their customers; and by keeping only those in their employ who are efficient and trustworthy assistants, and who take a personal interest in the business of the firm."

When the 1871 fire destroyed the Lake Street location, D. B. Fisk & Co. set up shop on West Washington before the embers had even cooled, despite suffering losses of nearly $300,000. After a brief layover on Clinton near Randolph, in 1873 the firm moved into a huge building, designed by John M. Van Osdel, at the southwest corner of Wabash and Washington. Its five stories and basement were filled from top to bottom. There was a floor to display hats; another to showcase cloaks, wraps, and other fancy items; another for straw goods; and yet another for flowers. At the very top sat the factory that created the "Fiskhats" that were in such demand from coast to coast. A report published about the leading members and businesses of the Chicago Board of Trade in 1885 - 86 marveled at the size of the workforce employed by the firm:

"The firm has brought its extended business into smooth working operation, with a thorough system of organization, and the large force of one hundred and fifty hands employed in the various departments, efficiently perform the duties required of them, while three hundred operatives find steady employment in the firm's factory."

After a bout with bronchitis, David died in 1891. He was known as a solid man, enthusiastic about Chicago, and devoted to his family. Despite membership in several clubs, "he found few pleasures so great as to draw him from his home," according to The Chicago Daily Tribune.

John E. L. Frasher took over as the acting head of the company, and with a steady hand made it an even bigger success. When he retired in 1905, *Millinery Trade Review* said: "To Mr. Frasher, possibly more than any other man, has been due the policies that have made this house as solid as Gibraltar." For a couple of years John's son, Edward, acted as Vice President, and Joseph J. O'Meara as President. In 1906, Robert H. Harvey, a doctor who'd married David Fisk's granddaughter, joined the company as treasurer. The next year, he led the firm. His middle name? Hatfield.

D. B. Fisk & Co. continued to grow. So, too, did its neighbor across the street, Marshall Field & Company.

Marshall had died in 1906, but he'd left his company in the more-than-capable hands of John Shedd, and by 1912 the department store needed more room. The big lot across the street looked pretty fine, and in 1912, Fisk and Field worked out a deal where Marshall Field & Company could have that corner lot for a new annex and D. B. Fisk & Co. would move a few blocks north and get a whole new building, two and a half times as tall as their current home. Win-win.

D. B. Fisk & Co. moved into their new headquarters overlooking the Chicago River on January 1, 1913. Local architect George L. Harvey continued Van Osdel's success and built another triumph of efficiency and design for the firm. A 1915 article printed in *American Angler* said: "It is one of the most complete buildings, from sub-cellar to roof, that has ever been put up for mercantile purposes." Inside it contained a baker's dozen of floors specifically designed for the country's biggest wholesale milliners. Made from fireproof materials, there was a sprinkler system and a complete ventilation system. Modern elevators, powered by an in-house electrical plant, shuttled employees and customers. Steel frame construction for high rises was standard in 1912, which meant large windows allowed natural light into the many floors of showrooms.

The company did swell during the roaring '20s with Dr. Robert Hatfield Harvey at the helm, but on November 3, 1931, a headline, followed by a one-paragraph article, in the Chicago Tribune said simply: "D. B. Fisk & Co. Plan to Quit Millinery Business." The company liquidated, but it wasn't done yet. Vice President Joseph Beckman rounded up former employees, salespeople, and executives and bought the name.

They moved out of their big building to a much smaller store and reduced their reach, but they still managed to survive for another couple of decades.

Other milliners moved into D. B. Fisk's efficient building, and several businesses used the space that had previously been filled by one. But by the 1950s, buildings weren't the only things losing their flourishes and frills. Fancy hats were out, too, and the high rise emptied entirely. By the end of the decade, a series of investors planned on converting the building into hotels. Finally, one succeeded, and the Oxford House Motor Hotel opened in 1960, but not before completely changing the look and feel of the building, both inside and out.

They gutted it, turning the show rooms and factory floors into hotel rooms with kitchenettes. They opened a split-level restaurant and a cocktail lounge and added meeting and banquet rooms and a two-floor garage.

Outside, Oxford House stripped the cornice and everything else, hanging a new curtain wall over the steel frame and masonry. Before the hotel opened on March 7, they'd received six hundred letters of inquiry for reservations, and the top floors and the bar weren't even done yet. The restaurant initially served French cuisine, then it became a discotheque, and then an Italian café with live music. For thirty years, the hotel welcomed tourists to its riverfront location.

In 1996, Oxford House began negotiations to sell. Kimpton Hotel Group had already snagged the former Bismarck Hotel with the idea of restoring it to its 1920s grandeur. The now unrecognizable D. B. Fisk & Co. would be a little more challenging, considering so many of its historical features had been removed. Instead of attempting to recreate a by-gone era, the renovation focused on developing a fashionable vibe, one that would be in keeping with the original tenant. On November 10, 1998, the swanky, hip Hotel Monaco Chicago opened. Gone were the kitchenettes; added were window seats overlooking the river, and goldfish. With the Shedd Aquarium acting as consultants, the hotel offered guests a companion goldfish during their stay.

D. B. Fisk & Company Today

Hotel Monaco tips a hat to its past while planted firmly in the present. In 2019, Kimpton Hotel Group remodeled the hotel again. Prior to this renovation, there'd been little reference to the building's history. This time around, they created allusions with things like hat hooks in the entrance to each room, hat boxes containing the honor bars, and large paintings of a chic woman in a fancy hat on each floor. They also teamed up with a local milliner, enabling guests to purchase one of their own, and a custom wine table with glass top displays items from D. B. Fisk & Co.'s past. The frills may have been stripped, but David B. Fisk's ghost, and the echoes of the successful firm he created, remains.

1916
Municipal Pier #2
Navy Pier

C hicago in the early 1900s was a mess, to put it lightly. Despite an official motto of "urbs in horto"—city in a garden—it was anything but. It was crowded. Dirty. Stinky. Think traffic is bad now? Fuhgeddaboudit. So many ships were coming into the Chicago River that you could barely cross it because the bridges were continuously being raised, and there weren't that many bridges in the first place. The Michigan Avenue Bridge didn't exist—Michigan Avenue north of the river didn't even exist. Getting "bridged" was an acceptable excuse for being late to work.

So a group of businessmen got together and made a plan. This plan was a civic ideal that would turn Chicago from a chaotic mess into the City Beautiful. The Second City, reborn from the ashes of 1871, would reinvent itself again. With the World's Columbian Exposition, Chicago had already proven that it could build beauty out of chaos and structure out of mud, but this time they would make it permanent. They even hired the same man to make it happen.

That man was Daniel Burnham. He's oft quoted for saying "make no little plans, for they have no power to stir men's blood," and while there's no proof he actually uttered those words, he certainly lived it. His dream of a new city was expansive, majestic, and would transform Chicago forever. After the 1893 fair, Daniel was in demand as a civic planner. Washington, D.C.; Cleveland, Ohio; and San Francisco, California hired him. So widespread was his fame that he designed plans for Manila and Baguio in the Philippines, too. He was still designing buildings while envisioning these orderly urban areas—it was while he was in Manila that Theodore Thomas cabled Daniel to applaud his design of Orchestra Hall.

On July 4, 1909, the Commercial Club of Chicago unveiled the epically detailed Plan of Chicago, co-authored by Daniel and Edward Bennett. Converting Chicago's lakefront from an industrial eyesore into a playground that was open to all was a vital piece of that plan. The trick, and this was an ongoing balancing act, was to satisfy the city's commercial interests with its social. The city that worked also needed to be the city that played.

The plan included the development of five piers in Lake Michigan. Two of those piers would flank the Chicago River. Not only would they greatly reduce the congestion of commercial ships into the river itself, but they would also provide a recreational space. It was the first time a pier would serve both purposes.

This wouldn't be easy. Lake Michigan was notorious for creating land along the shore where previously there had been water. In addition to landfill, Grant and Lincoln Parks owed much of their acreage to shifting sands. John Farwell added a pier to his four-acre property at the end of North Avenue in 1866 and ended up with fifteen more acres within six years. And Daniel's plan called for a pier that would stick more than half a mile into the lake. Make no little plans, indeed.

Daniel died in 1912, but the plan lived on and over the years, pieces of it began to take shape. Municipal Pier #2 was one of the first, and in 1913, the city chose Charles Sumner Frost as the architect. Charles, born in 1856 in Maine, graduated from MIT and worked with Peabody and Stearns in Boston before coming to Chicago in 1882. He partnered with Henry Ives Cobb and helped design the Palmer Mansion, the mock-castle that would drive the wealthy to the north side. After a decade of solo practice, he joined forces with Alfred H. Granger. From 1898 to 1910, Frost and Granger were the builders of railroad depots—they put up a whopping one hundred and twenty-seven buildings for the Chicago and North Western Railway alone. Of course, it helped that they'd both married daughters of Marvin Hughitt, the railroad's president. That experience gave Charles a unique perspective on building a space meant to keep people moving.

Charles was in charge of what would go on the pier. The pier itself would be the province of the uniquely qualified Edward C. Shankland. Not only was he the chief engineer of the Harbor and Subway Commission, Edward had also been Burnham's chief engineer for the World's Columbian Exposition. The plan he devised to keep the massive pier stable might have seemed like overkill: workers drove more than twenty thousand Oregon timber pilings between twenty and twenty-seven feet down. Steel tie-rods anchored the pilings, which were topped with a concrete foundation that supported the steel columns of the pier's buildings. A triple row of piles supported concrete dock walls; those were bordered with clay, rock, and sand and were buttressed by loose rock. That thing was not going to move...and it hasn't.

On top of the pier, Charles created a design that would pull the triple duty of serving freight, passenger, and recreational needs. On the west end, the neoclassical red brick Head House was decorated with terra cotta ornamentation of frogs, turtles, lilies, cattails, sheaves of wheat, and Native Americans. Two towers camouflaged a couple of sixty-thousand-gallon gravity tanks, which would feed the sprinkler system. On the east end, the Terminal Building held the information office, restrooms, first aid, a restaurant, and a rooftop garden. Next to that was a two-story open-air shelter, which connected to the concert hall, a stunning auditorium with exposed radial steel trusses formed in half-arches under a massive dome. Observation towers flanked this end.

In between these bookends, Charles built two sheds, each 2,340 by 100 feet with an 80-foot roadway in the middle. The first floor serviced freight, and the second floor serviced passengers, with a trolley running an elevated interior loop that could drop them straight at their gate. The whole thing was revolutionary, and was so anticipated that Chicagoans held an impromptu celebration: fifty thousand showed up on July 4, 1916, nine days before the official opening, when another twenty-five thousand appeared. And they kept coming, drawn by concerts, picnics, and promenades.

Within a year there was already a hint of its future conversions. When the U.S. entered World War I in 1917, Municipal Pier #2 became a military recruiting and training center, as well as a communication center—one of the east-end towers became a carrier-pigeon station. The pier also housed draft dodgers, and on one productive day, agents staked out both a Chicago Cubs double-header and a Barnum & Bailey Circus performance at the south side's White City Amusement Park. Between the two events, more than 200,000 young men were questioned and the dodgers were carted off to the pokey on the pier.

Recreational use continued throughout the war, but the 1920s were the pier's real heydey. While it was still used for freighters, it also became a full-fledged entertainment destination. There were live bands, plays, art exhibits, children's activities, fireworks displays, and airplane and motorboat races. In 1921, Mayor Big Bill Thompson kicked off the Pageant of Progress, a mini-world's fair. Over two thousand exhibits drew between one and two million people in a two-week period. It was such a success that they did it again the next year, but by that time the Mayor's track record of corruption, in addition to a transportation strike and pesky prohibition raids, dropped attendance in half. Still, the people came. Chicagoans could finally take full advantage of their city's greatest asset: Lake Michigan. Great Lakes cruise ships and excursion boats to Lincoln and Jackson Parks departed from the pier. The Goodrich Transit Company would ferry your car to Benton Harbor or Mackinac Michigan. There was even a merry-go-round. However, the automobile revolution was beginning to draw people away from the lake and towards the open road, and trains diverted freight from ships. From 1926 to 1931, steamship passengers dropped from 471,000 to 258,000. During that time, in 1927, Municipal Pier #2 became Navy Pier to honor the Chicagoans and Midwesterners who had served during World War I.

The Depression hit, but the pier adapted. It hosted trade shows, and during the 1933 - 1934 Century of Progress, ferried attendees to the fair. Then, World War II, and Navy Pier lived up to its name. It became a full-fledged Naval Training School, including two makeshift aircraft carriers converted from passenger paddlewheel cruisers. It made sense—Lake Michigan was safe from Axis submarines and bombers. More than 60,000 sailors, including up to 18,000 pilots, trained at Navy Pier, the most famous of which was future president George H. W. Bush.

After the war, the Navy moved out and the pier adapted once again. This time the War Assets Administration moved in and began selling surplus materials at auction. In a particularly odd placement, considering that this structure jutted into the lake, the Chicago Police Department's Traffic Division opened administrative offices, a garage, and a branch of traffic court. It operated there until 1955.

The end of the war and the passage of the G.I. Bill meant that lots of soldiers could now get a free college education, and boy did they want it. The demand was so great that the University of Illinois opened a branch in the unusual location of Navy Pier. Nicknamed Harvard on the Rocks, students could get a two-year education in arguably the oddest college campus in the country until 1965, when the school moved to Taylor Street. The school didn't take up the whole pier, though. There was still plenty of room for other business, especially business that hearkened back to one of the original goals of turning Chicago into a major inland port. As the St. Lawrence Seaway neared completion, a project that would enable vessels to navigate from the Atlantic Ocean to the Great Lakes, Major Richard J. Daley spearheaded a plan to turn Navy Pier into an overseas terminal. In 1958 the pier underwent a four-million-dollar renovation, adding berthing spaces for two ocean-going ships. The next July, Queen Elizabeth II and Prince Philip followed the new route and stopped for a quick thirty-one-minute tour of the pier's International Trade Fair. At first it seemed like Chicago could become an international port, and in the mid-1960s, more than 250 ocean liners docked at the pier. By 1974, however, there were only twenty.

These were tough years. McCormick Place Convention Center had opened in 1961 and taken away most of the trade shows that kept the pier afloat. The only respite was when the competition caught fire in 1967 and conventioneers had no choice but to return to the dilapidated, weather beaten, stripped down location. Things looked bad, but once again, Navy Pier rallied. This time, it was to celebrate the country's bicentennial. The city began a massive restoration, including landscaping and adding solar energy to heat the east buildings. In 1977, the City of Chicago declared Navy Pier a Chicago Landmark, and the following year it hosted the first Chicagofest. For the next four years, Chicagofest brought entertainers as diverse as Frank Sinatra, Kool and the Gang, Alice Cooper, and the Chicago Symphony Orchestra to Navy Pier. It would later become the Taste of Chicago.

Something was still missing, though. It was time to take a hard look at this big idea that had started as both a commercial and a recreation center. The solution was another renovation, one that would cement its status as a tourist destination and would reflect many of the experiences that people enjoyed during its golden age of the 1920s. The terminal sheds were destroyed; in their place, Festival Hall, Crystal Gardens, restaurants and shops and kiosks, a park with mini-golf and flying swings and towering above it all, a 146-foot-tall Ferris Wheel paying homage to Daniel Burnham's 1893 World's Fair. Summer fireworks blasted every Wednesday and Saturday to music. Chicagoans could once again take pleasure cruises. Concerts returned to the auditorium. The former Head House became home to the Chicago Children's Museum. Festival Hall drew trade shows and the Winter Wonderfest, and in 1999, the Chicago Shakespeare Theatre enticed fans of the stage.

It worked. The transformation was wildly successful, but many locals claimed it wasn't enough—even though they still came by the millions. Less than twenty years after that massive renovation, Navy Pier reinvented itself once again.

One thing that had been missing from the pier was, with the exception of the enclosed Crystal Gardens, any reference to Urbs in Horto. It had always been a concrete amusement park. This time around, it would be a softer, gentler, greener destination. Trees would line the dock and an undulating wave wall softened the hardscape and directed eyes to the new, taller Centennial Wheel and its climate-controlled gondolas. People could walk right up to the edge of the pier, giving them closer access to the water. Another thing that had been missing was the local feel. This time around, they recruited local restaurateurs. The pier also went the polar opposite of the Prohibition-era heyday and strolling with adult beverages in hand became acceptable—née, encouraged. When it reopened in 2016, Navy Pier's one-hundred-year anniversary, 9.3 million people decided that hey, maybe this was a pretty grand place after all.

Municipal Pier #2 Today

Navy Pier continues its early promise as one of Chicago's most popular, and free, destinations for a multitude of reasons, including its continued renovations. In 2020, Offshore opened, making Navy Pier the site of the World's Largest Rooftop Bar, according to the Guinness Book of World Records, and in 2021, Sable at Navy Pier became the landmark's first hotel.

Navy Pier has been repurposed, recycled, reinvented, and reinvigorated. It's been home to soldiers, prisoners, and students. It's been a driver of commerce, an innovator of entertainment, and a neglected by-product of happier times. Now, it's not only a reminder of what was, it's a vivid display of what happens when you make big plans.

1920
Michigan Avenue Bridge
DuSable Bridge

O n a sparkling mid-May day in 1920, three men stepped from an automobile and stood before a tiny red, white, and blue ribbon. Ropes held back the crowds as the gents uncovered their heads, one sweeping his signature cowboy hat to his chest. It just happened to be his birthday, and this was going to be one heck of a party. He pulled out the ceremonial scissors and snipped the silk streamer. Crowds cheered. A band played The Star Spangled Banner and airplanes flew overhead and threw leaflets to the crowds like so much confetti. Fireworks exploded, boats blew whistles and sirens, and the city erupted as one with a sense of gaiety and hope.

The Michigan Avenue Bridge was officially open.

The man with the hat was Mayor William Hale "Big Bill" Thompson and his companions were Board of Local Improvements President Michael J. Faherty and Chicago Plan Commission Chairman Charles H. Wacker. That day, those three may have been the face of this great accomplishment, but this project, this dream, was the result of a city with a plan that had been decades in the making.

Prior to May 14, 1920, the main thoroughfare between the north and south sides of the Chicago River was the inefficient Rush Street Bridge. This swing bridge, the fourth bridge in that location, was a bottleneck of epic proportions. Vehicles and pedestrians would queue up on either side and have to wait while the bridge swung to the center of the river to allow ships to pass, and then wait for it to swing back. Not only did this cause tardiness in the workforce, it was also quite the irritant when one wanted to attend the opera or go shopping at Marshall Field's. While the banks of the river were filled with industrial buildings, run-down homes, and railroads, further north wealthy residents like the Nickersons, the McCormicks, and the Palmers built mansions. In 1890, Mrs. Anna May, a northside resident whose father had been an early Chicago pioneer and whose husband, Horatio, was a Lincoln Park Commissioner, proposed a solution to the traffic jam: a tunnel. This wouldn't be a tunnel in the style of a dark, dank subway. This would be a grand boulevard that would just happen to go under the river.

Anna didn't suggest this on a whim. She commissioned a study, hired an engineer, tallied the cost to a million dollars, and figured out how to raise the money, "with a cool, calculating manner worthy of a financier," according to the *Chicago Tribune*. She projected they could complete it in time for the opening of the World's Columbian Exposition. That didn't happen, but discussions continued for years. General William Sooy Smith, the future chief engineer of the Chicago Public Library, dove into the "May subway" project and gave a rough cost estimate of a million and a half in 1891. Joseph Medill, *Chicago Tribune* Editor-in-Chief and former mayor of Chicago, lauded Anna's tunnel:

> "For our comfort the improvement will be of inestimable value. We have two ways of communication with the South Side, cable cars or walking. It is disgraceful now, the way we have to get from one side to the other. I had occasion to drive some friends over here the other day and coming down Michigan Avenue was caught in a swarm of trucks, trucks in front and behind and on both sides, and all in a great hurry. It made me nervous and I tried to keep the attention of my friends from our predicament. A tunnel is the best connection proposed."

A tunnel seemed the most viable option until 1902 when the first trunnion bascule bridge crossed Cortland Street. At its most basic, a bascule, French for see-saw, is a drawbridge. Adding the trunnion, or pivot point, with counterweights made lifting the leaves of the bridge a breeze. (Chicago likes to claim whatever it invents and this quickly became known as the Chicago Type Trunnion Bascule Bridge.)

This changed everything. For many people, from that point on only a bridge would do. Proposals flooded in, and while a tunnel was still a serious consideration in early 1903, by mid-year a new scheme was taking shape: the Boulevard Link. A May 31 editorial dreamt of a bascule bridge east of Rush Street that connected a wide boulevard thoroughly paved with asphalt. Gone would be the streetcar tracks to the south and warehouses to the north. In their place, stores would drive property values up and up and up. Mayor Carter Harrison IV thought it was a fantastic idea. He called it a "boulevard on stilts" and appointed six aldermen to a committee. The following mayor, Edward Dunne, was not so enthusiastic. Not to be put off, it was during Dunne's mayorship that the Merchants Club of Chicago, which would soon merge with the Commercial Club of Chicago, forged ahead with their own big dreams for the city. In 1906, they hired Daniel Burnham and Edward Bennett to turn those dreams into an actionable vision. Connecting Pine Street to the north with Michigan Avenue to the south via a boulevard link was an integral part of that Plan of Chicago.

Mayor Fred Busse, elected in 1907, was bully on the Burnham and Bennett plan, so he created the Chicago Plan Commission. Consisting of 325 businessmen led by chairman Charles H. Wacker, they were responsible for assessing the feasibility of and implementing the ideas presented in the plan, including the boulevard link.

This wasn't a simple matter of building a bridge. Michigan Avenue from Randolph to the river was a narrow strip. Same with Pine Street to the north. They'd have to widen both. There was only one problem: that land wasn't empty. It was crowded with warehouses, industrial buildings, run-down single-family homes and rooming houses, and railroad depots. The city passed ordinances and people fought them. For nearly a year, Judge Pond heard from objectors and their four-hundred lawyers and the city paid nearly $5,000,000 in assessments on more than 8,500 pieces of property.

A December 29, 1916, article declared that the last objection had been removed, clearing the final hurdle and optimistically predicting that the $10,000,000 improvement "should be completed inside of two years."

Next April, the United States entered World War I, and the government commandeered the steel that would have been used in the bridge. On April 15, 1918, construction on the link began, shortly after the first strains of a global pandemic hit the country.

Just like everything else in Chicago's no-small-plans mindset, this "link" would be no mere crossing. Not only would it be the widest bridge in the world, with six lanes and pedestrian walkways on the upper level, it would be a two-level thoroughfare, a double-deck bascule bridge across the Chicago river, the first of its kind ever built anywhere. It would take two years and one month for it to open, but even as Big Bill cut the ribbon while bands played, fireworks exploded, and decorated cars crossed the river, workmen continued apace on the lower level. Bare wooden scaffolding loomed at each corner instead of the four beautiful towers Bennett had designed, which were inspired by Paris' Alexander III bridge. The bridgehouses wouldn't be erected for another two years, and it would be six years after that for the sculptural reliefs.

Even in a town given to bombast, the effect of this bridge was immediate and could not be overstated. "Forged by twenty-four years of almost continuous endeavor, the Michigan boulevard link—the greatest single improvement in Chicago's history—will be opened to traffic today," a reporter stated. Traffic cops estimated 100,000 vehicles and 25,000 pedestrians crossed the river on the bridge's second day.

Within a year and a half property values had increased to $200,000,000 and the Drake Hotel, the London Guarantee & Accident Building, and the Wrigley Building were towering over Michigan Avenue. *Eight years of progress*, a January 1923, report from the notoriously hyperbolic Big Bill, declared: "The Michigan avenue improvement is responsible for the erection of these buildings, and from a commercial standpoint the completion of the boulevard link has developed a favorable site unsurpassed in any city in the world for office buildings, hotels, clubs, theatres, stores and shops... It is destined to carry the heaviest business and pleasure traffic of any street in the world."

William Wrigley Jr., who immediately saw the potential for the lot northwest of the new bridge and broke ground before the link was done, commissioned James Earle Fraser to create the sculptures on the two north bridgehouses. On one is *The Discoverers*, depicting Jolliet, Marquette, de La Salle, and de Tonti. On the other, *The Pioneers*, led by John Kinzie. The Benjamin F. Ferguson Monument Fund paid for the southern bridgetower sculptures. Henry Hering's *Defense* depicts a scene from the 1812 Battle of Fort Dearborn, and *Regeneration* celebrates the city's rebirth after the Great Chicago Fire.

Throughout the 1920s, North Michigan Avenue grew upward with new skyscrapers: Tribune Tower, Allerton Hotel,

Medinah Athletic Club, and the Women's Athletic Club. The neighborhood even had its own organization. Founded in 1912 to push along the boulevard link, the North Central Business District Association worked to create a consistent and profitable aesthetic, establishing what they hoped would become the "World's Greatest Thoroughfare." The district, with its tall buildings and retail character, didn't fare well during the Great Depression, and after the Second World War it was in need of a serious plan. Maybe not as serious of a plan as the one that created the thoroughfare in the first place, but it definitely needed to do something. Real estate mogul Arthur Rubloff, who led what was by that time called the Greater North Michigan Avenue Association, had just the thing: from the Chicago River to Oak Street, Arthur proposed stores, offices, a skating rink, parks, and promenades, and he would call it The Magnificent Mile.

It would become one of the greatest thoroughfares in the world, and it all began with a bridge.

Michigan Avenue Bridge Today

The Michigan Avenue Bridge was designated a Chicago Landmark in 1991. Not much has changed over the years, except the sidewalks and railings were replaced in 2009 to bring them back to their 1920s glory. In 2006, the McCormick Bridgehouse and Chicago River Museum opened in the southwest bridgehouse; it details the history of the river as well as gives visitors an inside peek at how the bridge works. On October 15, 2010, the bridge officially became the DuSable Bridge, named for Chicago's first non-native resident.

1920
The Drake Hotel

On January 17, 1920, Tracy and John Drake laid the cornerstone for their new hotel. It had been a decade since they opened the Blackstone and in that time the brothers had established a reputation as men who knew a thing or two about innkeeping. To be fair, that was expected. Their father, John Burroughs Drake, had been one of the most respected hoteliers of the nineteenth century and they'd learned from the master. It was probably no coincidence that Tracy and John chose that specific date to lay the cornerstone, considering it would have been their dad's 94th birthday.

The location was ideal—or at least it would be soon. Lake Shore Drive curved from north to east right in front of their lot. Oak Street Beach was on the other side. Mansions radiated west and north, including the extravagant Palmer Castle, which meant their neighbors were the kind of people who could afford to stay in luxurious hotels and who would want a convenient place for visitors. Perhaps the biggest draw for this particular location was that within four months the Boulevard Link would open, an innovative bridge that would connect the north and south sides of Chicago with a broad artery. Pine Street, as the one-lane dirt road was called from the Chicago River to Ohio Street, and Lincoln Park Boulevard, as the rest of it was called, would soon be widened and paved. When the Drake Hotel opened later that year, it would be sitting pretty on promenade-lined Michigan Avenue with a view of the lake and a direct line to the Blackstone, two miles to the south.

The land Tracy and John chose didn't exist when their father moved to Chicago in 1855. It was created out of whole cloth, or more accurately, out of sand drifts and landfill. Every time someone built a pier, the capricious lake would add a little more acreage to the shore. Chicagoans, being the creative opportunists that they were, realized that they could make something out of nothing, so the lake became a dumping ground with a purpose. That's how Grant Park grew, how Lincoln Park grew, and how enterprising entrepreneurs created the entire neighborhood of Streeterville.

Most of these entrepreneurs were your typical industrial barons, merchants, bankers, and real estate speculators, like the Palmers, who seemed to buy up chunks of the new land as soon as it stopped drifting. If it weren't for an upstart rapscallion with creative ethics, the neighborhood might have been called Palmerville. But George Wellington Streeter had big dreams and antics that filled Chicago's imaginations—and the headlines.

There are lots of legends associated with Cap Streeter, mostly hatched and promoted by the man himself. Variously known as a gunrunner, a circus promoter, a Civil War soldier, and a steamboat operator, he wove a romantic tale of being stranded by a storm in 1886. Fortuitously, it was a few hundred feet off of Superior Street. Being a sailorman of twenty-five years accustomed to living on boats, he and his wife, Maria, decided to stay right where they were. The lake did its thing, depositing sand around the shipwreck, and their little sandbar grew into acres. Everything was fine for a couple of years, but then the dumps of ash heaps and street sweeps from the shore began encroaching. Now all of a sudden, the landlubbers claimed that Cap was in their riparian right-of-way and he had to go. No way no how was he leaving. He declared his beach the District of Lake Michigan, a commonwealth of the United States, separate from Illinois and certainly not part of Chicago. Those rapacious scallywags would have to fight him if they wanted him to give up his land.

They tried. For years—decades—they tried. The first salvo happened in 1890 when N. K. Fairbank swore a writ of forcible detainer against Cap, who was arrested. The September 9 *Inter Ocean* report of the case was sympathetic towards the Streeters:

"All efforts to get the boat to float again proved futile, and the heavy surf scraped her keel upon the rocks and sand until she sprung a leak and floundered. She was allowed to remain where she was, and Streeter took up his abode on her with his family...But soon the need for new land necessitated the filling in of the lake not for World's Fair purposes, but to widen the possessions of N. K. Fairbank, who owns the land fronting on the lake shore for quite a distance along there...N. K. Fairbank now wishes through the aid of the law to dispossess the defendant of his property."

That greedy Fairbank! Trying to kick a man off of his gainfully gotten land. The nerve.

The nerve of George Wellington Streeter, that is. Two years later, in response to a suit brought by George against Fairbank, the Chicago industrialist claimed that Mr. Streeter had approached him in the spring of 1889. He said that Cap told him city authorities insisted he move his boat from Superior Street, and he wondered if he could move it onto Mr. Fairbank's property while he made the necessary repairs. Mr.

Fairbank said sure, but Cap didn't move it. Neighbors complained because the Streeters and their District denizens were so rowdy. Cap even had his wife locked up for insanity in 1891.

In this same court case, Mr. Henry Russer, the upstanding caretaker of the Newberry Estate, which sat within hailing distance of Streeter's scow, claimed in an official affidavit that it was all part of a grand scheme. The summer of 1890, the wily Cap confided to Mr. Russer that he planned on getting rich by squatting on the land and then claiming it as his own. He knew it would be expensive to fight the Fairbanks and their kind, so he invited Mr. Russer to invest. Mr. Russer "told Streeter that I regarded the scheme as crooked and upbraided him for repaying Mr. Fairbank's kindness to him in allowing him to remain on the land." Seven years later, Mr. Russer doubled down, saying that Streeter actually anchored his boat off of Superior in the hopes that it would get wrecked.

The whole thing sounds pretty far-fetched and doomed to fail, but you can probably guess by the fact that the neighborhood is named for the wretch that it worked. Kind of. The fight dragged on, and on, and on. Cap Streeter became a legend, frequently appearing on the front pages of newspapers. One headline said simply "Captain Streeter Again." A multi-page spread detailed the harrowing almost-battle of 600 Chicago policemen against the District of Lake Michigan's invading force of thirteen. The attackers were soundly routed when Lincoln Park Policeman William L. Hayes "spoiled everything by calmly ambling into the district alone and arresting the entire army of invasion. He took their cartridge belts away from them, kicked their mud fortifications down, and marched them off to the East Chicago Avenue Police Station." N. K. Fairbank died in 1903, but his nemesis lived on. There were gunfights, countless court battles, forged patents, and throughout it all, Streeter's stovepipe hat. In 1918, a judge finally ruled that Cap did not, in fact, "own 'The Deestrick of Lake Michigan'" but the fight continued, even after his death in 1921. So did his boat. In 1928, a harbor engineer finally announced that the ancient houseboat would be hauled out of Ogden Slip, and once it was dry enough, they'd burn it.

While all of this drama was playing out, Lake Shore Drive extended from Oak Street to Ohio Street and Streeterville, as it had been called since at least the May 9, 1899, edition of the *Inter Ocean*, marched inexorably towards its ritzy future. The Drake Hotel would be the shining, elegant capstone of North Michigan Avenue, tied to its sibling to the south not only by street name, but by architect. After Benjamin Marshall's award-winning design of the Blackstone, Tracy and John hired him to design this hotel as well. It was exactly what they wanted, and exactly what was expected. *The Hotel Monthly* quoted John Tellman as saying "I think that The Drake has no equal anywhere. The location is unsurpassed, and the construction and arrangements make it unquestionably the most wonderful hotel in the world, one which will not soon be imitated."

Benjamin, being a member of the Drakes' target market, certainly understood their clientele. Travel-weary guests wouldn't have to appear in the lobby disheveled and dirty. Before ascending a short flight of stairs, they could take a quick detour for a touch-up at the barber shop or the ladies' hairdressing parlor. Guests could send telegrams, make phone calls, and purchase cigars, newspapers, and train tickets in the lobby. The main floor was lined with walls of Bedford stone and floors of Tennessee marble. There were fountains, skylights, wrought-bronze chandeliers, and palm trees seemingly everywhere one looked, especially in the aptly named Avenue of Palms. The Drake Hotel appealed to transient guests as well as permanent residents. With shops and multiple restaurants, they could find almost everything they needed without stepping outside.

But they would step outside, because to the north was Oak Street Beach, and to the south was Michigan Avenue. Within a decade, the wide boulevard was lined with beautiful new skyscrapers. Now that the pesky Cap Streeter was gone, the neighborhood could become what Palmer, Fairbank, and the rest envisioned. A line of luxurious apartment homes, also designed by Benjamin, became the Drake's neighbors to the east along Lake Shore Drive.

The hotel's fame spread far and wide, aided in part because WDAP opened its radio studios at the Drake in 1922 after a brief stint at the Wrigley Building. Listeners as far away as the arctic circle could hear the strains of the Drake Hotel Concert Ensemble. Two years later, that station would become WGN. Everyone wanted to stay at the Drake, including celebrities and royalty. Cataloging those who stayed would basically be a list of every notable personality who ever came to Chicago between 1920 and today. (Slight exaggeration. Very slight.)

The popularity continued despite the crash of 1929, but three years later the Drakes declared bankruptcy and lost their hotel. Benjamin Marshall and Edwin L. Brashear took over, and that same year, the architect left another indelible mark on the Drake: he created the Cape Cod Room, America's first themed restaurant. An avid fisherman himself, Benjamin directed both the menu and the fantastical, New England-ish decor. The Drake changed hands again when Arnold Kirkeby leased it in 1937 (he would also lease the Blackstone and eventually purchase it). In 1940, he'd add the famous sign that quickly became an icon of Chicago's skyline. In 1946, Benjamin and Edwin got the hotel back.

The next year, Arthur Rubloff branded Michigan Avenue as The Magnificent Mile. The Drake Hotel, with its prime location and reputation for being magnificent itself, was poised to take advantage of that marketing campaign. For the next several decades the hotel maintained and expanded its reputation as the spot to see-and-be-seen in one of Chicago's ritziest neighborhoods—a neighborhood named for a scheming scofflaw in a stovepipe hat.

The Drake Hotel Today

The Drake, a Hilton Hotel Chicago, remains an anchor synonymous with wealth and luxury. Hilton International leased the property in 1980, and Hilton Hotel Group merged with their global cousin in 2006. The property's seen several renovations over the years, but all have attempted to maintain its original gilded splendor. The famed Cape Cod Room closed in 2017. Coq d'Or holds Liquor License #2, and guests feel like royalty with Afternoon Tea in the Palm Court.

1921
Wrigley Building

T he Wrigley Building rises above a bend in the Chicago
river like a beacon. Its cladding of terra cotta, with its
subtle gradient from gray to cream to gleaming white,
draws the eyes up, up, up to the soaring clock tower. In 1921,
newspapers called the building the "Jewel of Chicago" and

said it looked "like a snow palace, a tower of frost." Its beauty was a reminder of the shining White City of 1893, and while the visual effect was stunning, especially in a city plagued with pollution, perhaps the most surprising aspect was the lack of advertising. From a man who put an ad on every single streetcar in the USA and paid $104,000 a year for a sign in Times Square, this seemed distinctly uncharacteristic.

> "The strangest feature of this great cloud tickling monument to spearmint is that, although it will be the most commanding site in the middle west for a wonderful electric display of the virtues of William Wrigley Jr.'s chicle sticks, there won't be any advertising on the building." *Chicago Tribune, April 4, 1920*

Strange, maybe. Clever? Definitely. When it came to getting tongues wagging, William Wrigley Jr. knew what he was doing—and not simply because he sold chewing gum. "It was better advertising not to plaster my name on the building," he said. "People talk more about it. It is the unusual thing—the thing they didn't expect me to do."

William's whole life seemed based on doing what people didn't expect him to do. He was born in Philadelphia in 1861, the son of a scouring soap manufacturer. Young William wasn't exactly the scholastic type, and although he wasn't mean-spirited, his irrepressible nature got him kicked out of school on a regular basis. Every time he'd get in trouble, his father, William Wrigley, Sr., would write a note and the principal would let him back in. When he was eleven, William decided he'd had enough of that and took off for New York City. With the few pennies he had in his pocket, he bought some papers and became a newsie. When that grew tiresome, he ran errands for elderly strangers. And when that got old, working on a ship seemed just the thing, until he had to climb to the top of a rigging and discovered it was a bit too steep for his liking. A cook on another vessel fired him after one day of too-thick potato peels. Now and then William would send a postcard to let his parents know he was safe. After a few months of this adventure he headed back home, where Dad promptly re-enrolled him in classes. True to form, he was quickly kicked out—this time for throwing a spoiled pie at the side of the school.

> "No more letters from me," said his father. "Your school life hasn't been a success. We'll see how work strikes you."

Senior put him in the factory, stirring thick soap with a paddle, for $1.50 a week. Work seemed to suit William; the mischievous youth stayed at it for a longer stretch than he had at his studies, but after a year he had a better idea. At the age of thirteen, he proposed giving his paddle to someone else and he would go out on the road as a traveling salesman. "You're barely out of short trousers!" his dad objected. "I'm big for my age!" William replied.

William got his way.

Now *this* was something he enjoyed. He could be out on the road and meet new people. For six years he sold soap, often targeting the crankiest possible customers and charming them with his affable nature and his persistence. Then when he was nineteen, he and a friend hopped a train for the mining town of Leadville, Colorado. They only made it to Kansas City when they were forced to hop back off; William had put their tickets in his hat band, and after a strong gust whipped the hat out of the window, a conductor shooed them away. Despite being broke in a strange town for the second time in his life, William being William ended up selling stamps he'd borrowed on credit. By the time he was done he'd made hundreds, and he returned to Philly with presents in hand.

Back home, William resumed working for his dad, and this time he stuck around for a while. In 1885, he married Ada Elizabeth Foote, they had a daughter the next year, and in 1891 they moved to Chicago. He was thirty years old and he was still selling soap, but that was all about to change.

Competition was fierce, especially in a money-driven town like Chicago. When he realized merchants weren't buying his wholesale soaps because the five-cent retail price gave them no profit margin, he doubled it. They could sell each soap cake for ten instead, and to sweeten the deal, he threw in a free umbrella with every box. He then added a line of baking powder and gave away a cookbook. For every box of anything he sold, he gave away a free premium. Some offers were a big success. Others, like the tarnished silver-plated cologne bottles or the umbrellas with running dye, cost him every cent of profit, but each time he turned it around.

Finally he found the big one: chewing gum. What began as a premium became the product. He convinced his partner, Zeno Manufacturing, to change its formula to make the flavor last longer. According to the Chicago Landmark Designation Report, those flavors included Vassar, Sweet Sixteen, Peppermint, Lemon Cream, and Blood Orange. Then in 1893 he introduced stronger flavors at the World's Columbian Exposition: Juicy Fruit and Spearmint.

Those were a hit and William continued his tried-and-true tactic of offering premiums with every box, but what really turned Wrigley into a household name was advertising. He began with a few billboards in the South and gradually increased his activities, until in 1902 he bet it all—$100,000—on a huge campaign in New York City.

It didn't work.

He waited until he had another $100,000 and did it again. It didn't work that time, either. He moved upstate and plastered Buffalo and Rochester with billboards. That campaign paid off, so he figured he'd give downstate one more go and threw one and a half million dollars at the big city.

This time, it worked. His business tripled. In 1915, reasoning that anyone who could afford a phone could afford a pack of gum, he sent four sticks to every phone subscriber—all one and a half million of them. Four years later, there were seven million households with phones, and he sent them gum, too.

Advertising extended beyond direct mail and billboards. William also invested in recreational activities, and as a member of the Lincoln Park Commission he helped create Oak Street Beach. Outside of gum, he may best be known for his support of baseball. In 1916, he invested in the Chicago Cubs. By 1920, he was the majority stockholder.

One by one, selling his product at five cents a pack, William Wrigley Jr. became a very, very wealthy man. He bought a baseball team. He bought Catalina Island. And, he built one of the most gorgeous buildings in Chicago.

When plans began to solidify for the Boulevard Link, the bridge that would cross the Chicago River, William did what he'd done so many times in the past: he saw an opportunity and grabbed it. The lot had an odd shape, but its location meant that anyone on Michigan Avenue looking north, all the way from Twelfth Street, would see whatever was built there, as long as it was big and bright enough. He hired Graham, Anderson, Probst and White, successors to D. H. Burnham and Company. They gave the commission to Charles Beersman, and he crafted a unique building that would fit nowhere else and topped it with a tower modeled after Seville's Giralda Tower, each side fitted with a twenty-foot clock dial. It would be Chicago's tallest building, at least for two years, and Charles clad it in over 250,000 pieces of terra cotta in shades from creamy off-white to bright blue-white. At night, instead of advertising, reflectors illuminated the exterior, making it visible for miles. While the final cost more than doubled the $3,000,000 estimate, William had sold enough five-cent packs of gum to pay cash.

It was truly the house that chewing gum built.

In addition to being beautiful, the Wrigley Building was also the first Chicago office building with air conditioning, and when it opened on April 1, 1921, it was fully rented. William figured that was a good sign, so the next year he leased land to the north and began building an annex. Beersman designed this building, too, and it opened in 1924. The two buildings were originally connected by a street-level plaza and a third floor walkway. A fourteenth-floor walkway was added in the 1930s.

William died in 1932 and his son, Philip, took over both the chewing gum company and the Cubs. Philip was born in 1894, the year after his dad sold his first stick of gum, and entered the business at twenty. He had a similar knack for marketing and expanded both the company's product line and the baseball team's popularity. Philip, followed by his son, William, who took over in 1961, insisted on keeping that five-cent price for a pack of gum, and it wasn't increased until the early '70s.

Wrigley Building Today

A Wrigley led the company until 2006 when Bill Perez became the first non-family CEO and President. In 2008, Mars, Incorporated purchased the Wrigley Company, but they kept it independent and Wrigley now handles all of Mars' non-chocolate confectionery brands. In 2011, a consortium of investors purchased the building and removed a street-level screen wall between the two towers, creating an open-air plaza. The Wrigley Company moved out in 2012, but its name, and the legacy of its charismatic founder, remains on the building built by nickels

1921
Columbian Museum of Chicago
Field Museum

E dward E. Ayer almost took "No" for an answer. If he had, there might not be a Field Museum of Natural History, and if there was a museum, it certainly wouldn't have the same name.

The idea for the museum began with a letter to the *Chicago Tribune* on May 31, 1890. It had only been three months since Congress selected Chicago to host the World's Fair, and only a month since the Senate concurred with that choice. The Columbian Exposition would take place in less than three years, and while the city was madly preparing, Frederick Ward Putnam, the fair's future curator of anthropology, suggested that it would be a good idea to collect the exhibits when it was over. As a Harvard professor of American Archaeology and Ethnology, he thought "such a collection would form a grand beginning for a permanent ethnological museum which would grow in importance and value as time goes on." The *Chicago Tribune* called it an "interesting suggestion."

Others thought Mr. Putnam was on to something, and in November of 1891 he was invited to present the idea of a World's Fair memorial museum to the Commercial Club of Chicago. Being a group of prominent money-makers, the men must have appreciated the efficiency of having the exhibits already in their city, exhibits that would normally require expensive expeditions. The *Inter Ocean* thought it was a "Startling Suggestion." William T. Baker, one of the club's founders, thought it was a great opportunity.

It was a great opportunity, but before they could take advantage of it they had to create the fair in the first place. After a mad dash that defied all expectations, the White City opened on May 1, 1893. That summer another letter to the Tribune suggested a museum, and newspapers and others rallied around it. By August the fair was in full swing and the Exposition directors had a little room to breathe, so they created a three-man committee to ascertain public interest. The next month the State of Illinois incorporated "The Columbian Museum of Chicago."

The interest was there, but the problem was money. How were they going to pay for all of these exhibits? Commercial Club members were a philanthropic bunch, but a museum of the grandeur they envisioned would be prohibitively expensive. Unless they could get someone to pony up a million bucks.

Edward began a steady promotional campaign and talked up the museum whenever and wherever he could—at his clubs, at social outings, at card games, you name it. He was like a kid tugging on every rich man's shirt sleeve; if you were a "leading citizen" of Chicago and Edward got near you, you were going to hear about the museum. George Pullman, Norman Ream, and James Ellsworth joined him in these efforts. Every person of wealth was fair game, but they all targeted one man in particular: Marshall Field. The merchant prince was the richest man in Chicago, and while he wasn't stingy with his philanthropy, a million dollars was a hefty commitment even for him.

Edward approached him every chance he got, even during fishing trips. Every time, Marshall said no. Or, as Edward recounted, he said "I don't know anything about a museum and I don't care to know anything about a museum. I'm not going to give you a million dollars."

Undaunted, Edward kept asking. And asking. And asking. So did his friends. About twenty of them met a month before the fair ended to figure out what they needed to do, and they realized that the Panic of 1893 meant they wouldn't be able to get the money they needed without a big donation from Marshall. Without his help, the only option would be to raise what they could, buy what they could, get donations of exhibits where they could, and put it all aside until things improved. They soon had a second meeting and Edward, who wasn't at the first, told them that plan was impossible. An astounding ninety percent of the natural history materials, such as feather-work and leatherwork, would essentially disintegrate if they weren't stored properly. He basically said to forget the idea of a museum, but to go ahead and raise funds to at least buy some of the collections. Then they could divide what they had and give them to the University of Chicago, Northwestern, Beloit College, and University of Illinois. Edward would give his own substantial "Indian" collection to the University of Chicago, or dispose of it in any other way that the members of the committee thought best.

It was discouraging, to say the least. But that night, James Ellsworth sent Edward a letter and asked if he'd see Marshall one more time. The next morning, even though he didn't think it would do an "atom of good," Edward was waiting for Marshall when he arrived at his office. Frank Lockwood recounted the conversation in *The Life of Edward E. Ayer*:

"Marshall Field, I want to see you tonight after dinner."

"You can't do it," he replied, "I have a dinner party and shall be late."

"Well, the next night."

"No, I have another engagement then."

"Well, I have to see you right away; it is important."

"You want to talk to me about that darned museum," was his reply to this.

"Yes," I admitted.

"How much time do you want?"

I replied, "If I can't talk you out of a million dollars in fifteen minutes, I'm no good, nor you either."

He got up, closed the door, came back, and said, "Fire ahead."

Edward asked Marshall if he'd ever heard of a man named A. T. Stewart. Marshall hadn't. Well, there you go. A. T. Stewart was a greater merchant than even the merchant prince himself, Edward said, and nobody'd heard of him. He'd been forgotten in a mere twenty-five years. Did Marshall want that to happen to him?

That had his attention. Edward went on (and on) to detail why the museum would be important, what it would mean to millions of people, how many children could receive an education unlike any they'd be exposed to without this museum. After forty-five minutes, Marshall told him to get out. Edward then pulled the personal favor card and asked his friend to meet him the next day at the fair to show him exactly what they were hoping to buy with his money. Fortunately, George Pullman had already told Marshall that he'd been astounded when Edward had done the same with him. Edward, Marshall, and Marshall's brother Joe toured the fair and the next morning, Marshall gave him a million dollars. Edward had done it.

With that money secured, George Pullman and Harlow Higinbotham each gave $100,000. Mrs. George Sturges gave $50,000. Edward donated his Native American collection, valued at $100,000. Eleven hundred people donated their Exposition stock, which added another $1,500,000 to the kitty. Chicago was going to get its museum.

The fair closed October 30, 1893, and the museum committee gobbled up as many collections as it could purchase and stockpiled them in the one permanent building on the grounds. Tiffany's gems and pre-Columbian gold ornaments, exhibits in the fields of agriculture, botany, forestry, anthropology, and mining, plus their display cases, all made their way into the Palace of Fine Arts, along with collections from Paraguay, Peru, Africa, the South Sea Islands, and British Columbia. Putnam's grand beginning and Baker's great opportunity were quickly becoming a reality.

After installing heat in the built-for-summer building so they could work through the winter, by December there was a preliminary plan for the exhibits, which needed to be divided, counted, listed, and organized. Hall by hall, the collections began to take on the semblance of a museum. In January 1894, the board of trustees elected Edward as the museum's president. On May 21 they changed the name to the Field Columbian Museum, honoring their primary benefactor for his "Princely Munificence," and on June 2, the doors officially opened. Edward Mason, President of the Chicago Historical Society, said the museum was "the monument of the Exposition, holding many of its best exhibits, housed in the most beautiful of all its beautiful edifices and perpetuating its central idea. It is the lasting flower of that glorious summer to which we look back as to an enchanted dream."

When Mr. Mason completed his remarks, President Ayer arose and with a raised gavel said: "I now declare the Field Columbian Museum open."

The dream was now a reality, but it would be a quarter of a century before the museum found its true home. Acquisitions grew rapidly and scientists traveled the globe to expand the museum's collections. Free public lectures, like "Cats and the

Lands they Inhabit" and "Structure and Natural History of Sharks" drew capacity crowds. Marshall's interest didn't wane after the initial legacy-assuring investment, and he continued to donate to the museum. In November 1905, the institution became the Field Museum of Natural History and the scope was officially limited to the fields of anthropology, botany, geology, and zoology. Two months later, Marshall died, bequeathing a whopping $8,000,000 to his namesake institution. Half of that was earmarked for a building, but they had to pick a site for it within six years.

That would prove to be an issue. They had a spot, right on the lake front in the middle of Grant Park. They'd picked it out years before Marshall's death. It was such a great location that the people of Chicago actually voted to pay a special tax to fund building both the museum and the Crerar Library in that spot. Everybody wanted it there. Even the *Chicago Tribune* was optimistic, declaring on December 29, 1907, that "before the year 1910 dawns the Field museum will rise from the level of the lake front to stand as a monument to the late merchant prince and as an example of the highest development of modern architecture."

Everybody wanted the museum in Grant Park, except for Aaron Montgomery Ward. He fought, and fought, and fought to keep the park forever open, clear and free. Daniel Burnham didn't care what Ward wanted and he put the Field Museum smack in the middle of Grant Park in his 1909 Plan of Chicago. Well, Ward didn't care what Burnham or the Commercial Club or the taxpayers of Chicago wanted. That park was supposed to be open. Legally, Ward was right, and case after case proved it. By 1910, people were so frustrated that they proposed making an island a hundred feet east of shore. The Illinois House of Representatives said yes. Ward, and the courts, said no.

Well, now what were they going to do? In 1911 they resolved to just build the darn thing in Jackson Park, north of the existing location. They weren't thrilled about it, but they couldn't simply stay where they were because the old Palace of Fine Arts was falling apart and to repair it would be prohibitively expensive. (The building would later be rescued and become the Museum of Science and Industry.) In 1911, Illinois Central Railroad and the south park board came to an agreement that gave the people of Chicago the shoreline from the southern end of Grant Park to Jackson Park. The Field Museum of Natural History could now be built at the end of 12th Street.

It didn't happen right away. There were several years of delays, but while they awaited confirmation museum officials ordered supplies, including the mountain of Georgia marble they'd need as well as steel. Construction finally began July 15, 1915. What that really meant was they began installing derricks to drive the 9,921 piles they'd need for the foundation. They were building on made land and they'd have to shore it up several more feet before they could even begin constructing the building, which took more than a year. In 1918 enough had been completed that they could begin gradually dismantling exhibits and readying them for the move. The museum in Jackson Park closed February 1920 and wouldn't reopen for over a year.

Moving the exhibits, which included the original windfall secured from the Columbian Exposition as well as nearly thirty years of acquisitions and expeditions, required precision and care. There were hundreds of display cases and millions of specimens, from the miniscule to a pair of mammoth elephants. Somehow they completed the task in just thirty-four days, with total damage valued at only $1,250. Then came the task of installing them in the new behemoth. Designed by Graham, Anderson, Probst and Young, the building and its graceful caryatids were directly inspired by the Erechtheion, a Greek temple dedicated to Athena and Poseidon. The sculptor of the robed women was Henry Hering, the same man who would carve the reliefs on the Michigan Avenue Bridge southern bridge towers. On May 2, 1921, the Field Museum of Natural History opened, with thousands of Chicagoans lining up to enter.

Marshall wasn't the only Field to lend his money and support to the museum. His son, Marshall Field II, was a trustee. His grandson, Marshall Field III, gave around eight million to the museum between 1925 and 1949 and funded expeditions. His great-grandson, Marshall Field IV, was also a trustee, as was his brother, Joseph. Stanley Field, Marshall's nephew, was President and chairman of the board for more than fifty years before his death in 1964. Stanley had shepherded his uncle's namesake through the whole search for a permanent location, the construction and subsequent move, two world wars, and a Great Depression. Under his tenure, the museum's name changed once again to the Chicago Natural History Museum to more closely identify as a public institution. Stanley announced it on the museum's fiftieth anniversary.

After he died, Trustees voted to honor the contributions of the family and change the name back to Field Museum of Natural History.

Columbian Museum of Chicago Today

Ever since its grand beginning as a great opportunity, the Field Museum has been one of the premier museums in the world. Its dedication to the accumulation and dissemination of knowledge continues unabated. Today the number of specimens and artifacts in its collection exceeds forty million, more than can be displayed in any person's lifetime. The museum also continues to fund expeditions with more than 150 scientists and researchers traveling anywhere and everywhere to document life from billions of years ago to today.

1921
The Chicago Theatre

W hen Balaban and Katz opened The Chicago Theatre
on October 26, 1921, eager and hopeful moviegoers
swarmed State Street. Lines formed as early as two
o'clock, a full three and a half hours before the scheduled
opening. By six, crowds wrapped around the block, and a force
of two hundred patrolmen and thirty mounted sergeants tried
to keep the masses in order. Chicago was simply mad for

movies, and Balaban and Katz's reputation for grandeur was well-established with their Central Park, Riviera, and Tivoli theaters on the west, north, and south sides of the city.

Chicago's fascination with moving pictures began with the Columbian Exposition when they first saw Anschutz's Elektrotachyscope at the 1893 World's Fair. It didn't take long before Chicagoans would invent projectors: George K. Spoor the Kinodrome and William N. Selig the Selig Polyscope. Soon nickelodeons provided inexpensive entertainment. According to The Chicago Theatre's Chicago Landmark Designation Report, in 1902 there was one "five-cent theater" in the city directory. By 1913, there were 606. Most of these were storefront theaters; they were easy enough to set up since you could buy everything you needed in the Sears, Roebuck catalog.

Balaban and Katz, who would become the premiere movie palace providers in the Midwest, began because a family got the movie biz bug. Israel and Augusta Balaban were Bessarabian Jewish immigrants who owned a grocery store in a run-down neighborhood on the near west side of Chicago. It was a hard business, especially with eight mouths to feed. Unsold stock would go bad, and Israel would often extend credit to customers who couldn't pay immediately. The eldest son, Barney, helped pay the bills with a $25 a week job at a cold storage plant, and Abraham, or A. J., worked at a wool mill for $10 a week. A. J. got a second job singing at The Kedzie, a nickelodeon, and his sister, Ida, accompanied him on the piano. The siblings realized that this was the business to be in. They took Mom and she caught on immediately. Show biz was way better than the grocery biz. For one, there would be no spoiled product. For another, and most importantly, people paid cash, and they paid before they even saw what they were getting. What a magical concept.

They quickly roped in the whole family and Barney and A. J. pooled their savings of $175 to lease the storefront. It was a rough little nickelodeon. Seats consisted of camp chairs and the screen was a sheet. The Balabans immediately classed up the joint by replacing the sidewalk barker, hired to harangue

238

passing pedestrians, with a more soothing violinist. They even installed an electric fan to cool their customers, but it was so loud it could only be run between reels. Barney kept his better-paying job at Western Cold Storage Company while managing the business side of things, keeping overhead low by pressing his younger brothers into service. A. J. was the front man and booked the films and sang; Ida played the piano. Dad was the janitor; Mom the matriarch oversaw them all.

The Balabans were hooked. They decided to go big, ending their lease at the tiny storefront so they could build a full-fledged movie theater a block away. When it opened, the Circle hinted at the future amenities the family would provide patrons, including a pipe organ, a four-piece orchestra, and a service to watch baby carriages and alert the mom when the babies within them fussed. Vaudeville acts performed between short one-reel movies. The talent of the talent steadily increased, with A. J. hiring the likes of Sophie Tucker and the Marx Brothers. When they decided to build an even grander movie house, A. J. brought in his friend Sam Katz. Sam had also played piano at neighborhood nickelodeons, and he and his father, Morris, invested in theaters. By the time Balaban and Katz partnered, Sam had attended Northwestern University, John Marshall Law School, and owned three theaters with his dad. In 1917, the Katz and Balaban families joined as well when Sam and Ida married.

After a visit to Ringling Theater in Baraboo, Wisconsin, the in-laws hired its architects, brothers Cornelius and George Rapp, to design the first true Balaban and Katz showcase movie palace. This dazzling new theater was everything that nickelodeons were not. Opening October 27, 1917, Central Park was majestic, seating 2,800 people in a lavishly decorated auditorium. The introduction of a cantilevered balcony meant no columns to block the sightlines. A horseshoe mezzanine enabled more intimate seating closer to the stage, and the exterior terra cotta embellishments and the interior ornate chandeliers, tile flooring, and plasterwork created a true escape, an escape that was sorely needed during the height of World War I. Barney had left his job at the cold storage company by this time, but his experience came in handy. Central Park was the first movie house to offer air conditioning, which also made it the first theater to stay open year-round. An ad proclaimed the theater "Removes the Temper from Temperature," with its "fresh and exhilarating air, chilled to any degree of coolness necessary to our patrons' comfort."

The building itself was entertaining, but this was, after all, a theater. In addition to cinema, Balaban and Katz presented orchestral and live acts. New Yorker Frank Cambria directed these themed shows, setting the stage for all future Balaban and Katz productions.

Next came the Riviera in the north side Uptown neighborhood, and the Tivoli in the south side's Cottage Grove. With west, north, and south covered, it was time to open downtown.

Balaban and Katz found an L-shaped lot that wrapped around one of Chicago's oldest buildings. This odd configuration became a blessing because it meant the theater would be wider than it was deep, providing the illusion of intimacy despite a capacity of thousands. They again hired Rapp and Rapp, the brothers who had designed their previous three movie palaces and would be their architects of choice for all future projects.

The Rapp brothers outdid themselves, creating a Neo-Baroque French Revival temple to entertainment on State Street. This was to be the "largest, most costly and grandest of the super deluxe movie palaces built up to that date." With its six-story Arc de Triomphe-inspired entrance and its three-story lighted marquee, the "Wonder Theatre of the World" promised luxury, and what Balaban and Katz promised, they delivered.

The thousands who gained entrance that opening night of October 26, 1921, were greeted with a five-story lobby designed to resemble the Royal Chapel at Versailles. Patrons could mingle along the balcony and mezzanine level promenades. Even the grand staircase, modeled after that of the Paris Opera House, brought a touch of France to Chicago.

240

The auditorium itself rose seven stories to a dome covered in murals by Louis Grell and lit by crystal chandeliers. Yet, it had a feeling of intimacy. A November 5, 1921, Billboard article about the opening proclaimed: "The greatest marvel, perhaps, is the architectural triumph achieved in bringing so many seats so close to the stage. Despite the great size of the theater proper, there are still wide, roomy promenades on three sides of the auditorium. Here, amid paintings, sculpture and imported furniture, one may sit and look at the performance, across grilled railings and beside fluted marble pillars." None other than Charles H. Wacker, chairman of the Chicago Plan Commission, presided over the opening night's ceremonies.

And, oh, what ceremonies they were. Patrons poured into the grand lobby, serenaded by a string quartet. When it was time to be seated, 125 crisply uniformed ushers showed them to their places. The fifty-piece Chicago Theatre Symphony Orchestra played an overture, which was followed by an operatic scene from "Faust," which was followed by a solo by famed organist Jesse Crawford on the Mighty Wurlitzer. There were short films and a musical pageant all about Chicago. Finally, they presented the feature film, *The Sign on the Door*, starring Norma Talmadge.

This extravagant, extensive program was not reserved solely for opening night. Future patrons were entertained from start to finish with orchestral overtures, newsreels, and entertainers. There'd be an organ solo and a full stage production before the featured picture. They even provided childcare, making it easy for parents to enjoy a day at the movies.

In September 1922, The Chicago Theatre welcomed jazz artists to the stage for Syncopation Week. Jazz found a ready audience, and even after the talkies arrived, the theater survived both that change and the Great Depression by bringing in acts like Jack Benny, Ethel Waters, Cab Calloway, Judy Garland, Tommy Dorsey, and Benny Goodman. In 1926, Famous Players—Lasky Corporation, which would become Paramount Pictures, bought a controlling interest in Balaban and Katz. The result was Paramount Publix Corporation, a cinematic powerhouse that combined a production company with physical theaters, creating a vertical monopoly that the U.S. Supreme Court dismantled in 1948.

The 1933 Century of Progress Exposition prompted the theater's first renovation and consisted mainly of redecoration. They hired Louis Grell to paint over his original murals, replacing the French themes with Greek and Roman deities. During World War II the programs switched to patriotic shows and motion pictures, and Frank Sinatra and Danny Kaye performed on stage.

The 1950s saw both a reduction in attendance and the theater's glamour. Another renovation, which the nomination for National Register of Historic Places called a "carefully done but artistically inferior remodeling that was typical" of the decade covered the grand staircase and window with drapes. Flower boxes with plastic foliage replaced bronze torches. False ceilings covered the vaulted lobby. All of the Louis XIV furnishings disappeared, replaced by chrome and coral chairs and built-in benches capped with Formica end tables. This "Streamlining for a Palace of the 20's," as it was called, didn't help. By the end of the decade, stage acts were discontinued entirely.

Without live entertainment, there was nothing to set the downtown movie palace apart from its growing suburban competition, and in 1973 shows returned to the stage. It was a thumb in the dam and owners Plitt Theaters, a descendant of Paramount Publix, the company that absorbed Balaban and Katz, wanted to demolish the former flagship. Despite the building's landmark designation in 1981, Plitt was undeterred and applied for a demolition permit the following December. This demolition would include the adjacent Page Brothers Building, which had been designed by the city's first architect and at the time was believed to be the last in downtown Chicago with a cast-iron front. After heavy negotiations, a private/public partnership with the city, and the devoted attention of attorney Marshall Holleb, in 1985 the Chicago Theatre Preservation Group purchased the buildings and renovations of both National Historic Landmarks began.

This renovation corrected the travesty of the 1950s whitewashing, removing false ceilings, restoring original artwork, and generally bringing the theater back to its golden days. They replaced the rusting three-story "Chicago" marquee and its archaic wiring with a replica. In less than a year, The Chicago Theatre reopened with five nights of Old Blue Eyes himself, three decades after his previous appearance.

The Chicago Theatre Today

In its prime, Balaban and Katz operated more than 125 movie palaces, 50 of which were in Chicago. Since reopening after its third restoration on September 10, 1986, The Chicago Theatre has been a mainstay of live performances, featuring among other renowned acts Sting, Aretha Franklin, David Letterman, Dolly Parton, Prince, and Diana Ross. For decades it's been a tradition for performers to make their marks backstage and the walls are covered in autographs, including Dean Martin's and Bob Hope's. The Mighty Wurlitzer, with its 29 ranks, is itself an historic landmark. Madison Square Garden Entertainment purchased the building in 2007. In 2011, the Chase Bank logo replaced the Balaban and Katz symbol at the top of the marquee. While this corporate sponsorship ruffled some feathers, Preservation Chicago considered it a small price to pay to ensure this landmark would be secure.

The Chicago Theatre remains a shining example of early 1920s lavish flamboyance. As the National Register of Historic Place Nomination Form concluded: "To millions of Chicagoans, the Chicago Theatre is the world's 'Wonder Theatre'."

1923
London Guarantee &
Accident Building
LondonHouse Chicago

T he south side of the Chicago River at Michigan
Avenue, where Fort Dearborn used to be, is one of the
most well-marked spots in the city. There are brass
rectangles that say "Site of Fort Dearborn." On the northwest

corner of the intersection, near the bridge tower, is a plaque letting you know the fort had been built in 1803, destroyed in 1812, rebuilt in 1816, and destroyed again in 1856. A stone scroll on the bridge tower, titled *Defense*, tells the story of the 1812 Battle of Fort Dearborn, although decades of Chicago weather have made it barely legible. At the base of the building on the southwest corner of Michigan and Wacker there's another plaque: "Here stood Old Fort Dearborn 1803 - 1812." And above tall doors on the same building, between Corinthian columns, there's yet one more—a bronze engraving depicting the stronghold with the words "Fort Dearborn; Destroyed 1858" on the left and "Office Building; Erected 1922" on the right.

In case you missed it, THIS IS WHERE FORT DEARBORN STOOD.

What stands there today is a 1923 skyscraper that, according to the Chicago Landmark designation report, "is one of the few and best examples of Beaux-Arts style classicism." The former office building, now the LondonHouse Hotel, is one of four 1920s-era anchors of Michigan Avenue and the Chicago River. Noted for its irregular shape and its distinctive cupola, the London Guarantee and Accident Building is a piece of architectural eye candy that invites sightseers to stop and gawk at its "harmonious and refined designs" and "restrained classical detailing."

This location, and the site of de Sable's trading post across the river, mark the beginnings of Chicago. The last vestiges of the old fort burned in 1871 and the next year wholesale grocer William Hoyt built a warehouse on the lot. He had to conform to the plot's odd shape, dictated by the north-south direction of Michigan Avenue, the diagonal skew of River Street, and a narrower stretch along Front Street, which faced the river. With easy access to ships plus the railroads east of Michigan Avenue, it was an ideal location for a grocer. However, history needed to be marked. The Chicago Historical Society suggested that need to Mr. Hoyt, and he commissioned a fifteen-foot high, six-foot wide marble tablet. Its installation on May 21, 1881, was accompanied by all the pomp and circumstance one might expect from such an august commemoration. State guards marched to the spot, forming up along Front Street and offering military salutes. The Chicago Historical Society opened with a call to order, W. M. Hoyt & Co presented the tablet, and Eugene J. Hall read his poem, "The Memorial of Fort Dearborn." A band played and the Honorable John Wentworth delivered an address, and the entire assemblage concluded with a departing march.

In 1908, W. M. Hoyt announced plans to vacate the lot, which prompted calls for the space to be public property. There were talks of a municipal museum, an ornamental fountain, or both. Those ideas may have been lost in the whole hubbub of the City Beautiful/Plan of Chicago movement; in 1917 a billboard covered the tablet, although the advertisement was quickly removed after William Hoyt, from his winter home in Florida, and the Chicago Historical Society, specifically its librarian Miss Caroline M. McIlvaine, made lots of noise about the desecration. In his defense, Thomas Cusack, the owner of the company that erected the billboard, hadn't even known a tablet existed. (This may not be the same marker, as the article mentions a bronze tablet and Hoyt's was marble.)

Hoyt's building was torn down to make way for the Boulevard Link, the bridge that would connect Michigan Avenue to the south with Pine Street to the north. In its place, architect Alfred S. Alschuler designed a showpiece. London Guarantee and Accident Company, an English company that insured merchant ships, wanted an American headquarters, and this plot provided access and visibility. Alfred, however, had his work cut out for him. It wasn't just the odd shape of the lot itself. Hoyt had adapted to that fifty years earlier, and across the river, Graham, Anderson, Probst and White tailored the Wrigley Building to fit a lot with similar constraints. Alfred's biggest issue came from a stubborn resident.

This new building wasn't merely a commercial interest; it was to be the forerunner of a cleaner, more beautiful riverfront and part of a broad new double-deckered boulevard. That meant everything on the south banks had to go. There was only one problem: a two-story, 24-foot by 50-foot brick building squatted almost in the center of the Michigan Avenue frontage, and its owner refused to sell. Well, John W. Keogh, the owner, *would* sell, but he was going to get paid. "Offers were made Mr. Keogh," said an October 20, 1921, article in the *Chicago Tribune*, "which made even the real estate brokers gasp, but he asked a little more."

John S. Miller, who owned the rest of the site and was building the skyscraper, said "Too high." Alfred, the architect, said no problem, and that it would actually improve the $4,000,000 project:

> "Keogh's lot is so small he cannot possibly build higher than three or four stories and we will always have the benefit of the air and light over his roof."

Alfred carved in a lightwell, and even when John decided that he would sell, two months before they broke ground, the architect drew in five stories where Keogh's building had been and kept the air shaft.

The cornerstone ceremony for this multimillion-dollar skyscraper took place on December 3, 1922, and it was an even grander affair than Hoyt's commemoration more than forty years before. Anywhere from a thousand to fifteen hundred people attended, and while it didn't have the flying confetti or marching bands of the Michigan Avenue Bridge opening, it was still quite the event. The Chicago Historical Society held court and created an agenda that left no doubt of the location's significance. Fort Sheridan not only sent a military band, but also fifty-five soldiers, the same number who'd attempted to escape the fort in 1812. Mayor "Big Bill" Thompson, Alfred Alschuler, and members of the Chicago Historical Society spoke, and General George Van Horn Moseley gave the principal address. Also in attendance were direct descendants of Captain John Whistler, the officer who designed and built Fort Dearborn and led its soldiers until 1810. Whistler's great-grandson William Robert Wood laid the cornerstone. Chicago

Historical Society librarian Miss Caroline M. McIlvaine, who in 1907 had insisted the offending billboard covering Hoyt's tablet be removed, interred a time capsule with the help of Whistler's great-great-granddaughters Catherine and Margaret Joy. The copper box contained Whistler's blueprint for Fort Dearborn, a letter he'd written to his boss Col. Jacob Kingsbury, and a piece of timber from the second iteration of the fort.

London Guarantee and Accident moved into their new building in 1923, and the next year the Lake Shore Trust and Savings Bank awarded Alschuler the Gold Medal for excellence in design. Charles E. Fox, president of the Illinois Society of Architects and partner of Benjamin Marshall, sat on the jury.

For 23 years, London Guarantee and Accident occupied their marquee, but in 1946 they sold it to the Michigan Wacker Building Corporation. Future tenants included Stone Container Corporation and Crain Communications. In the 1950s, '60s, and '70s, jazz greats, like Ramsey Lewis, Marian McPartland, and Sarah Vaughan, filled up The London House on the first floor. The WLS studios occupied the fourth floor from 1960 into the 1980s, and for a time that's where Paul Harvey told listeners *The Rest of the Story*. At one point, executives installed a basketball court on the 21st floor.

In 1987, the Commission on Chicago Landmarks submitted Alschuler's skyscraper for designation. The owner of the building was letting it go to seed and didn't want the historic status. He lost, and on April 16, 1996, the London Guarantee and Accident Building became an official Chicago Landmark.

London Guarantee & Accident Building Today

Today this magnificent building is a 452-room luxury lifestyle hotel. Oxford Capital Group, the same investors that converted Marshall and Fox's 168 North Michigan into Hotel Julian, purchased the property in 2013 and renamed it LondonHouse Chicago. The name is a nod to the original owners and to the jazz club, and "house" is a synonym of hotel. Enter through the original lobby, with its travertine marble walls and vaulted rotunda, for a sense of the grandeur of the original building. For a truly epic experience, head to the rooftop under that distinctive cupola.

1924
The Chicago Temple

A t the top of a neo-gothic skyscraper across from Daley Plaza is a steeple. It's an unusual sight, not really something you expect to see in the heart of the Loop, but inside is a church whose Chicago beginnings date back to before the city was a town and which has stayed on that same corner, in five different buildings, for more than a hundred and eighty years.

In the late 18th and early 19th centuries, Methodist clergy in America traveled the young country on horseback, preaching wherever people congregated. The routes for these circuit riders could be up to five hundred miles. It was a rough life, and nearly half of traveling preachers before 1847 didn't reach the age of thirty. In 1825, Jesse Walker visited what would become Chicago for the first time, even though he was fifty-nine years old and had been riding the circuit for nearly a quarter of a century. The old preacher became determined to bring his church to a place whose population consisted mainly of soldiers stationed at Fort Dearborn and a few traders. "Chicago got into Walker's mind and clung to it like a cockle burr," said Almer Pennewell in *A Voice In the Wilderness: Jesse Walker, "the Daniel Boone of Methodism."*

Within six years of that itinerant minister's first visit, Chicago had its own Methodist congregation. Meetings were held in a log cabin on the west side of the river and it didn't take long before they needed more room. More people were settling north of the river, so in 1834 they built a church at North Water and Clark Street. Jesse died the next year, but his church grew with the town around it. Within a few short years Chicago's population exploded from a few hundred to four thousand. Most of the action seemed to be south of the river, so the Methodists moved again. This time they decided not to build a new church. They had a perfectly good one that was only a few years old, so they floated it across the river and rolled it on logs to Clark and Washington Streets.

This was to be the first of five buildings on that corner. In 1845, John Van Osdel designed a second, replacing the frame church with one made of bricks and topped with a 148-foot spire. Thirteen years later, in 1858, The First Methodist Episcopal Church of Chicago, as it was by then officially known, took a different approach. This third building combined the practical with the spiritual, and architect Edward Burling incorporated two floors of tenants in the new four-story structure. This hybrid meant that retail shops and other occupants could help pay the rent. It was a fairly simple brick building, and the only way you could tell a church was inside was to read the sign on the outside.

Then, the fire of 1871 reduced building number three to ashes. Instead of picking up and leaving, which would have been the easy thing to do, the congregation chose once again to rebuild on that same spot, by this time known as "The Methodist Corner." Edward Burling, joined by Dankmar Adler before he partnered with Sullivan, designed another multi-use structure for the Methodists and they stayed in it until the roaring twenties.

They got a good fifty years out of building number four, but the city was growing vertically and, once again, the church needed more space. It would have been understandable if the congregation left for the suburbs, or at least moved out of downtown. Post World War I fear and a real estate boom in the Loop made it seem like the logical thing to do, but nope. They'd been in that spot that long, they'd stay a bit longer. Back in 1904, Arthur Dixon, Esq. wrote in *Northwestern Christian Advocate*: "Who would dare think of removing the old mother church and obliterating the last remaining token and link which binds the active present to the sweet, glorious memories of the past?"

Who would dare, indeed? Everyone was building up, and up, and up, and the First Methodist Church joined in, hiring Holabird and Roche to design a skyscraper. Called the City Temple during construction, their new showcase became known as The Chicago Temple upon completion in 1924. Although the church had skipped the steeple with the previous two buildings, they topped their skyscraper with a spire and a cross, and for the next few years it was the tallest building in Chicago.

Inside, the first four floors were dedicated to the sanctuary and various chapels and church offices. The main sanctuary, all four stories of it, was lined with stained glass windows depicting both traditional biblical scenes and more local Chicago themes. At the altar was a wooden carving of Jesus crying over Jerusalem. The fifth through the twenty-first floors were leased, mostly by lawyers because of the proximity to government buildings. Clarence Darrow was once a tenant.

Near the top of that towering spire is the parsonage, the three-story residence of the senior minister. Above that, soaring four-hundred feet above street level in what was originally the bell tower, is the Sky Chapel. After drugstore founder Charles Walgreen died, his wife, Myrtle, wanted to honor his memory by donating a chapel to their church. Dedicated April 13, 1952, on Easter Morning, the chapel is a tiny place of worship that only has room for about forty people. A series of sixteen stained glass windows illustrates both the church's and the city's past. The wood, including beams that cover structural braces forming a Saint Andrew's cross, came from the Walgreen's farm in Dixon, Illinois. It's all carved beautifully, but of particular note is the piece on the altar, which is a companion to the carving in the main sanctuary. In the Sky Chapel, Jesus is weeping over the Chicago of 1952, and you can plainly see the Wrigley Building and Tribune Tower.

The Chicago Temple Today

The Chicago Temple remains the home of the First United Methodist Church and the sanctuary is open to all. Upstairs, below the Sky Chapel, is a tiny museum that tells a brief history of Methodism. Outside, east of the building is a plaza containing Miró's Chicago, by Catalan artist Joan Miró i Ferrà. On the wall of the building itself is an often overlooked feature that's worth a stop: a series of stained glass storyboards. They tell the history of First United Methodist from Reverend Jesse Walker's first arrival to the construction of their fifth building on this very spot.

1925
Union Station

1848 was a big year for Chicago. The Illinois and Michigan Canal finally connected the Great Lakes to the Gulf of Mexico. The first telegraph message was received (from Milwaukee). Far-sighted merchants founded the Chicago Board of Trade. And, the Galena and Chicago Union Railroad opened. All these developments fueled the growth of the city. The impact of all of these was profound, but the railroad's influence on the wealth and population of Chicago was immediate and far-reaching. Even though the city had been steadily growing in the eleven years since its incorporation, the explosion that happened with the advent of railroads soon made it the fastest growing city in the world. Trains made it easier and faster for people to travel, and travel they did. To some, lured by the promise of land with the acquisition of the Oregon Territory or the gold fields of California, Chicago was a stopping point on the way to somewhere else. Thousands, however, stayed. Between 1848 and 1858, the city's population increased from around 20,000 to 90,000. By 1871, more than 300,000 lived in Chicago. In the years after the Great Chicago Fire, the population grew to more than half a million people, and the city's recovery was due in large part to trains.

By 1908, nearly two and a half million people lived in a city that was incorporated a mere seventy-one years before.

This growth was not just due to shuttling people from one place to another. Trains improved the transportation of grain, beef, hogs, and lumber—basically anything that could be loaded onto a car—and enterprising businessmen quickly saw the potential for riches, from the trains and railroads themselves, to the land those tracks would cross, to the warehouses built to house the products shipped to and fro, to the transported goods. Within four years of the Galena and Chicago Union Railroad's beginning (which never did make it to Galena) four more railroads came to Chicago. By 1856, there were ten railroads and 3,000 miles of track, tracks which shaped the city: when the Illinois Central Railroad wanted to run trains along the shoreline to get to the river and its boats, the city convinced it to build a breakwater. That breakwater would help create Grant Park.

Rapid and unchecked growth led to enormous riches, fantastic pollution, and crowding. Downtown was already geographically bound by the lake and the river; with all of those trains it also had to contend with tracks and depots taking up valuable real estate. When the Commercial Club of Chicago set out to design their dream city with Daniel Burnham and Edward Bennett, cleaning things up was a big priority. That meant consolidating several of those competing railroads into one Union Station.

Plan of Chicago's Chapter V opens with: "Chicago has been made largely by the railroads, and its future prosperity is dependent upon them." Burnham, Bennett, and the rest took this seriously, and it wasn't solely for financial reasons. "Let the man who undertakes this problem think of the hundreds or even thousands of people who must habitually use the given station," the plan pleaded, "and let him do his utmost to bring into being for these people something that shall be a joy to them." The Plan, presented by the Commercial Club in 1909, covered parks, streets, harbors, piers, museums, boulevards, bridges, and more, all with an eye towards creating a city that would be both efficient and beautiful. They wanted the same for their train depot.

Daniel Burnham began designing the new Union Station, but he died in 1912. His company became Graham, Burnham and Company, a partnership between his sons and Ernest Robert Graham, among others, and they took over. This wasn't a simple matter of designing a depot and building it, which on its own is a complicated endeavor. Existing businesses had to work together in an industry that was notoriously competitive. But, as the Plan said:

> "Whatever concessions may be called for, they will be found insignificant when compared with the great gain which will result to the transportation systems themselves from creating here in the central metropolis of the United States a complete system of handling both freight and passenger traffic so as to promote the convenience of the people, and to enhance the commerce of the city of Chicago."

This massive civic project required the straightening of the river, broadening of streets, and demolition of existing buildings, which meant the city had to pass ordinances to make it all happen. In 1913, five competing railroads joined together to form Chicago Union Station Co. Finally, work began on March 16, 1915.

It would be a decade before Union Station opened. The process crawled because the trains had to keep moving. Plus there were labor strikes, shortages of labor and materials during World War I, and a period of more than two years when the government took over the railroads entirely. A depression followed the war, threatening to grind Chicago's plan to a halt.

But Chicago wasn't called the Windy City for nothing, and the same "I Will" spirit that brought the 1893 World's Columbian Exposition to the city kept the plan alive. One of the biggest boosters was Charles H. Wacker, chairman of the Chicago Plan Commission. In *An Appeal to Business Men,* published in 1921, he detailed Chicago's previous "herculean accomplishments," including raising the streets, creating parks and boulevards, rebuilding from the fire, hosting the world's fair, and building a $65,000,000 drainage canal. He wrote:

> "We are prepared. Are we going to falter and suffer consequent failure? Are we now, for the first time, going to tarnish the I WILL spirit of Chicago? No!! The public spirit of the citizens of Chicago, evidenced time and time again ever since the city was founded, still lives, and therein lies the promise of the future."

For Charles, this went beyond mere transportation. Public improvements would avert bread lines and soup kitchens, promote city growth, increase property values, and foster "citizens sound in body, mind, and morals."

In *The Chicago Plan, a Brief Review of Its Development, Projects And Accomplishments,* Marshall Field & Company complained that one-third of downtown traffic was blocked by "railroad land," but due to the genius and enthusiasm of the Plan and its boosters, "Chicago bids fair to become one of the world's best organized and most beautiful cities."

Work on Union Station resumed in earnest in 1922 and was completed in 1925. When the station opened, *Railway Age* published a twenty-two page article dedicated to the $75,000,000 project. It was the only double-stub station in America, which meant that tracks coming from two different directions ended at the terminal. Cars, new in 1909 but more common when the station opened—wouldn't block street traffic because there were interior driveways and vehicle platforms. Graham, Anderson, Probst and White, the successor firm to Graham, Burnham and Company, designed a headhouse and concourse that were neoclassical on the outside and Beaux-Arts on the inside. All four of the named partners had worked for Daniel Burnham, so his vision could be considered safe with them.

Chicago was the undisputed rail center of the United States, and now it had a station worthy of that status. The Bedford limestone headhouse filled an entire city block between Adams Street and Jackson Boulevard with a massive colonnade fronting the west side of Canal Street. Inside, passengers waited for trains under a barrel-vault skylight in a room lined with buff-colored Roman travertine marble and Corinthian columns. Henry Hering, artist of the Field Museum's caryatids, created *Night* and *Day*, female statues that overlooked the passengers as they walked across pink Tennessee Marble. The women, one holding an owl and one a rooster, represented the railroads' motto of "Service Around the Clock." Passengers could dine at Fred Harvey or Gold Lion. Men could get their shoes shined and their hair barbered. Women could relax in their own lounge furnished in American walnut upholstered with blue silk mohair.

The headhouse connected to the concourse with a tunnel under Canal Street, and that's where passengers could get their tickets, make telephone calls and send telegrams, and drop off and pick up their baggage. The Concourse was also grand, feeling more like a cathedral than a train station.

After a decline during the Great Depression, ridership increased to its greatest numbers during World War II, with more than a hundred thousand daily passengers, many of them soldiers. Air travel and the Interstate Highway system caused a precipitous drop in train travel in the 1960s. By the end of the decade the Concourse was demolished and a new office building constructed above the tracks. It seemed like passenger trains might be doomed, but in 1971 Amtrak began operations. The quasi-public corporation guaranteed inter-city rail travel across the country. Amtrak acquired full ownership of Union Station in 1984. There were some minor renovations in the 1990s, including removing the tar that had covered the Great Hall skylight since World War II.

Union Station Today

Union Station is the third busiest railroad terminal in the United States, with about 120,000 passengers daily. In 2012, Amtrak unveiled a Master Plan to both renovate and modernize the historic station. They restored the Grand Staircases in 2016, using marble from the same Italian quarry as the original. The former Women's Lounge became the Burlington Room, and the new Metropolitan Lounge opened for premium Amtrak customers. In 2018, Amtrak completed a $22 million renovation that focused on the Great Hall. Two dozen chandeliers and the grand skylight were restored and repaired, and Henry Hering's statues were restored and illuminated. The former Fred Harvey restaurant space, which has been closed since a 1980 fire, is slated to be an upscale food court.

1925
Tribune Tower

I t takes gumption to open your skyscraper's design to a competition. Of course, it helps if you seed the playing field by paying your favorite architects to participate, and it certainly doesn't hurt if you're the one judging the entries. Then it's not just gumption; it's a publicity bonanza.

260

The *Chicago Tribune* was no stranger to gumption, or to publicity. When the paper announced its $100,000 contest for a new skyscraper in 1922, publisher Robert R. McCormick had been printing "The World's Greatest Newspaper" on the masthead for eleven years. The paper's 75th anniversary and a need for more space provided a perfect opportunity for an international competition that would keep people talking for the next century. It would also keep the paper in one place for a while: since first rolling off the presses in 1847, The *Chicago Tribune* had lived in seven different buildings—eight if you include the temporary quarters after the 1871 fire.

The paper's first offices were in a single room on the third floor of a building at Lake and LaSalle Streets. In 1849, they moved a block away to a spot above Gary's grocery at Clark and Lake. The next year, the Tribune moved to another spot on Lake Street, this time in the Masonic Building. Two years after that, the paper took over two floors in the Evans Block, which was on Clark between Randolph and (you guessed it) Lake.

For the next seventeen years, through the Civil War and beyond, The *Chicago Tribune* stayed put, but in 1869 it was time to get their very own building. Editor-in-Chief Joseph Medill, who'd been running the paper since 1855, hired Edward Burling. This time they moved away from Lake Street, and the architect designed a four-story building of Joliet limestone at Dearborn and Madison.

It was supposed to be fireproof. It wasn't, although it didn't burn completely to the ground during the Great Chicago Fire. After missing just two days at press, Medill and staff resumed operations in temporary headquarters. In 1872, Burling, with his new partner Dankmar Adler, built them a five-story building on the same lot and used some of the interior pieces that had survived. An October 9 article in the Tribune said that this building was "intended to be *really* fire-proof this time." (Emphasis added.) Fortunately, they didn't find out whether it was or wasn't, and they didn't need another structure until the turn of the century, three years after Medill passed away in 1899.

This time around they thought seventeen stories should be enough for at least a few generations. They weren't. In less than two decades the paper moved printing operations to a new plant north of the river and across the street from the recently opened Wrigley Building, and they still needed more space. That's what happens when you're The World's Greatest Newspaper.

If they needed to move—again—they were going to go big. Really big. On June 10, 1922, on the *Chicago Tribune*'s 75th birthday, a full-page ad announced $100,000 in prizes to architects. The goal was "to erect the most beautiful and distinctive office building in the world." First place would get half of that prize money, second place would get $20,000, and third place $10,000. The remaining would be divided equally among ten specially invited architects. These included Jarvis Hunt, who'd designed their printing plant; Holabird and Roche, who'd designed their current building; D. H. Burnham and Co, because how could they not; and a New York pair named Howells and Hood.

Requests for applications poured in from all over the world, and when all was said and done, the Tribune received 285 sets of drawings, 115 of which were international submissions. To prevent bias, the architects submitted their designs anonymously. That was probably a good thing, since two of the top three designs were by specially invited architects. Third place went to Holabird and Roche and first place, to Howells and Hood.

The jury of co-publishers (and cousins) Robert McCormick and Joseph Patterson, along with Edward Beck, Holmes Onderdonk, and Alfred Granger voted unanimously for the Neo-Gothic tower, and while most agreed that it was a beautiful building, a few, including one vocal and unsurprising critic, thought that another design was better and would leave a more enduring legacy. Finnish architect Eliel Saarinen's simpler and more modern tower spoke to one person in particular: Louis Sullivan. The famed form-follows-function architect was thoroughly disgusted with the jury's selection. He believed that the second prize design should be placed first, "where it belongs by virtue of its beautifully controlled and virile power," and that the first place winner should be "demoted to the level of those works evolved of dying ideas, even as it sends forth a frantic cry to escape from the common bondage of those governed by ideas."

Leave it to Louis.

The misanthrope might have been surprised to learn that John Mead Howells approached it from the same sensibility as he did. At the dinner honoring the winners, Howells said: "Your building must express its use and its construction...Mr. Hood and I have tried to set aside any itching for the original for fear of the fantastic, and we have striven only for a straight solution of that most worth while in American problems—the American skyscraper."

Their straight solution took plenty of turns with a three-story arched entryway featuring an elaborate stone screen of Aesop's Fables. Sculptures, like that of a howling dog for Howells and Robin Hood for Hood, illustrated a distinct sense of play. Grotesques—comically distorted figures—decorated the building: a whispering man represented the snideness of rumors, while a shouting man the volume of a hot story. Inside, the travertine marble walls in the lobby, which became known as the Hall of Inscriptions, were etched with quotes emphasizing the necessity of freedom of speech

The *Chicago Tribune* absolutely loved it. They touted its beauty in their paper, and they kept touting it. A 1929 article said the tower was as "delicate as a lady's hand and as firm as a man's." A 1943 souvenir booklet for people who visited the "Home of the World's Greatest Newspaper" opened with:

> "Words cannot describe the beauty of the Taj Mahal. Man fails to voice the true impression of the magnitude of the Great Pyramid. To say that Tribune Tower is a stone skyscraper which is square in plan and isolated on all sides is to describe a Brahms symphony as a musical composition written for a number of instruments. To appreciate the music of this great master you

must hear it. To appreciate the symphony in stone which is Tribune Tower you must see it, experience it, live in the same community with it."

It's surely no coincidence that the booklet specifically mentions the Taj Mahal and the Great Pyramid. In another move that was guaranteed to generate publicity, and not a little controversy, McCormick came up with the idea to embed pieces of landmarks in his tower, and those two wonders of the world made the cut. The legend is that while he was covering World War I he'd picked up a piece of a cathedral in Ypres, Belgium, that had been bombed by the Germans. As the new tower was under construction, he thought fragments of important buildings would be a cool way to decorate the building, so he sent a note to his correspondents asking them to try to get pieces of history, "by honorable means." Thirty-one are listed in *Pictured Encyclopedia of the World's Greatest Newspaper*, published in 1928, including pieces from China's Forbidden City and Great Wall, France's Notre Dame, Greece's Parthenon, Norway's Trondjhem {sic} Cathedral, and David's Tower in Jerusalem. More were added over the years until at one point there were 150. The provenance of most of them can be established, but there are a few that might have been obtained through less-than-honorable means.

Additions for WGN (World's Greatest Newspaper) radio and television were built in 1935 and 1950. Many of the historic stones are embedded in those additions.

Tribune Tower Today

The *Chicago Tribune* stayed in its monumental tower for nearly a century. In 2016, Tribune Media sold Tribune Tower and the historic building has been converted to condos.

1926
Bismarck Hotel
Allegro Royal Sonesta Hotel

L ike so many other Chicago Landmarks, The Allegro
Royal Sonesta Hotel Chicago can trace its beginnings
to the 1893 Columbian Exposition. This landmark's
story began when Emil Eitel, the oldest of eight siblings,
arrived in Chicago from Stuttgart, Germany in 1890. The next
year his brother Karl followed him to the states and the two
started their own company, naming it—what else—Eitel

Brothers. They imported wine, beer, and liquor, and during the fair they represented several German companies exhibiting items as diverse as jigsaw blades, bandages, and harmonicas. The brothers also saw a fantastic opportunity, and it would write their future. Millions visited the World's Fair and they needed someplace to stay, so the brothers converted an apartment building at Cottage Grove and 63rd Street into a hotel with a hundred and fifty beds.

And that was all she wrote. The year after the fair Emil and Karl bought the Germania Hotel at Randolph and Wells and renamed it the Bismarck Hotel. It only had fifty beds, but the following year they bought the building next door and doubled the capacity. They capitalized on their Teutonic heritage—appealing to a German clientele, serving German food, decorating with German furnishings, and naming it after the first German chancellor—and it was an unmitigated success. In 1894, Emil and Carl, with a C, were listed in *The Chicago Blue Book of Selected Names* as members of a German social club. In the 1897 directory, Emil and Karl, spelled correctly with a K this time, were listed as two of those "Prominent Residents." The brothers knew what they were doing: Chicago in the late 19th century was fairly swimming with Germans. By 1900, one of every four residents had either been born in Germany or was the child of someone who had been. The Eitels created a place that felt like home.

In 1898 their brother Robert immigrated to Chicago, and Max followed in 1901. Business was booming, enough so that plans for a new, bigger hotel made the papers as early as 1906, even though it wasn't realized until much later. In 1918, the Eitel brothers briefly changed the name of their property because of anti-German sentiments during World War I. More than five thousand suggestions were submitted and they decided on Randolph Hotel, but within a few years the name was back to Bismarck.

By the 1920s the Eitels had spent 30 years in the hospitality business and it was time to step up their game. They decided to raze the building at Randolph and Wells and build a whole entertainment complex. There would be a bigger and better

Bismarck, a luxurious theater, and an attached office building. They owned the whole block, so why not?

They hired another set of brothers, George and Cornelius Rapp, to design the project. As the official architects of theater magnates Balaban and Katz, Rapp and Rapp had an established reputation for creating beautiful and complex spaces. This project would entail redesigning the Bismarck Hotel while adding Palace Theatre and Metropolitan Office Building.

The New Bismarck Hotel opened June 7, 1926. The block had changed since the Eitels purchased the Germania more than thirty years before; the location was now buttressed by an El station practically at their door, the new double-decker Wacker Drive a block away, and a widened LaSalle Street ferrying financial sorts right next to their new office building. Whether through savvy or coincidence, the brothers had struck again.

Even a publication as familiar with hotels as *The Hotel Monthly* was impressed. Their 1927 feature exclaimed "There is so much that is 'different' in the Bismarck Hotel that we are at a loss for words to explain." The grand stairway and its polished brass lighting fixtures, designed by another Eitel brother, Albert. The colored glass double windows, the terrazza lobby floor, the artfully-arranged furniture. The Walnut Room, with its namesake timber grown in America and carved in Germany. That room's chandeliers were also designed by Albert, who had to give the final OK before the project could even begin. The lobby of the Palace Theater was "the most impressive room of its kind in America." Even the office building was a success; seventy percent of it was rented before construction was completed.

The new Bismarck opened in the middle of Prohibition. On April 7, 1933, beer with 3.2% alcohol by weight was legal again in Illinois and at 12:01AM, the Bismarck Hotel tapped the first legal keg of beer in Chicago. Most hotels didn't participate because they didn't want to take the chance the Volstead Act wouldn't be repealed if people went overboard after fourteen years of "abstinence," but the Eitels knew their people. "Its

German-American clientele had been considered and ... the patrons were entitled to say a few 'prosits' as soon as the government authorized them to." Eight months later, the Bismarck would jump the gun by opening taps at 4:00PM Central—Utah didn't cast the vote that ratified the 21st Amendment until 4:30PM.

Oh well.

The Eitels, which now included Karl's son Otto, managed the Bismarck until 1956, when Otto sold to Arthur Wirtz, future owner of the Chicago Blackhawks. The hotel went downhill, although its proximity to City Hall made it a popular haunt of the Cook County Democratic Party, and especially of the boss himself. Mayor Richard J. Daley was such a regular he had his own table with a private phone in the Walnut Room. Bill Kimpton took over the hotel in the late 1990s. It would be the boutique hotelier's first foray in Chicago, and he renovated the old Bismarck as the Hotel Allegro. The hotel was renovated again in 2015, this time highlighting the hotel's 1920s art deco era, including those Albert Eitel-designed star chandeliers.

Bismarck Hotel Today

In 2020, Sonesta International Hotels Corporation purchased Hotel Allegro from Kimpton Hotels, renaming it Allegro Royal Sonesta Hotel Chicago. The hotel continues to carry the grandeur and eloquence of the 1920s Bismarck, from the grand staircase entrance to the lobby and the light fixtures designed by Albert Eitel. Local artists are highlighted in a rotating "Artist Window" series. The hotel is cyclist-friendly; complimentary bikes for guests make it easy to explore downtown Chicago.

1926
Oriental Theatre
James M. Nederlander Theatre

O nce you've established a reputation for creating elaborate movie palaces, each more grand than the last, there's only one thing you can do: make the next one even more elaborate, more over the top, more exciting, more exotic. That's exactly what Balaban and Katz did with the Oriental Theatre. Opened on May 8, 1926, it was "more oriental than the orient," "the spirit of the Orient in gay mood," and filled with "hasheesh dream decor." In the midst of Prohibition, a trippy theater must have seemed like just the ticket.

It had been five years since Balaban and Katz opened The Chicago Theatre and they were due to make a splash. The theater owners partnered with the Freemasons, who needed a new building, and the two seemingly disparate interests created a twenty-four story office building, and behind it, a seven-story theater topped with eight floors of Masonic halls. The location was the site of the infamous Iroquois Theater, which opened on November 23, 1903, and suffered a devastating fire a few weeks later that killed several hundred people. That fire made a permanent impact on theater safety laws, requiring automatic sprinklers, exit lights, and fire alarms, and flame-resistant scenery, props, and curtains. Doors also had to open outwards with push bars instead of doorknobs or handles. The building itself reopened as Hyde and Behman's music hall the following fall, and in 1905 became the Colonial Theatre before it was razed in 1924. The building wasn't completely removed, however. According to the National Register of Historic Places Nomination Form, "The Oriental retains the flame scorched south and west stage walls of the Iroquois. Marks still indicate locations of the Iroquois dressing rooms on the south wall."

Everything else was completely new. From the outside, the New Masonic Temple and Oriental Theatre looked like your relatively standard skyscraper with a strong base followed by floors of uniform office space and topped with a cornice. However, because this was a Rapp and Rapp-designed building, there were also gargoyles, serpents, a three-story grand window over the entrance, and a lighted marquee.

But inside...nothing could prepare audiences for what they'd see behind that marquee. Brothers Cornelius and George Rapp built an entire world, an ode to India that was a marked departure from their previous nods to European classicism. *Suburbanite Economist* called it a "glorious, barbaric thing of color, color, color." Patrons entering the theater were greeted by elephants everywhere: propping up wall lights, supporting foyer tables, fortifying throne chairs.

There were buddhas and princes and princesses, and inside the auditorium, an Indian dancer one and a half stories tall posed in a gilded niche. A giant silver dome, inset with a deep blue and green flower medallion, rimmed with seahorses and goddesses, soared above it all. The architects themselves described the decor as "intricacies of Eastern magnificence, grotesque dancers and Indian animal figures, resplendent with lights behind colored glass around ornate shrine-like niches." Even the Wurlitzer organ participated—painted in bright red lacquer (described as "chinese red") and trimmed with black, it was emblazoned with crimson firebirds.

They needed an act just as enticing, and they got it in Paul Ash. Paul was the syncopation darling. Part jazz musician, part comedian, he'd been performing to sold-out audiences at McVickers Theater until Balaban and Katz swooped him up with an exclusive contract. And, oh what a contact it was. The redhead signed on for a million bucks over five years—an unheard-of amount in 1926. Paul was worth it. His last year at McVickers he performed a record-breaking 1500 shows and, according to the *Palatine Enterprise*, had "the largest and most loyal following of any stage artist in the world." A contract of that size came with restrictions, of course. Paul couldn't change his face or get plastic surgery of any kind, and he must keep his hair long and wavy. A small price to pay for a cool mil.

Winning Paul from the competition was such a coup that the Rapp brothers built a "magic flying stage" specifically for him and his merry-mad musical gang. This ingenious contraption could move up, down, and sideways, enabling scene changes that previously would have been impossible. Paul and his band needed them; he was more than the leader of a big band. He and his troupe were Performers who crafted themed shows. They opened the Oriental with "Insultin' the Sultan." Another show brought audiences to the Hawaiian isles. "Russian Jazzki" was set in Moscow, and Paul became "Paulski Ashovitz" for the duration. *The Daily Herald* described that program as "summery fluffiness," despite the snowy setting.

The Oriental's opening was an unmitigated success. *Forest Park Review* reported: "Never in the history of the theatre in Chicago has a new playhouse opened to such tremendous enthusiasm as has greeted the new Balaban & Katz Oriental theatre...The Oriental broke all attendance records."

Paul and company earned their keep. During that first week, they performed five and six shows a day to capacity crowds. "Almost 100,000 persons entered 'the gateway to the orient.'"

After a while, all of those performances got to him, and in February 1928, Paul Ash collapsed on stage. By May of that year he was off to Broadway. Despite not completing the five year contract, he seemed to leave on good terms since he was reported to return to the Oriental that September for a limited engagement.

Paul may have left, but the show must go on, and the Oriental lit up its marquee with names that are known to this day: The Three Stooges, Al Jolson, Cab Calloway, and Duke Ellington, to name a few. In 1934, a young lady by the name of Frances Ethel Gumm took the stage with her sisters. According to one story, and there are several, comedian George Jessel noticed the audience laughing when he introduced The Gumm Sisters and suggested they change the name to Garland. Whether this was inspired by his friend Robert Garland, a garland of flowers, or Carole Lombard's character Lily Garland in *Twentieth Century* is anybody's guess. Either way, the twelve-year-old became known as Judy Garland, and the next year Metro-Goldwyn-Mayer gave her a contract.

Live performances brought people in, but at its heart, the Oriental was a movie palace. Like other theaters, once television became more popular and readily available it didn't seem worth the effort to head downtown to watch a movie. Audiences declined throughout the fifties and sixties until the Oriental hit rock bottom. Preservationists tried to rescue it by adding it to the National Register of Historic Places, but despite being entered in 1978, the theater closed down three years later. With the building crumbling around it, the lobby became "Oriental Electronics," a retail television and radio store, an almost final ignominy as it sold the items that helped lead to the theater's demise.

The Oriental's rescue came with the city's plan to revitalize the Loop. What had heretofore been considered a pie-in-the-sky dream would become a reality. "Amazing Return of the Oriental", in the January 12, 1996, *Chicago Tribune*, said "Suddenly, the North Loop is on the verge of achieving what many once thought impossible—a Broadway-style theater district along Randolph." The rebranded, renovated, and renewed Ford Center for the Performing Arts Oriental Theatre opened October 18, 1998, with the Chicago premiere of *Ragtime*. Two years later, New York impresario James M. Nederlander created Broadway in Chicago, kicking off what would be a three and a half year run of *Wicked*. In 2017, the New Masonic Temple became the Cambria Hotel Chicago Loop - Theatre District.

Oriental Theatre Today

James M. Nederlander was one of the most powerful theatrical producers in the United States. Nederlander Organization, begun by his father in Detroit in 1912, is still one of the largest theater and music venue operators and is the second largest owner of Broadway theaters in New York. Acknowledging that the word "Oriental," with its objectifying and racist overtones, was problematic, the theater was renamed in 2019 for Mr. Nederlander, who had passed away in 2016.

That same year another theater opened inside what had been the New Masonic Temple. West Coast-based Teatro Zinzanni planned to bring their circus-themed dinner theater to Chicago. The only problem was, they needed a place to pitch their spiegeltent (a large traveling pavilion), and Midwest winters aren't exactly conducive to a venue made of wood and canvas. Broadway in Chicago president Lou Razin happened to know about a big huge open auditorium in the Cambria Hotel, one of what had originally been several masonic halls. With ten auditoriums on four floors, none of them with visible supports, the National Register of Historic Places Nomination Form considered it a masterpiece of engineering. To lead producer Stanley Feig, it was Teatro Zinzanni's new home.

1927
The Stevens Hotel
Hilton Chicago

S ometimes a hotel is just a hotel. It's a place to sleep for the night, and that's all it was ever meant to be. But sometimes, a hotel is an obsession. One particular hotel was the obsession of two men and their fixations had contrasting outcomes: For one, it was a heralded achievement, but for the other, it became the cause of scandal and suicide.

James W. Stevens wanted to build the biggest hotel in the world, and on March 4, 1922, *The Economist* reported that he was going to do just that. It would be twenty-five stories, have three thousand rooms, and cost fifteen million dollars. It would have magnificent lounges, shopping along Michigan Avenue, and a grand staircase. Most of all, it would be beautiful. A March 7 editorial in the *Chicago Tribune*, a clipping that would make its way into a copper box buried in the cornerstone, precipitately named it the World's Greatest Hotel.

The plan was audacious, but James, or J. W., already owned the largest hotel in the city. He'd built the Hotel La Salle in 1909 and his son Ernest ran it so successfully that occupancy rates were near one hundred percent. His other son Raymond helped him run Illinois Life Insurance Company. J. W. and his brother had founded that company and it made them rich. It also helped fund those hotel dreams, funding which would prove to be their downfall within a few short years. Raymond wasn't so sure about the hotel, but Ernest was all in, and the family created The Stevens Hotel Company and sold bonds to pay for the behemoth.

The Stevens opened May 2, 1927, and it was a magnum opus. Two thousand windows overlooked the new Buckingham Fountain. Sixty-one miles of carpet covered the floors. The entrance featured two grand staircases, one on each side, with travertine walls and columns. Three of Ernest's sons, including future Supreme Court Justice John Paul Stevens, were models for two bronze fountains. Opening night guests received gifts carved with replicas of the fountains: the north fountain appeared on book ends for the ladies, and the south fountain on ash tray paper weights for the gents. It took seven freight cars just to bring the glassware from Bryce Brothers in Pennsylvania, and the switchboard needed seventy-five telephone operators—more than a town of twenty-five thousand people would require. The Grand Ballroom was so grand that ten two-story five-room houses could fit inside.

The first guest to sign the register was Vice President Charles Dawes. The second, Cuban President Gerardo Machado. And on the third day, three thousand movie types, including Cecille B. DeMille, filled the Grand Ballroom for the

Motion Picture Association Ball. During those festivities, flappers almost lost their tassels over Milton Sills, a University of Chicago professor of psychology and philosophy turned actor who was apparently quite the dreamboat. They mobbed him in the lobby and they mobbed him in the ballroom, until the president of the Movie Owners' Association had to select who would fill Milton's dance card.

From their entrance through the grand hall until they entered their rooms, guests would be helped by no fewer than nine people. Once they were settled, there was no reason to leave. While at the Stevens, guests could pick up necessities at the twenty-four-hour drug store, find reading material at the lending library aided by a University of Chicago librarian, buy flowers and jewelry and ice cream, watch a movie, go bowling, and buy clothes and toys for the kids. Men could see a barber; women could go to the salon. Starting in 1930, if the weather cooperated they could play 18 holes of miniature golf on the rooftop. Even their bathrooms were special, with taps for hot, cold, and ice water.

They could even have surgery in one of the two operating rooms in the on-site hospital.

It was an auspicious beginning. At first it seemed this self-contained city within a city would be a huge success, drawing celebrities like Charles Lindbergh and Amelia Earhart. Unfortunately, when the roaring twenties ended, so did J.W.'s dream. The market crashed and he and Ernest tried, desperately, to save their hotel. Their desperation was so extreme they made the horrible decision to give the hotel loans from their insurance company. In 1932, only five years after the World's Greatest Hotel had opened, more than fifty banks closed and the Stevens filed to place both of their hotels in receivership. Then Illinois Life failed. In January 1933, J. W., Raymond, and Ernest were indicted for conspiracy and embezzlement. In March, J. W. suffered a massive stroke from which he'd never recover. Shortly after, Raymond committed suicide. That October, a jury convicted Ernest. The next year, the Illinois Supreme Court overturned his conviction, but the damage was done. In 1942 the U.S. Army bought the hotel for six million, stripping it of its amenities and comforts. Ten thousand soldiers moved in, crammed four to a room, and the Grand Ballroom became the mess hall. The government didn't use it long, selling it for a little over five million in September 1943 in a convoluted transaction that included Blackstone and Drake Hotels owner Arnold Kirkeby and, in the background, Stephen Healy. In November, Kirkeby partially reopened with 1,100 available rooms but by January 1944, Healy owned the Stevens Hotel.

Waiting impatiently was another man who wanted the World's Greatest Hotel, a man who had been building up his wealth and his reputation as a formidable hotelier. Conrad Hilton had already tried to get the Stevens Hotel, buying mortgage bonds in the late '30s, but then the Army beat him to it. By early 1945 he decided he'd waited long enough and he headed to Chicago, determined not to leave until he owned the Stevens Hotel.

That would prove to be tricky, because Stephen Healy was a slippery little sucker. Conrad thought he had a deal multiple times, but Stephen would renege and ask for more money. When Stephen disappeared after the third negotiation, which would have netted him a million dollars in profit, Conrad's friend Willard Keith took matters into his own hands. Willard had had enough of the Chicago winter and wanted to get back to California, so he trudged into the snow, found Stephen, and told him that Conrad was tired of his shenanigans and would just buy the Palmer House instead.

Conrad got the Stevens. He ended up paying seven and a half million for it, but he got his hotel. Ten months later, he got the Palmer House, too.

He turned Chicago into his headquarters and the Stevens Hotel into his flagship, and it began to live up to its early promise, helped along by Conrad's celebrity status. (He was married to Zsa Zsa Gabor, after all.) Beginning in 1948 and for twenty-one years, families would flock to the Boulevard Room to watch the ice frolics, an indoor ice-skating show. Guests included everyone from Babe Ruth to Ray Charles to Elizabeth Taylor, who for a brief time was married to Conrad "Nicky"

Hilton, Jr. At a meeting on November 19, 1951, that Conrad did not attend, the Board of Directors voted to change the name from Stevens Hotel to The Conrad Hilton.

The hotel attracted politicians, including Presidents Truman and Eisenhower and Senator John F. Kennedy, and cinematic royalty like Bette Davis and Lauren Bacall. On July 6, 1959, official royalty in the form of Queen Elizabeth II arrived in Chicago aboard HMY Britannia. She and her husband, Prince Philip, were celebrating the just opened St. Lawrence Seaway, which opened the Great Lakes to oceangoing vessels from the Atlantic. "The city hasn't been as excited since someone caught the mayor in the Everleigh Club—the city's leading bordello—back in the days when Chicago was a bawdy frontier town," said a special correspondent to *The Indianapolis News*. The Conrad Hilton hosted the Queen and twelve hundred of her closest friends for dinner during her whirlwind fourteen-hour visit to Chicago. The Imperial Suites, which had been built in 1956, offered one of the best views of the city from their rooftop location; Her Royal Majesty was able to relax for a few minutes before and after the banquet in a spot where guests used to play miniature golf.

In the 1960s The Conrad Hilton reduced the number of rooms to 2,400 by increasing their size, and expanded their convention capacity by adding a new complex. The lobby got a touch-up in 1968. That same year the Democratic National Convention turned into a disastrous clash between anti-war protestors and Chicago police in Grant Park, which was essentially the hotel's front yard. In an attempt to keep tear gas and "stink bombs" out of the lobby, the hotel decided to lock the doors. Only problem was, they couldn't find the keys because the doors hadn't been locked since the hotel opened thirty years before.

In 1970, the elevators were converted from manual operation to automatic. During that decade, downtown Chicago declined and The Conrad Hilton had the same issues as the rest of its South Loop neighbors. Namely, this was no longer a desirable location. By 1978, the hotel's future was uncertain, and while demolition was considered, Hilton made the decision to renovate. This was the World's Greatest Hotel, after all. In 1984, they closed the hotel down for a year and spent $185 million dollars to ensure it would live up to its legend. They reduced the number of rooms to 1,543. The hotel had already lost its status as the world's largest in 1964 when Soviets built the Rossiya in Moscow; now it was just about offering a better experience for the guests. According to *Chicago's Grand Hotel: a History of the Hilton Chicago,* "old-world craftsmen painstakingly restored the 24-karat gold leaf, crystal, and marble appointments, and also the original oil paintings." Italian restorer Lido Lippi, who would restore the Palmer House's frescoes in the '90s, spent seven months cleaning and repainting the Hilton's. The Tower Ballroom, located at the very, very top, was converted into the Conrad Hilton Suite, an extravagant apartment with a balcony overlooking Grant Park, a private kitchen, a library with pool table, and a grand salon with a fireplace. It even had its own helipad, although that's no longer available. Prime ministers, kings, rock stars, movie stars, and presidents, both American and Mexican, have stayed in the two-story five thousand square foot palace.

When the hotel reopened October 1, 1985, it was re-christened Chicago Hilton and Towers. In 1998, it became Hilton Chicago.

The Stevens Hotel Today

While the former Stevens Hotel is no longer the World's Largest, continued renovations keep the Hilton Chicago current while respecting its storied past. A $150 million renovation in 2017 included updates to meeting spaces as well as creating specialty suites and a significant restoration of the Conrad Hilton Suite. The Imperial Suites got a major touch-up in early 2020. As an anchor of Chicago's skyline, Hilton Chicago is one of the city's most recognizable buildings, aided by its appearance in several television shows and movies, including *ER*, which used the helipad; *The Fugitive*; *My Best Friend's Wedding*, and *Road to Perdition*.

1929
Medinah Athletic Club
InterContinental Chicago

M ichigan Avenue just north of the Chicago River is
architectural eye candy. There's the gleaming white
Wrigley Building on the west, the Tribune Tower

with its flying buttresses on the east, and beyond that is the InterContinental Chicago, an art deco skyscraper with a distinctive yellow dome. That dome is the crown of a madcap building that's the embodiment of the organization that created it.

In the midst of the roaring twenties, Chicago's Shriners decided they needed their own athletic club. Sure, they could have gone to the Chicago Athletic Association, but that was filled with fuddy-duddies and the Shriners were anything but. An offshoot of the Freemasons, the Ancient Arabic Order of the Nobles of the Mystic Shrine, as the group was officially known, was all about having fun. As in, that's why the order was created in the first place. In the 1870s a small group of New York Freemasons, including actor Billy Florence and Walter Fleming, M.D., felt that the fraternity, while worthwhile, was a bit too stoic for their tastes. After attending a party hosted by an Arabian diplomat during a trip to France, Billy was inspired by the event's "exotic style, flavors and music." When he got back home he suggested an Arabic theme to Walter. The good doctor, who was savvy in the ways of Freemason rituals, agreed, and between the two they created their own fraternity based on fun, fellowship, and philanthropy. They weren't complete rebels, though—you had to be a third-degree mason before you were eligible to become a Shriner.

By the early 1900s, the group had spread across the country and into Canada, Mexico, and Panama. In 1912, the Chicago Shriners built their Medinah Temple with a 4,200-seat auditorium and topped with an onion dome, and in June 1925 they laid the cornerstone for a new Shriners' Hospital for Crippled Children at Oak Park and Belden. In November of that year, the Fez-wearing gents announced their next big project: the Medinah Athletic Club. This "towering clubhouse" would be designed by Walter W. Ahlschlager. (Ostensibly he won a design contest, but he was considered a shoe-in. It probably didn't hurt that he was a member of the club.) The architect described it as "a tower of the Orient, a Saracenic tower, proudly piercing the sky with its gold pear shaped dome and many minarets." In addition to offering all of the expected amenities of a men's athletic club, it would also have hotel rooms. The entire tower, all forty-plus stories of it, would only be open to members and their guests.

The tower would be a fitting home for the "party animals of Freemasonry," as CBS reporter Mo Rocca would later call the Shriners. In an era when the goal of entertainment was escape, Ahlschlager, who'd designed the Roxy Theatre in New York, created a vertical version of 1920s opulent movie palaces. From its onion dome to the three Sumerian guards on the twelfth floor to the friezes a few stories below them, the Medinah Athletic Club would bring the Middle East to Michigan Avenue. Those friezes, envisioned by theater designer George Unger and carved by Leon Harment, represented the stages of construction: Contribution, or the gathering of materials; Wisdom, depicting a ruler conferring with his counselors and architects; and Consecration. According to a September 16, 1928, article in the *Chicago Tribune*, the latter shows a priest "sacrificing a white bull whose blood will be mixed with crushed grapes and poured into the earth." While the Shriners didn't sacrifice any livestock, they did install a time capsule. Inside they placed a copy of the article announcing the building, a roster of all the members, and photos of the officers, among other historical knick-knacks. Some of the men were also memorialized on the outside of the building— Unger used faces of club members as models for the characters in the friezes.

Once a Shriner entered, he stepped into a world of whimsical time travel. There was the Hall of Lions, set in ancient Assyria, and King Arthur's Court, a smoking lounge decorated with murals that depicted the Medieval king's timeline. That room also had the bonus of hidden panels where booze could be stored - it was Prohibition, after all. The Spanish Tea Court brought him forward to the time of King Ferdinand and Queen Isabella. Any women who chose to enter this male sanctuary had to use a separate entrance, and they had to be chaperoned anywhere the ceiling wasn't painted blue, which was most places. The time travel continued even for the ladies, though; their Renaissance Room reflected the elegant era of Louis XVI, and included a loggia overlooking Michigan Avenue.

The athletic facilities for these fun-loving party animals were a playground of "ooh ooh ooh! You know what else we need? We need miniature golf!" and so they had it. Way up on the twenty-third floor, the Shriners could attempt to avoid water hazards as they went for a hole-in-one. There were the standard amenities, like a running track and a gymnasium, but they also had a bowling alley, and an archery range, and a shooting range, and a two-story boxing arena. They added a swimming pool, but instead of doing something easy like installing it in the first couple of floors, Ahlschlager put it on the fourteenth—above the Grand Ballroom and its 12,000-pound crystal chandelier. It wasn't just any old place to swim laps. It was a glorious bathing stadium, with seats for spectators, a fountain of Neptune, gorgeous Spanish majolica tiles, and stained glass windows decorated like fish scales.

Many years later, architecture critic Paul Gapp would call the limestone-skinned building a "belovedly extravagant architectural concoction." That extravagance made the persistent and oft-repeated rumor that the dome was designed as a dock for dirigibles plausible. However, an extensive search of newspaper archives failed to unearth a single reference to either plans for or use as a dock. Sometimes, as was the case with their Medinah Temple, a dome might be just a dome.

A few months after this man cave to end all man caves opened, the economy closed. The stock market crashed October 24, 1929, but the Shriners were able to hold onto their private, members-only club for an incredible five years, even with low occupancy. In 1934, the building was turned into apartments until developer John Mack bought it in 1944 and reopened it as, coincidentally, since it had no connection to future owners, the Continental Hotel. Three years later, the Sheraton chain bought it and renamed it the Sheraton. In 1961, they built a 26-story tower to the north. The Radisson took over in the late 1970s, but it was only open for a few years before it became the Hotel Continental. Then it closed, too. Finally, Inter-Continental bought the property and invested millions. They turned the north tower into their budget brand, the Forum Hotel, which opened in 1989, and the historic tower opened as the Inter-Continental in 1990.

The restoration was, as the Tribune's Gapp said, carried out with great skill. Fortunately, they could see exactly what it used to look like because a former member heard about the renovation and donated his 1930 Scimitar, the club's yearbook. Even with that visual aid, returning the club to its original magnificence took some doing. In the years since the Shriners had left, someone had slathered paint and plaster over just about everything that made the place unique. Not only that, a thief had stolen eight original paintings from an elevator lobby outside the Renaissance Room. To remove the paint in the Hall of Lions they used finely-ground corn husks; any other method would have been too corrosive. Lido Lippi, the master painter who'd consulted on the restoration of the Sistine Chapel and, closer to home, restored the frescoes in the Hilton Chicago and would soon do the same for the Palmer House's ceiling, did his magic at the Inter-Continental. Not only did he restore nearly forty paintings in the Grand Ballroom, he also recreated those that had been stolen.

Medinah Athletic Club Today

In the mid-1990s, InterContinental got rid of Forum and merged the towers into one hotel. In the years since, they've invested millions in multiple restorations. The result is a luxurious hotel that's a trip into a time machine.

1929
Carbide and Carbon Building
Pendry Hotel

T he Carbide and Carbon Building is unique in Chicago. Its green terra-cotta tower with shining black base and golden summit stands out in a skyline of muted shades of beige and gray and the occasional white. The legend goes that the Burnham brothers designed it to resemble a champagne bottle's green glass topped with foil. That's a fitting description and it makes sense considering the building was completed nine years into Prohibition, but the origin is less fanciful. Instead of being inspired by booze, this noteworthy skyscraper is an illustration of the evolution of buildings and how architects, in the best tradition of scientists, build on the works and ideas of others.

New York-based Union Carbide and Carbon wanted a Chicago presence, and they selected the Burnham brothers to make it happen. The brothers were the sons of *that* Burnham, the legendary force behind the White City and co-author of the Plan of Chicago. Hubert and Daniel Jr. both began working at their dad's firm not too long before his death in 1912 and had gotten quite a bit of experience in the years since.

The brothers followed different paths to their father's company. Hubert graduated from the US Naval Academy in 1905 and served as an officer for six months before resigning and returning to Chicago. After a brief stint with D. H. Burnham & Co., he moved to Paris to attend École des Beaux Arts, the school that had molded the 1893 World's Fair and so many of Chicago's prominent architects. He attended intermittently, graduating in 1912. Daniel Jr. chose at first to be a Harvard man for a couple of years, but then in 1907 he left to study with his father in Europe before coming back to Chicago and entering the firm on the construction side. According to Daniel Sr.'s biographer, fellow architecture legend Peter Wight, by 1909 Junior was the Assistant General Superintendent of his dad's firm.

When Daniel Sr. died, the firm became Graham, Burnham and Co., and Hubert and Daniel Jr. were partners with Ernest Graham. The brothers left in 1917 to form D. H. Burnham Co. and their dad's company then became Graham, Anderson, Probst and White.

By the time Union Carbide and Carbon hired Hubert and Daniel Jr., the brothers had already built several high rises in downtown Chicago, but none were as distinctive as this one would be. An article dated May 13, 1928, said: "Although color is fast becoming an important factor in the sale of most American products, owners and architects have overlooked to a noticeable extent its use in buildings. The Carbide tower, however, will be an exception, for D. H. Burnham & Co. have designed a structure to be entirely in green and gold, with a black base."

Union Carbide and Carbon believed in architecture as advertising and their new building would be their calling card. The philosophy was an extension of the architectural concept that a building's form should be based on its function. The physical shell can convey the inhabitants' stability, creativity, luxury, and even, as was the case with the Medinah Athletic Club, a sense of frivolity. Since Union Carbide planned on using the lobby to showcase the products of its subsidiaries, they wanted something that would grab people's attention.

They certainly got it.

The Burnham brothers' design may have been unique in Chicago, but its inspiration can be traced back to the Tribune Tower design contest. Many considered Eliel Saarinen's second place concept to be the true winner and it was widely heralded. Even one of the winning architects, John Hood, who with his partner Raymond Howells would build the neo-gothic Tribune building, thought it was pretty cool—so cool that their American Radiator Building in their home of New York City was inspired by Saarinen's design. They differentiated it not only with more ornamentation on the building's setbacks and crown, but also in the color. Sheathed in black brick and accented with gold, it was meant to symbolize coal and fire.

Daniel Jr. and Hubert took that idea and ran with it. The color scheme reflected their client's earth-based products, and the artistic renderings of leaves in the exterior design symbolized carbon's origin from the decay of prehistoric plants. As the submission to the Commission on Chicago Landmarks said in 1989 - 1990, "Simply put, Union Carbide takes elements from the earth and air and makes them into chemicals." That covered a whole range of products. In the earlier years, the company made its money with the invention of the D cell battery and things like Glad bags, Simoniz car wax, and Prestone antifreeze. By the time of the landmarks commission report, United Carbide and Carbon's products included radio isotopes, welding equipment, and sausage casings.

The Burnham Brothers, who officially changed their company name in 1928, created a showstopping, 1920s Art Deco illustration of luxury and success. Elegant, glamorous, and eye-catching, the tower was sheathed not in gold paint, but in 24-karat gold leaf. The lobby was an elaborate display case of finely ornamented bronze and black Belgian marble.

The setting for this vertical commercial was chosen specifically because of its prominence, which could be directly attributed to Daniel H. Burnham. That section of "Boul Mich" was widened in preparation for the Michigan Avenue Bridge, an integral part of the Plan of Chicago that connected Michigan Avenue to the south of the river with Pine Street to the north in 1920. The bridge encouraged the development of one of the most beautiful boulevards in the world and enabled the construction of the Wrigley Building, Tribune Tower, the Drake Hotel, and London Guarantee and Accident. The Carbide and Carbon Building, while completely different from its neighbors, fit right in.

The skyscraper remained an office building until 2001, when Hard Rock Hotel converted it. It was a long, slow, expensive project. By the time they opened on December 31, 2003, the bill exceeded $100,000,000. After a successful run, including many years as the official hotel for Lollapalooza, the Hard Rock closed in 2017. It reopened in 2018 as St. Jane Chicago Hotel, named for the legendary Jane Addams. That iteration was only open for two years when the world was hit by COVID-19. Like many businesses, St. Jane didn't survive, closing in October 2020.

Carbide and Carbon Building Today

The Carbide and Carbon Building reopened as another hotel in 2021. Montage International purchased the landmark in late 2020 and converted it into Pendry Hotel, a brand of luxury boutique properties.

1929
Civic Opera Building

L yric Opera of Chicago is such an institution that it seems its existence has always been a given. But just like the Chicago Symphony Orchestra and the Field Museum surmounted multiple difficulties in their early years, establishing a permanent opera company was no easy task.

And since this was opera, its drama was on an even grander scale, almost Wagnerian in scope.

Chicago wanted opera. With the popularity of the Grand Opera Festival in 1885, Ferdinand Peck confirmed that desire. He hired Adler and Sullivan to build an amazing, acoustically perfect theater, even though the city had no company of its own and had to rely on traveling productions to get its fix. The Auditorium opened in 1899, providing Chicago with its very own opera house - yet it still had to wait for the Metropolitan Opera and, later, the Manhattan Opera Company to visit from New York.

That was a wholly unacceptable situation to *Chicago Evening Post* music critic Karleton Hackett. In early 1909, he began making noise that Chicago needed its own opera company. He appealed to the city's civic pride, of which it had plenty to spare, pointing to the Chicago Symphony and its Orchestra Hall as an example of what Chicago could do when it decided it wanted something. Karleton's publisher, John Shaffer, agreed with him.

John not only agreed, he jumped right in. While Karleton appealed to the public through his writing, John began chatting up his fellow men of means. It didn't take long before Oscar Hammerstein (not the famous lyricist, but his grandfather), the cigar-making founder of the Manhattan Opera Company, expressed interest in helping Chicago get its opera. He'd already created a successful competitor to the powerful Met. He told John it would cost about half a million dollars to start a company in Chicago. John said he'd raise it, on the condition that there be a seven-member board of directors, three of whom had to be Chicagoans.

Why, of all the nerve. In *How Grand Opera Came to Chicago*, C. J. Bulliet recounted: "Mr. Hammerstein 'almost flew into a rage,' ... and informed the Chicago publisher that he never had had any directors, and that he managed his businesses alone. He would not consider for a moment, he said, having anybody from Chicago on a board of directors for a Chicago opera."

John wasn't about to put his city's opera in the hands of someone like that. The next day, the Met's Otto Kahn sent John a cablegram claiming he could guarantee Chicago a first-class opera company in a modern theater. On Otto's word—he was the director of the Metropolitan Opera, after all—John reached out to forty-nine wealthy men, and every single one pledged the requested $5,000. Then he met with Otto and his connections in New York and they secured another $235,000.

Although Otto had suggested a new theater in his cablegram, the two decided that they'd use the one they had. Not only was the Auditorium beautiful and acoustically perfect, renting it would have the added bonus of preventing Oscar Hammerstein from being able to bring his company to Chicago and compete the way he did in New York. All they had to do was pay $100,000 to secure the lease. Otto wrote a check.

Chicago had gotten its opera from New York, and now it would get its opera company *because* of New York. The *Chicago Tribune* announced the good news on November 4, 1909, and on November 3, 1910, Chicago Grand Opera Company opened its first season with Verdi's *Aida*.

In the first few years there were some minor disagreements that made the papers, but trouble was brewing and it came to a head in 1913 when Andreas Dippel, general manager and artistic director, quit. Despite much protestation from Andreas and from Cleofante Campanini, the general music director, that everything was fine, the consensus was that the two got in a feud. With the support of Harold McCormick, president of the Chicago Opera Company, Cleofante assumed control of the orchestra as well as the opera company—and was the business manager to boot.

Later it came out that Mrs. Edith Rockefeller McCormick, Harold's wife, offered to pay any deficit that might occur as long as Cleofante was in charge. Well, there was a deficit alright. The company lost a quarter million dollars during the 1913 - 1914 season and ended up filing for bankruptcy. Because of that and World War I, there was no season the next year, but the following year the company reformed as the

Chicago Opera Association and Harold McCormick was still president and Cleofante was still in charge. By 1916, John Shaffer was so fed up with this arrangement that he wanted out entirely. There was no board of directors anymore and it was "no longer a Chicago grand opera company owned and financed by citizens of Chicago, but a McCormick-Campanini opera company."

Edith moved to Switzerland in 1913 to be treated by and study with Carl Jung, but she and Harold continued to pay the opera company's losses until the couple finally divorced in December 1921 after living apart for eight years. That last year Soprano Mary Garden produced the opera's most lavish season to date. As the "Directa," she ran a deficit of over one million, and the McCormicks paid a whopping $600,000.

The future of Chicago's opera company was in the air again, but Samuel Insull was waiting in the wings. In yet another reorganization, the Civic Opera Association elected the utilities magnate as its president, General Charles Dawes and Richard Crane Jr. as vice presidents, Charles Hutchinson as treasurer, and Stanley Field as secretary. They also had a finance committee, which included John Shedd. These were big names in both Chicago's business and cultural philanthropy circles. It seemed like the opera would have firm footing for once, especially since this new board of highly successful businessmen wasn't going to do anything until they'd secured a guarantee of $500,000 per year for five years. They got it, and instead of relying on a handful of rich people, this time they had 2,200 subscribers. The season opened November 12, 1922, with *Aida*.

The opera still ran at a loss. Samuel's solution was to build the Civic Opera Association its own theater topped with an office building. Rents from those offices would pay for any deficits. He bought a giant site along the south branch of the river and hired architectural favorites Graham, Anderson, Probst and White. The firm created a building with a tall tower and two wings, a design that maximized rental space while providing ventilation for the large auditorium. The result resembled a throne, and would give rise to speculation that

Samuel wanted it that way so he could metaphorically turn his back on the east (despite the fact that New York was the reason Chicago had an opera company in the first place).

The Civic Opera Association christened its new auditorium on November 4, 1929, with a performance of—what else—*Aida*. It was only six days after the stock market crash that plunged the country into the Great Depression, but that Monday evening opening brought a sense of wonder to the city. An Associated Press story that appeared around the country said: "On a site where less than a century ago wolves bayed at the moon on the marshy flats along a lonely little stream cutting windswept prairies has appeared this forty-five-story tower of marble, gold, steel and bronze to provide the youthful city by the Inland sea with the world's most luxurious and sophisticated home of song." In *Forty Years of Opera in Chicago*, Edward C. Moore described the theater as a rose-colored grotto with the "most scientifically constructed stage in the world."

> "Everything was beautiful, everything was spacious, everything was ingenious beyond all telling."

A few weeks after the opening, New York journalist Pierre V. R. Key said of Samuel: "In six years he has transformed a shaky institution into one now entering its fullest estate."

In a couple of years, it would all come crashing down. The Civic Opera Company gave its last performance on January 30, 1932. Samuel's financial house of cards also collapsed, wiping out not only himself, but also hundreds of thousands of shareholders. He resigned from his companies, including Commonwealth Edison and Peoples Gas, and sailed for Europe. In Paris he found out he was under investigation so he fled to Greece, which had no extradition treaty. In his absence, both a Cook County and a federal grand jury indicted him. Samuel was arrested in Turkey and jailed in Chicago. He was universally reviled, until in 1934, a jury found him not guilty on all charges.

During this time, in the depths of the Depression, Chicago was still trying to keep its opera dreams alive. Out of the ashes of the Civic Opera Company came the Chicago Grand Opera Company in 1933. Two years later, after the man who'd given them a home was acquitted, what was now the Chicago City Opera company offered him an inscribed key declaring him "the father of grand opera in Chicago." He accepted. On July 16, 1938, Samuel Insull died, penniless, in Paris.

In 1940, Chicago's opera reorganized yet again, calling its sixth iteration the Chicago Opera Company. This version would last for six years, but when it closed, the city wouldn't have a resident opera company for almost a decade.

This time, the company wasn't founded by businessmen. This time, a 28-year-old force of nature named Carol Fox picked up the operatic mantle. Despite training in Europe, her own dreams of performing weren't to be, so she joined with conductor Nicola Rescigno and fellow thwarted musician Lawrence Kelly to bring opera back to the Civic Building's stage. In 1954, Lyric Theater of Chicago opened with Bellini's *Norma*, and Maria Callas made her American debut. After some disagreements, Lawrence and Nicola left the next year and founded the Dallas Opera, but Carol stayed, renaming the company one final time to Lyric Opera of Chicago.

Carol resigned in 1980 and was succeeded by her assistant manager, Ardis Krainik, whose leadership brought the company out of financial peril. Since then, Chicago's resident opera has not only survived under the helm of William Mason and then Sir Andrew Davis, it's become one of the premiere companies in the world—and it tends to keep the drama on the stage.

Civic Opera Building Today

The Civic Opera Building remains the home of Lyric Opera of Chicago. In 1993, the company purchased the theater and backstage space and began extensive renovations, including refurbishing the seats for the first time ever. With the theater closed in 2020 - 2021, the company took the opportunity to replace those seats, providing better sightlines and more leg room.

1930
Adler Planetarium

Most cultural institutions begin because of lofty ideals. Someone wants to make the world a better place by enriching the experiences of others, usually through art, in all its forms; beauty; and understanding. By the mid-1920s, Chicago was already the beneficiary of several philanthropically minded souls, and it had an art museum, an opera company, an orchestra, and a museum of natural history, all of which were recognized and respected. These institutions instilled wonder and could take a person beyond the humdrum of daily life, opening whole new worlds. When Max Adler decided the city needed a planetarium, his ideals were even loftier than most. Some might even say they were astronomical.

In 1930, few people had seen a planetarium. That's because they were brand-spanking new: Carl Zeiss invented a projector that would display an accurate image of stars and planets on a dome in 1923 and Munich's Deutsches Museum opened the first planetarium the same year. This was the same museum whose hands-on exhibits, including a working coal mine, had so intrigued Julius Rosenwald's son that the Sears magnate decided to create an interactive science museum. When a friend of Max Adler's gave him a brochure about the new planetaria in the German museum, he was intrigued; as a recently retired executive who'd made millions, he could do something about that curiosity.

Max Adler was a businessman, but he didn't start out that way. Born in Elgin, Illinois, to Jewish-German immigrants, he was all set to be a world-class violinist, even studying abroad to improve his skills. He was good. He had talent. But, after awhile, he realized he didn't have "it." He understood musicians, however, and what they were looking for. That included a young woman named Sophie Rosenwald. She shared an interest in music, and the two discovered they shared an interest in each other. They married in 1897, and that same year her brother invited Max to join him in a young mail-order business. The new brother-in-law had been with the company for two years and it was growing like gangbusters. Max took him up on the offer and began by merchandising musical instruments. He realized that merchandising appealed to him, and he could succeed in this business in a way he never could in music.

And succeed he did. Sears, Roebuck and Company made millionaires out of both Max and his brother-in-law, Julius Rosenwald. Both men would use their millions to make the world a better place. One of the ways Julius did this was to create the Museum of Science and Industry. Max gave Chicago, and the United States, its first planetarium.

After Max's friend had given him the Deutsches Museum brochure, he went to Munich to check it out. He took his wife's cousin, Ernest Grunsfeld Jr., with him so they could see what would be involved. Ernest was more than just family; he was an architect who had graduated from MIT and studied at École des Beaux Arts. On June 7, 1928, newspapers announced Max's gift of half a million dollars to the South Park Commissioners for a planetarium. The concept was so new that the article had to explain what it was:

> "The planetarium is a device designed to give the average person an opportunity to study the heavens. It is so arranged that the instructor or operator can bring into the planetarium 'sky' a view of the heavens as they appear at any given time, such as when the Egyptians viewed them or as they will appear hundreds of years hence. By working the apparatus the workings of the sky throughout a year can be reproduced in the space of a few minutes time."

In July, *New York Times* science writer Waldemar Kaempffert, who would become the first director of the Museum of Science and Industry, announced "America is to Have a Planetarium" in a feature that described the history of astronomy itself and the wonders of Carl Zeiss' new projector. "Thanks to Max Adler, a retired businessman, a magnificent building is to be erected on an island in Lake Michigan," he reported. "Within that structure the finest of all planetaria is to be installed by 1930."

The island Waldemar referenced was manmade and was supposed to be the northernmost of a series of five proposed in the Plan of Chicago. The 19th Annual Report of the Chicago Plan Commission remarked that Max's gift to the city would be constructed on "island No. 1," which would be connected to the mainland by an ornamental bridge. With its neighbors the Field Museum, open since 1921, and the Shedd Aquarium, still under construction, Adler Planetarium would complete the triumvirate of man's natural existence: earth, water, and sky.

That alone was a lofty goal, but Max saw a bigger picture. At the dedication of Adler Planetarium and Astronomical Museum, he shared the vision that had prompted him to make this gift:

"The popular conception of the universe is too meager; the planets and the stars are too far removed from general knowledge. In our reflections, we dwell too little upon the concept that the world and all human endeavor within it are governed by established order and too infrequently upon the truth that under the heavens everything is interrelated, even as each of us to the other." Philip Fox, the first director of the planetarium, put it even more plainly: "We hope that the planetarium, in short, will result in more law and order in mundane, earthly affairs. And we hope, too, that it will help to show that there should be no cleavage between individuals, nations, and races."

The building itself was completely different from its neighbors and their Georgia marble. Ernest designed a dodecagon—a twelve-sided polygon—to represent the months of the year, sheathed in rainbow granite. A copper dome topped the planetarium and the museum wrapped around it. The Zeiss projector was the star of the show, but also impressive was a large display of historical navigation, astronomical, and mathematical instruments. Max had purchased a collection of more than five hundred pieces from Amsterdam art collector Anton Mensing, and it immediately established the new institution as a place that would appeal to serious astronomers as well as those who were merely curious.

At the close of the first year, more than 600,000 people had visited. That was good, but attendance picked up dramatically in 1933 and 1934; the planetarium was a very fitting welcome to the Century of Progress Exposition, made even more so by an esplanade constructed by the National Terrazzo Mosaic Association. Patterns at the bottom of twelve shallow pools symbolized months of the year.

When Waldemar Kaempffert left the Museum of Science and Industry in 1937, Philip Fox took his place as director, which opened up the top spot at Adler. Maude Bennot, who had been the assistant director, filled it. According to the *Encyclopedia of American Biography* from 1941, she was the "only woman in the world to head a major planetarium." She held that position until 1945.

Max Adler passed away in 1952. Out of the major benefactors whose donations would be the primary funding for four of Chicago's biggest museums, Max was the only one who would see his legacy come to fruition. Marshall Field, John Shedd, and Julius Rosenwald all died before their museums opened. After Max's death, his son Robert organized the Chicago Planetarium Society, a non-profit to help fund and promote Adler Planetarium. In the late 1950s and throughout the '60s, with Sputnik and the ensuing space race, more and more people would visit to learn about the universe beyond, and by the early 1970s it was time for an expansion. They added a lower level with another theater, classrooms, a library, dining facilities, and more. The only downside was that they had to rip up those terrazzo mosaics from the Century of Progress. In 1977, Chicago got its first public telescope with the Doane Observatory. A renovation in the late 1990s added sixty-thousand square feet. The Atwood Sphere also moved to the Adler at that time. It's the oldest sky simulator in the world, designed in 1913 by Wallace Atwood for the Chicago Academy of Sciences. Over the next two decades, the museum continued to increase its capacity and capabilities, made easier by some multimillion-dollar donations.

Adler Planetarium Today

As knowledge of the universe beyond has increased with the speed of light, Adler Planetarium has kept pace with innovative initiatives like their high-altitude ballooning program and launching a nano-satellite into space. With the closure of the museum due to COVID-19, it opened up virtually to encourage people to explore the universe from home. In a move that Max surely would have approved of, Adler Planetarium used its 3-D printers to produce nearly six thousand face shields for medical personnel. The museum also donated its powerful sky show servers to the Rosetta@home project, which uses idle computers to model proteins for disease research, exemplifying Adler's belief "that under the heavens everything is interrelated."

1930
John G. Shedd Aquarium

I t was December of 1923 when Chicago learned that it would be getting an aquarium. A rumor leaked that John G. Shedd was going to donate two million dollars for that purpose, and John was known as a pretty generous guy. He'd contributed six figures to the Young Men's Christian Association, gave $50,000 to the Smith college development fund, and was an early and consistent supporter of the arts, not to mention his work helping to bring the Plan of Chicago to life. The papers called the aquarium an early Christmas gift, and in January the *Chicago Tribune* published a preliminary drawing of the new museum. It would sit just east of the Field Museum of Natural History. It was a perfect location, not only because it was right on Lake Michigan, but because it would continue the combined legacies of Marshall Field and the man who succeeded him.

John Graves Shedd was born on a New England farm in
1850. One winter he and his brother were out sugaring, or
tapping trees for syrup. John fell while carrying a yoke of
heavy pails filled with the sticky substance and it leaked into
his boot. While his brother laughed, John decided then and
there that he would quit. The next June, shortly before he
turned seventeen, he made good on his word and found a job
at a grocery in Bellows Falls, Vermont. His pay may have only
been $1.50 a week, plus room and board, but he'd gotten off
the farm and he wouldn't go back. After a year he returned to
his hometown of Alstead, New Hampshire, where he found a
job at James H. Porter's general store and met the proprietor's
niece Mary. When John was twenty-one he took a job at
another dry goods store, this time in Rutland, Vermont, but a
fire burned the store down after he'd only been there for three
months. Benjamin H. Burt hired the young man and doubled
his pay. Even though Mr. Burt would leave a lifelong
impression on John, enough so that he kept a portrait of
Benjamin in his office until he retired, the ambitious young
man had big dreams. Within a year he made his way to
Chicago, determined to work for the biggest store in town.
That store was Field, Leiter and Company.

"What can you do?" Marshall Field asked.
"Sir, I can sell anything," was John's reply.

Marshall hired him.

The two had no way to know this, but they'd followed
extremely similar paths. They'd both grown up on New
England farms and realized as teens that was not the life for
them. They began working at dry goods stores at the age of
seventeen, and when they turned twenty-two, they both
moved to Chicago, showed up at the most prosperous store in
the city, and were hired on the spot.

John quickly made himself indispensable. If he'd proven
himself after five months he was supposed to get a raise from
ten dollars a week to twelve. Marshall was so impressed with
the young man that he bumped it up to fourteen. A few years
later, John returned to Alstead long enough to marry Mary,

the niece of his one-time employer, and the couple came straight back to Chicago. In 1893, John became a partner of what was by then Marshall Field & Company, and in 1901 he was the vice president. When Marshall died in 1906, there was no question that John would take over as the company's president.

In addition to his role at Marshall Field & Company, John was also a director of several banks and railroads; combined, these activities made him very, very wealthy. He was the kind of wealthy that could drop a couple million dollars to give his city another cultural asset. He decided on an aquarium because, according to the *Guide to the John G. Shedd Aquarium*, written by director Walter H. Chute in 1933, "His choice was influenced by the belief that an aquarium would provide instructive entertainment for a larger number of individuals than any other type of institution." His condition was that the South Park board provide the site and create a fund for maintenance. The board agreed, and the Shedd Aquarium Society was established with two hundred members.

Graham, Anderson, Probst and White, who had designed the Field Museum, and was therefore the only firm for the job, designed an octagonal palace with a Doric exterior similar to the natural history museum's. The building's bill would be another $1.25 million on top of the already donated two, and John provided it.

John never got to see his gift to the city. The groundbreaking wouldn't happen until 1927 and he died the year before from appendicitis. Construction was completed on December 19, 1929 and on May 30, 1930, the John G. Shedd Aquarium, a "magnificent marble home for fish," officially opened its doors.

The entire building, encased in white Georgia marble, was an ode to aquatic life. The *Guide* described it thus: "Fishes, turtles, shells and invertebrates, all modeled from life, are seen on every hand. Even the marble wainscoting was especially selected and was set in place with the markings so matched as to give a wave effect. At the far end is a lofty archway, in the center of which is hung an interesting clock having aquatic animals in place of numbers."

The Shedd was the world's largest and the only inland aquarium with saltwater. The building itself accommodated five different water environments: heated and chilled saltwater; and heated, chilled, and natural fresh water. Fresh water was easy enough to get; they could pump it in from Lake Michigan. The salty stuff was a little more challenging. Before they could add any animals, twenty railroad cars made eight trips to Key West, transporting over a million gallons of seawater.

Then they had to get the animals. Fish are notoriously bad travelers, so the Pullman Company created a special "collecting car" dubbed Nautilus. One end of the train car was outfitted with a berth, galley, and living quarters for six men. The rest of the car was a traveling miniature aquarium. "During a normal collecting season the Nautilus travels more than 20,000 miles," the *Guide* detailed. "It has visited in a single season Boothbay Harbor, Maine, Los Angeles, California, and Key West, Florida, as well as many points nearer home." The Nautilus would be used until 1959.

John's belief that the aquarium would be popular was quickly proven right. Between June 30, 1930, and December 21, 1932, more than ten million people visited the museum. On May 21, 1931, alone, 78,658 entered its doors. Most of those visitors came on Thursdays, Saturdays, and Sundays, when admission was free.

The first thing people would see after entering was a forty-foot pool in the Rotunda. It was a makeshift swamp, home to turtles, snakes, frogs, and the like, with rocks covered with ferns in the middle. Six wings extended from the center like spokes, and each wing was a different gallery. There were exotic creatures such as electric eels from South America, Japanese salamanders, and Hawaiian goatfish, and more familiar species from the Great Lakes. In 1971, the first big change occurred when they replaced the pool in the rotunda with the Caribbean Reef. This 90,000 gallon circular tank brought the tropics to Chicago. That same year the Shedd acquired its first research vessel, which was replaced with its second in 1985. In 1991, they added the Oceanarium, known since 2010 as the Abbott Oceanarium, a habitat for Pacific Northwest marine mammals including dolphins, beluga whales, California sea lions, and sea otters. Below the Oceanarium, Magellanic and rockhopper penguins live in the Polar Play Zone, designed to replicate the Falkland Islands. Wild Reef, added in 2003, recreates a Philippine coral reef, considered the most diverse underwater ecosystem in the world, with twenty-six interconnected habitats. The addition of the Oceanarium and the Wild Reef more than doubled the aquarium's original size.

Shedd Aquarium Today

John G. Shedd's gift to the city continues to delight and attract millions each year. Not only is it a home for thousands of species, Shedd Aquarium also has an Animal Response Team that rescues, rehabilitates, and releases animals. The aquarium is a Smithsonian affiliate, an accredited member of the Association of Zoos and Aquariums, and is active in conservation and research around the globe.

1930
Chicago Board of Trade Building

O n January 6, 1836, Chicago trustees ordered constables to remove all buildings from public streets.

Let that sink in for a moment.

In 1836, people were erecting buildings in the middle of the street, and enough people were doing this that trustees had to issue an order for their removal.

Three years after its incorporation, the town of Chicago already had a couple of hotels and a few houses of worship. It had been platted. George Dole began shipping beef and pork in 1832, presaging the Midwest's future role in feeding the world. Chicago had plans. But in the meantime, people were ignoring all sense of civility and putting up buildings in the middle of the street.

The chaos was the product of a quickly changing world. In the mid-1830s and into the 1840s, people were heading not only to Chicago and other frontier towns, but to the rural areas beyond them. It didn't take long for settlers to realize they'd landed on some pretty fertile ground. After harvest, getting their crops to places like Chicago that had buyers and options, albeit limited, for distribution was hampered by bad roads, no roads, and generally poor traveling conditions. Nevertheless, farmers braved the mud and muck to try to sell what they'd grown.

Once they got there it was a madhouse. Farmers charged different prices and merchants paid varying fees. Farmers would go from one buyer to another, hoping to get the best rates. Then there was the whole issue of prices fluctuating due to supply and demand. Abundance after harvest meant prices would be rock bottom, and often the farmers couldn't sell everything they brought and the overage would get dumped into Lake Michigan. In late spring and summer, when the previous fall's harvest stocks had run out, prices would skyrocket.

Merchants had their own issues. There was no weight standard and quality was all over the place. One farmer could have a sack full of beautiful winter wheat, and the next could be half sand. In *History of the Board of Trade of the City of Chicago*, Henry Taylor said: "Every one of the grain dealers in the early days was forced to become a speculator whenever he bought a wagon load of grain from a farmer, or sold a cargo to be shipped by lake."

Some sort of order was desperately needed, and when 1848 rolled around it was about to get worse. Not only were both the Illinois and Michigan Canal and the Chicago and Galena Railroad set to open that year, but there was also a campaign to build plank roads, turning dirt trails into something navigable. Suddenly it would be a lot easier to get herds of livestock and wagons filled with bushels of wheat to the market. But then what?

Two men who were intimately familiar with the hazards of the current laissez faire situation had the idea to create an organization that would regulate the madness. Grain broker W. L. Whiting and Thomas Richmond, who was in the grain elevating business, decided what Chicago needed was a Board of Trade. This board would be made up of men who appreciated the necessity of consistent weights and quality, and possessed an understanding of supply and demand. They put out a call for interested merchants and had their first meeting March 13, 1848, in rooms over Whiting's offices. That meeting set up the organization and they adopted a constitution and appointed a committee that would draft the by-laws. They next met the first Monday of April in their new offices above Gage and Haines' flour store. The group had already grown to a board of eighty-two members, including Chicago's first mayor, William B. Ogden, and Gurdon Hubbard, who'd built the city's first stockyard.

While the Board of Trade didn't have any legal standing, it did accomplish quite a few things that first year, including the appointment of inspectors of fish, provisions, and lumber and submitting plans for a system of uniform banking. The second year, the board promoted rebuilding the bridges which had been destroyed, regulating tolls on the canal, extending the telegraphic facilities (which had made their debut in 1848), and improving the harbor.

Despite this early promise, membership dropped and they had to keep moving their offices. By 1854, the Board was on its fifth location. Attendance at the meetings was so bad that people had to be bribed with free crackers, cheese, and ale. That worked a little too well, and they installed a "doorkeeper" to "keep out the loungers who were attracted by the free lunches."

That's right. The Board of Trade hired a bouncer.

Those free lunches did the trick, though, and in 1856 they didn't need them any more. Three years later, there were 542 members on the rolls. In 1858, they established a grain inspection program, taking care of one of the issues that had prompted the formation of the board a decade before. *Origin, Growth, and Usefulness of the Chicago Board of Trade* said of this system: "Under the old-time methods of transporting grain in bags, and its delivery at the various railroad depots, or by canal or water-ways, a general system of inspection was well-nigh impracticable, and was perhaps unnecessary. But the tremendous growth of production made a change in the method of handling grain indispensable, and to this point, years since, the transportation of grain in bulk...necessitated a change in the method of handling and storing; and out of this grew our vast {grain} elevator system. It became impossible, therefore, to keep each shipper's grain by itself, and there grew up at once a necessity for fair and equitable inspection."

In February 1859, the Illinois General Assembly passed articles of incorporation that granted the Board of Trade legal authority to administer oaths, compel attendance of witnesses, and make judgments in arbitrations. The Board now had some teeth.

During the Civil War, it used them. An 1882 *Chicago Tribune* article about the Board of Trade's new building detailed the organization's history and mentioned that when the "Rebellion" started, the board made supporting the Union a condition of membership. "Resolutions were offered providing that no new members should be elected who had not subscribed to the oath of allegiance, but this proposition was so modified as to deny the rights of membership to any applicant suspected of disloyalty until he could prove that such suspicions were unfounded."

Using their powers for the good of the city and the country worked well, and by the time the war was over they needed more room. They took possession of bigger quarters inside the new Chamber of Commerce building in April of 1865, and they were so excited the festivities lasted three days. They probably would have stayed there for quite some time, but the fire of 1871 forced them to move yet again. They rented a room on Franklin, and according to *Origin*, "the Board of Trade there opened, not for speculation, but for the noble purpose of aiding those who were only less fortunate than themselves in losing their courage." As quickly as possible, though, they returned to the business of speculation, and a year later the Board moved into the new Chamber of Commerce building.

Within five years, "this historic arena had grown too small for the contests of the gladiators of trade" and they began talking about getting their own building. After some legal maneuvering, the Board secured the lot where LaSalle Street terminated at Jackson and hired W. W. Boyington of Water Tower fame. They moved into their new ten-story building with its 322-foot tower on April 29, 1885, solidifying what would be known as Chicago's financial district.

That building served the Board for forty years. By the 1920s they grew out of it and they jumped into the skyscraper frenzy that had taken over downtown Chicago. They wanted to keep their spot at the foot of LaSalle, so they decided to demolish their Boyington building and replace it. While they waited for their newer, bigger highrise, they hired Holabird and Roche to build temporary quarters on Clark Street. When they were ready for their new home, both William Holabird and Martin Roche had died, and the firm had reorganized as Holabird and Root, for William's son John and John Root's (of Burnham and Root) son John Jr.

The Chicago Landmark designation report stated that John Holabird and John Root Jr.'s "Chicago Board of Trade Building is one of the finest examples in the United States of the Art Deco-style setback skyscrapers of the 1920s." The linear style emphasized a building's height, and the setbacks, required by zoning laws, added geometric interest. Like the

Carbide and Carbon Building and New York's American Radiator Building, the Board of Trade was influenced by Eliel Saarinen's second place entry in the Tribune Tower design contest.

Over the entrance is a clock face, flanked by two hooded figures. The sculpture on the left represents a Babylonian man holding a shaft of wheat, and on the right is a Native American with a stalk of corn. The most famous figure on the building is way at the top. Artist John Storrs sculpted a 6,200-pound, solid aluminum statue of Ceres, the goddess of grain, and she overlooks the city from six hundred feet above the sidewalks. The Chicago-born sculptor explained why Ceres has no face in an article from May 30, 1930: "Because of the great height at which it will stand the matter of detail did not have to be taken into consideration. The outline of a woman's figure is suggested rather than rendered exactly."

Chicago Board of Trade Building Today

In 2007, the Chicago Board of Trade (CBOT) merged with Chicago Mercantile Exchange to form CME Group. The Chicago Mercantile Exchange had previously been the Chicago Butter and Egg Board, which was a spinoff from the CBOT. Inside, some traders still practice what's called open outcry, a method of trading commodities using a combination of shouting and hand signals. Electronic trading has risen dramatically, however, and the Board of Trade Building is one of the few places where open outcry is still used to trade.

1930
Merchandise Mart
theMART

I t's difficult to comprehend just how big the Merchandise Mart is. You can say it's four million square feet. You can know it was once the largest commercial building in the world. You can mention that there are six and a half miles of corridors, that the initial plate glass order would stretch for seven miles, and that thirty thousand people enter through its doors every weekday, but none of that sinks in until you stand in front of it and look left, right, and up. Even then, the sheer scale can escape you.

James Simpson, president of Marshall Field & Company, was the force behind this massive building. Like John Shedd, Harry Selfridge, and Marshall Field himself, he was another top-level executive who started at the bottom as a young man and worked his way up. James was only seventeen when he began working at Marshall Field's as a clerk. The Scottish immigrant, who'd been in the states since he was six, so impressed Marshall that he made James his confidential clerk (basically a private secretary) within a year. In 1906, James was promoted to second vice president and assistant to John Shedd, who'd been appointed president after Marshall's death in January of that year. Eleven years later, James moved up to first vice president, and when John retired in 1923, James took the top spot.

Marshall Field & Company had always had a robust wholesale wing. Marshall's early partner, Levi Leiter, wanted the company to be wholesale only and get rid of retail altogether. Marshall disagreed, got rid of Levi instead, and managed to grow both. In the late 1880s he had Henry Hobson Richardson build him a sturdy wholesale warehouse that took over a city block. (That building would inspire another massive project, Adler and Sullivan's Auditorium Building.) Hobson's Marshall Field Wholesale Store would serve the company for over forty years, but by the mid-1920s, James Simpson had even grander plans.

At first, this new building would be the company's wholesale showroom. At a projected cost of fifteen million dollars, it was a big project. But plans changed. What if they invited other distributors to join them? This rising-tide-raises-all-ships concept was unusual in a cutthroat industry, but it caught on, and incredibly, especially since the world's economy was already in the Great Depression, when the Merchandise Mart opened in 1930, it was eighty-two percent occupied.

Instead of stocking wares on shelves, distributors would display their goods in showrooms. James knew it worked on the retail side; Marshall Field & Company had created model homes on their eighth floor, decorated with items you could purchase in the store. The new Merchandise Mart would do this on a grand scale for retailers looking for the next hot items. Having multiple distributors in one location made those retailers' lives easier. It was like a giant shopping mall for store owners.

The location for the building was a specific choice. Not only was the plot adjacent to where the city's very first trading post had been, providing a connection with the not-too-distant past, at the time it was littered with unsightly railroad tracks. Since James was the chairman of the Chicago Plan Commission, succeeding Charles Wacker, erecting a modern building would continue the plan's goal to beautify the city.

Those tracks, however, posed a challenge. The plot was the site of Chicago and North Western Railway's old Kinzie Street station, and the railroad still owned the land. Marshall Field & Company ended up buying the air rights, the second building in Chicago after the Daily News Building to use the new type of real estate transaction. That gave them the right to build over the tracks, and the only actual land they bought were 458 individual parcels, one for each of the caissons that supported the foundation.

Field favorites Graham, Anderson, Probst and White designed an art deco, rhomboid-shaped complex that was eighteen stories tall with a twenty-five story tower. While ornamentation was limited, the tower was encircled with fifty-six Native American chieftain heads, in honor of that very first trading post. Underneath, those train tracks delivered carloads straight to and from the building.

Marshall Field & Company moved in on May 5, 1930. They took up four whole floors, which left plenty of room for the other eight hundred distributors. There was also space for an entirely different type of tenant: radio stations. An Associated Press article from October 30 dubbed the building Radio City. "It is the new midwest headquarters of the National Broadcasting company on the nineteenth and twentieth floors of the Merchandise mart...Described as the 'last word' in broadcast facilities, it really is a two-floor radio penthouse containing more than 66,000 square feet." In the late 1940s, NBC began broadcasting television shows, and when it converted to an all-color station in 1956, the world's first station to do so, it was from their studios at the Merchandise Mart.

Not long after his thirty-million-dollar mart opened, James Simpson left his role at Marshall Field & Company. He was already a director of Commonwealth Edison and other companies led by Samuel Insull. In 1932 when the utility companies collapsed and Samuel resigned—and fled to Europe—James took over, and James McKinsey replaced him as the head of Marshall Field.

During the world's fair of 1933 - 1934, the Merchandise Mart was touted as a tourist attraction. *A Century of Progress Exposition Authorized Guide to Chicago* extolled its virtues:

> "The lobby is embellished by nineteen murals representing market places of the world, the work of Jules Guerin," who was well known as the illustrator of the Plan of Chicago, and would also paint the murals in the Civic Opera Building. "National Broadcasting Company have studios on the nineteenth and twentieth floors. At night the building is an outstanding sight on the river, lit up as it is with powerful banks of lights. Not more than a hundred years ago this site was occupied by Wolf Tavern."

Despite the Merchandise Mart's propitious beginning, the Depression took over and in 1935 Marshall Field had to divest itself of its wholesale wing. Tenants moved out, leaving acres of empty offices. During World War II, the United States government filled some of them, leasing space for the treasury department, the department of the interior, and other divisions. Then, in 1945, Joseph P. Kennedy, the former ambassador to Great Britain, bought the Mart. At first the purchase price was undisclosed, but it later came out that the Boston financier had gotten it for sixteen million. It had cost more than thirty million to build fifteen years before.

That sale did triple duty: it enabled Marshall Field & Company to pay off millions in debt; it funded Joseph's political aspirations for his sons, paying for John F. Kennedy's campaigns for senator and then president; and, it gave the landmark building a new lease on life.

The November 14, 1945, issue of the *Chicago Tribune* reported that the Mart was "nearly 100 percent occupied, with more than 900 tenants and a daily working population of about 20,000 persons." It was truly a city-within-a-city, with its own police force, post office, dentist, druggist, physician, bank, telegraph office, railway exchange office, several restaurants, retail clothing stores, a florist, a dry cleaners, and a liquor store. "In addition," a United Press article dated August 26, 1945, said, "the building boasts a chamber of commerce, a weekly magazine, the Merchandise Mart Review, three complete dress factories, barbers, shoe repairers and beauty salons."

Those curious about the inner workings could take tours. In 1953, Joseph commissioned bronze busts of eight significant American merchants, including Aaron Montgomery Ward, Julius Rosenwald, and, of course, Marshall Field himself. Erected on pedestals along the river and facing the building, the sculptures are known as the Merchandise Mart Hall of Fame.

A modernization campaign in the 1950s and '60s meant the removal of those noble chieftain heads, to be replaced by concrete plates. An entrance canopy was added in 1962. In 1977, Skidmore, Owings & Merrill built the Chicago Apparel Center on the west side of Orleans Street, and in 1988, Helmut Jahn connected the two with a pedestrian bridge. The 1980s saw another renovation, and at the end of the decade that entrance canopy was removed and the display windows, which had been painted over, were restored. In the '90s, Joseph's grandson Christopher Kennedy began managing the mart, and after the Kennedy family sold the building to Vornado Realty Trust in 1998, Chris stayed on as president of Merchandise Mart Properties, Inc. from 2000 to 2012. During his tenure, there were so many green initiatives that the building received LEED (Leadership in Energy and Environmental Design) Silver Certification in 2007. The building was awarded Gold Certification in 2013 and 2018.

Merchandise Mart Today

In the 21st century, theMART, as it's now known, has gone through more renovations and restorations. Jules Guerin's murals, which encircle the top of the lobby with scenes of marketplaces from around the world, were thoroughly cleaned in 2014. Restaurants and specialty shops fill the first two floors, and the rest of the building is a mix of tech companies, interior designers, architects, manufacturers, small businesses, and Fortune 500 companies. LuxeHome invites the public to shop showrooms like retailers of yore, and the Design Center is the world's largest design marketplace.

1932
Chicago Historical Society
Chicago History Museum

T he title page of *A Brief History of the Chicago Historical Society*, published in 1881, tells a story:

Organized 1856.
Incorporated 1857.
Collections Destroyed, October 9, 1871.
Re-organized, 1872.
Destroyed second time, July 14, 1874.
Re-organized again, 1877.

It's a very Chicago story. Of planning and building, of setbacks, of re-building, of more setbacks, and of re-building, again. It's a story of a museum, but it's also a story of a people and a city that won't give up.

The Chicago Historical Society's story begins in 1856, when Reverend William Barry suggested creating an association to preserve history. He was joined by prominent citizens, including the city's first Mayor, William B. Ogden, and J. Young Scammon, who published Chicago's first newspaper. The society incorporated in 1857, only twenty years after the city itself had done the same. Chicago was so young it didn't have much history of its own, but that wasn't a problem. The charter included the preservation of American's past as well as that of Chicago, Illinois, and the Old Northwest.

At first, the society met and stored their collections in Walter Newberry's building at the northwest corner of Wells and Kinzie. In 1868, the year Walter died while at sea, the Society finally got its own building, billed as a perfectly fire-proof structure, at Dearborn and Ontario. According to *A Brief History*, by then the Society had amassed over one hundred thousand documents. Their catalog included "nearly complete" records of the "United States Government, in every department, from its organization down to the present time" as well as documents and publications of the Territorial and State Governments of Illinois and laws and legislative records for all the Colonies.

It also included Abraham Lincoln's final draft of the Emancipation Proclamation. The President had donated the draft to the organizers, who were all women, of the North-western Soldiers' Fair so they could sell it to raise money for wounded Civil War soldiers. The Chicago Historical Society purchased it for a sum of $3,000 and added the proclamation to its collections.

On October 9, 1871, that document, and every other piece of history collected by the society, went up in flames.

Organizations from all over the country came to the Chicago Historical Society's aid, donating documents to help them build up their collections again. The New England Genealogical Society provided temporary storage in their new fireproof Boston headquarters until the Society could find a safe place. Mr. Scammon, one of those founding members of the Society, provided space in his offices at 209 North Michigan.

Then, on July 14, 1874, disaster struck again. Another fire ripped through the city, and although it wasn't nearly as deadly as the fire three years prior, it still destroyed forty-seven acres; burned eight hundred and twelve structures, including eight churches and four hotels; and killed twenty people. Many of the displaced were African Americans, Jewish immigrants, and prostitutes. Mr. Scammon's building, containing the historic documents accumulated by the Chicago Historical Society since the fire of 1871, burned, and they lost their collections again.

For the next few years, the Chicago Historical Society slowly gathered historic documents. After two catastrophic losses, the thought of starting over once more must have been daunting, but they continued to hold meetings, take care of any donated materials, and request help from other historical societies. In 1877 the society moved into its second building at Dearborn and Ontario, a temporary structure that would serve them until 1892 when they put everything into storage and laid the cornerstone for their new, permanent, fireproof building. That building, designed by Henry Ives Cobb, who would later design the Chicago Varnish Company and Newberry Library buildings, is still one of the most recognizable structures in Chicago's River North neighborhood. Both a Chicago Landmark and a National Historic Landmark, it stands at the corner of Dearborn and Ontario in imposing Gothic might, covered in granite and topped with gargoyles.

Over the next thirty-two years, the Society acquired more and more collections, the most significant occurring in 1920 when they purchased thousands of documents from the estate of Charles F. Gunther. An eccentric businessman who made his money selling candy, especially caramels, he was passionate about collecting items from the Civil War and anything to do with Abraham Lincoln. At first, he displayed his items in a private museum above his candy store, but then he transported an entire Confederate prison from Richmond, Virginia, to Wabash Avenue. Some of his items, like the Garden of Eden Serpent Skin, were obvious frauds. But others, like Lincoln's piano, his carriage, and the bed on which he died, plus the table on which General Lee signed the terms of surrender—those were real. Mike Conklin, staff reporter at the *Chicago Tribune*, wrote in an August 12, 2001, article: "Russell Lewis, director of collection and research, credited the acquisition in transforming the Chicago Historical Society from a library 'with a smattering of local and regional artifact' into a major museum."

With their growing collection and a desire to open to the public, the Society needed a new home. They chose a large lot in Lincoln Park, where the graveyard used to be, and hired the architecture firm of Graham, Anderson, Probst & White. For this project, the firm, which had previously designed the Civic Opera Building, Field Museum, Shedd Aquarium, and the Wrigley Building, took a departure from their Beaux-Arts portfolio. The Chicago Historical Society would be evolving from an organization devoted to research and preservation to a public museum, so they designed a Georgian colonial building with red brick and stately columns. The Works Progress Administration (WPA) built the museum in exactly one year, from the groundbreaking on May 19, 1931, to move-in on May 19, 1932.

The unveiling revealed one of the most modern museums of its kind. An illustrated handbook from 1935 described the Society's new home, with its "innumerable innovations" that would soon become standards in museum design. The Chicago Diorama Gallery, for example, used electrical buttons to allow visitors to illuminate detailed scenes, from its beginnings as a frontier town, to the Chicago Fire, to the World's Columbian Exposition of 1893. Period rooms evoked episodes of America's past: the Spanish Exploration Room walled with crushed coquina rock from St. Augustine, the oldest city in the United States; a reproduction of Paul Revere's Boston house; yellowed maps covering the French Exploration Room; and the British Colonial Room and its Pennsylvania dining room straight out of 1775. Also from Pennsylvania was the Foyer, a direct copy of the foyer of Philadelphia's Independence Hall. There was a Western room, a Civil War room, and a Victorian room. There was even a "typical" Chicago parlor of the 1850s, showing what life was like when the Society began.

Forty years after the move to North and Clark the Chicago Historical Society needed more space, so they hired Alfred Shaw and Associates to design an expansion, which was clad in limestone. In 1988, Holabird and Root expanded the museum again, covering the previous limestone addition in red brick to provide a more unified exterior. The firm also added a curved-glass end that gives the building a more modern appearance from the south.

Chicago Historical Society Today

In 2006, the Chicago Historical Society changed its name to the Chicago History Museum, completing the transition begun in 1932 when it moved into its final home. Today its collections include approximately 22 million specimens. Since those can't all be displayed at once, they often have special exhibits.

Imagining Chicago: The Dioramas does a dual job as both an artifact itself and a look at the city's history through the lenses of 1932 curators. *Chicago: Crossroads of America* takes you back to the city's roots, beginning with the origin of the name, introducing the first residents, and showing you what Fort Dearborn looked like. There's even timber from the second fort in the display. The hall also covers Chicago's architectural, societal, industrial, entrepreneurial, and musical highlights and lowlights. You can see the Pioneer, the first locomotive to roll on those city-changing tracks in 1848, and step inside L Car #1, which transported fair-goers from downtown to the 1893 World's Columbian Exposition.

Abraham Lincoln is prominently featured, with both an exhibit on the man himself, as well as what Chicago would have been like when he came to visit.

There are several online resources. The Great Chicago Fire details what happened before, during, and after the conflagration, and offers suggested walking tours. The Encyclopedia of Chicago is the digital version of their comprehensive print resource, and Digital Chicago is a collection of projects developed at Lake Forest College. These include subjects like Mapping the Blues and The Assassination of Fred Hampton. You can also access the *Chicago History* magazine archive from 1970 to the present.

The Chicago Historical Society, now the Chicago History Museum, continually expands its collection of documents, maps, manuscripts, prints, photographs, and more. It continues to tell Chicago's story.

Maps

MAPS! My mom insisted I include maps. She's right, of course. What's a book about landmarks if there are no maps?

These are very basic and are intended to give you an idea of where each landmark is located, and where you can find it in relation to the other landmarks. Poor Museum of Science and Industry is all by itself, but as one friend and fellow Chicago-lover said, it's probably used to that.

Landmarks are listed by their original name followed by their current name, where applicable. I've also included the address so you can look it up on a real map and get directions if you'd like.

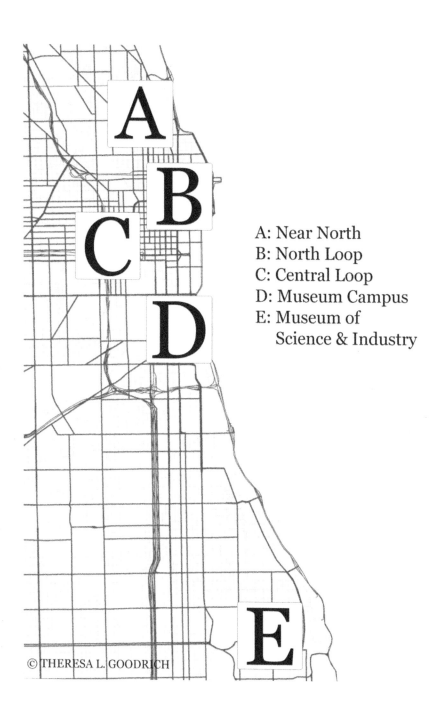

A: Near North
B: North Loop
C: Central Loop
D: Museum Campus
E: Museum of
     Science & Industry

© THERESA L. GOODRICH

A. Near North

North Avenue

Lake Shore Dr

Division Street

Chicago Avenue

Grand Avenue

© THERESA L. GOODRICH

A. Near North

1. Lake Park (Lincoln Park); 2001 N. Clark St.
2. Chicago Historical Society (Chicago History Museum); 1601 N. Clark St.
3. Charnley-Persky House; 1365 N. Astor St.
4. Newberry Library; 60 W. Walton St.
5. Drake Hotel; 140 E. Walton Pl.
6. Water Tower; 806 N. Michigan Ave.
7. Nickerson Mansion (Driehaus Museum); 40 E. Erie St.
8. Tree Studios; 4 E. Ohio St.
9. Medinah Athletic Club (InterContinental); 505 N. Michigan Ave.
10. Merchandise Mart (theMART); 222 W. Merchandise Mart Plaza
11. Chicago Varnish Company (Harry Caray's Italian Steakhouse); 33 W. Kinzie St.
12. Wrigley Building; 400 N. Michigan Ave.
13. Tribune Tower; 435 N. Michigan Ave
14. Municipal Pier #2 (Navy Pier); 600 E. Grand Ave.

B. North Loop

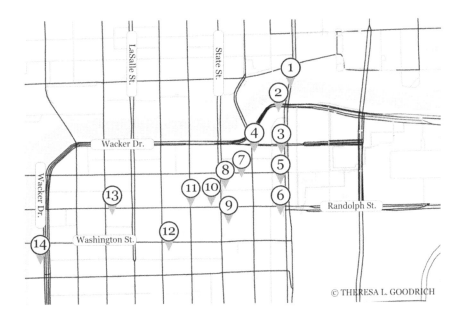

© THERESA L. GOODRICH

B. North Loop

1. Michigan Avenue Bridge (DuSable Bridge);
   333 N. Michigan Ave.
2. London Guarantee (LondonHouse Hotel);
   85 E. Wacker Dr.
3. Carbide & Carbon (Pendry Hotel);
   230 N. Michigan Ave.
4. D. B. Fisk & Co. (Hotel Monaco); 225 N. Wabash Ave.
5. Federal Life Insurance Building (Hotel Julian);
   168 N. Michigan Ave.
6. Chicago Public Library (Chicago Cultural Center);
   78 E. Washington St.
7. Page Brothers Building; 177 N. State St.
8. The Chicago Theatre; 175 N. State St.
9. Marshall Field & Co. (Macy's); 111 N. State St.
10. Oriental Theatre (Nederlander Theatre);
    24 W. Randolph St.
11. Bryant Block (Delaware Building); 36 W. Randolph St.
12. The Chicago Temple; 77 W. Washington St.
13. Bismarck Hotel (Hotel Allegro); 171 W. Randolph St.
14. Civic Opera Building; 20 N. Upper Wacker Dr.

C. Central Loop

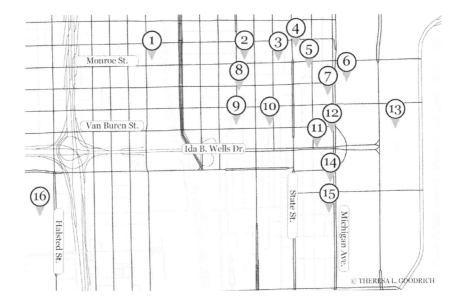

C. Central Loop

1. Union Station; 225 S. Canal St.
2. New York Life Insurance Building (Kimpton Gray); 122 W. Monroe St.
3. Majestic Theatre (CIBC Theatre); 18 W. Monroe St.
4. Schlesinger & Mayer (Sullivan Center); 9 E. Madison St.
5. Palmer House; 17 E. Monroe St.
6. Art Institute of Chicago; 111 S. Michigan Ave.
7. Orchestra Hall (Symphony Center); 220 S. Michigan Ave.
8. The Rookery; 209 S. LaSalle St.
9. Chicago Board of Trade; 141 W. Jackson Blvd.
10. Monadnock Building; 53 W. Jackson Blvd.
11. Auditorium Theatre; 50 E. Ida B. Wells Dr.
12. Studebaker Brothers (Fine Arts Building); 410 S. Michigan Ave.
13. Lake Park (Grant Park); Congress & Columbus
14. Blackstone Hotel; 636 S. Michigan Ave.
15. Stevens Hotel (Hilton Chicago); 720 S. Michigan Ave.
16. Hull House; 800 S. Halsted Ave.

D. Museum Campus

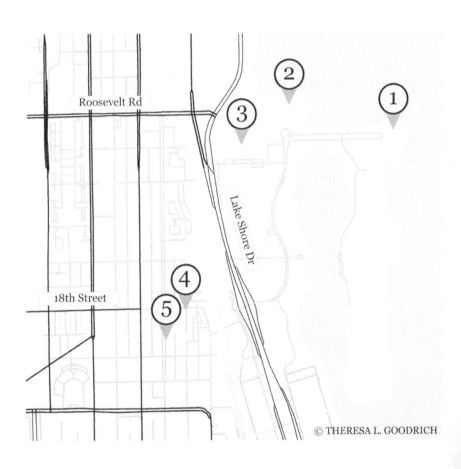

D. Museum Campus

1. Adler Planetarium; 1300 S. Lake Shore Dr.
2. Shedd Aquarium; 1200 S. Lake Shore Dr.
3. Field Museum; 1400 S. Lake Shore Dr.
4. Glessner House Museum; 1800 S. Prairie Ave.
5. Clarke House Museum; 1827 S. Indiana Ave.

E. Museum of Science & Industry

1. Palace of Fine Arts (Museum of Science & Industry); 5700 S. Lake Shore Dr.

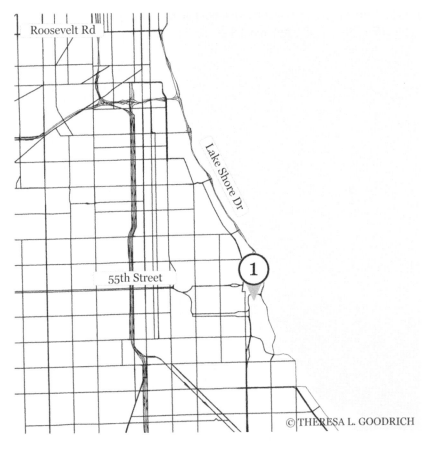

How Living Landmarks was Made: Select Sources

Research is one of my favorite, favorite things to do, which means writing this book kept me in my happy place for extended periods of time. I've visited every one of these landmarks, taken several tours, and pre-pandemic, stayed in every hotel except for The Drake. The on-the-ground research was vital and I'm glad I was able to do so much of it before we went into lockdown.

I'm also grateful for the incredible amount of material that's available online. So much information has been digitized that, while I couldn't dive into the collections at the Newberry Library, the Chicago History Museum, or the Art Institute of Chicago, I could locate primary source materials through many of the sources listed below as well as other online repositories.

Discovering the history of these landmarks required investigative skills (I knew that journalism degree would come in handy) and digging deep to find things like annual reports from the Chicago Historical Society or the original *Plan of Chicago*. I spent many a happy afternoon diving into newspaper archives. Tip: do not do this if you have to be anywhere any time soon. Browsing ads and articles from the 1800s is *fascinating*.

It was fun, but it was also time consuming and sometimes aggravating, especially when I began to wonder if I was procrastinating so I wouldn't have to actually write. But then, more often than not, that one last search would reveal some cool little tidbit that would direct how I'd tell the story. Every time I'd nail down a fact or either confirm or refute a rumor

I'd do a little dance. That kind of stuff makes my journalist heart happier than unlimited time with an unabridged dictionary. Being confident I knew what really happened—or at least what was reported at the time—gave me the freedom to tell each landmark's story in a way that is honest and, hopefully, entertaining.

Because this book is about the stories, I haven't included footnotes or endnotes. Those can be distracting, and I didn't want to pull you out of these captivating tales. Plus, listing every resource would practically double the size of this book—and it's already pretty lengthy.

Below I've listed a few of my go-to sources. These and more are listed on the Resources page of livinglandmarksofchicago.com. Also on the website are detailed sources for each landmark, and you can find those on the landmark's individual page. You can find a link to a page with all of the landmarks from the navigation menu.

Please note that since these sources are online, they're subject to change or disappear entirely.

Chicago Architecture Center

The Chicago Architecture Center should be the starting point for anyone interested in Chicago's buildings. In addition to their incredible tours, especially their famous river cruises, their online database offers summaries of many of the city's most significant landmarks. *architecture.org*

Chicagology

Chicagology "is a study of Chicago history with a focus on the period prior to the Second World War." The site features newspaper articles, magazine excerpts, and editorial summaries about historic buildings, people, and lots of other things, like Prohibition, horse racing, and the Chicago park system. *chicagology.com*

Chronicling America

Sponsored by the National Endowment for the Humanities and the Library of Congress, this site provides "access about historic newspapers and select digitized newspaper pages." Newspaper pages date back to 1777. *chroniclingamerica.loc.gov*

City of Chicago Landmark Designation Reports

Most of the landmarks in this book are designated Chicago landmarks. The official reports usually include information about the architect as well as a description of the building. There's often a section on the context of the landmark. For example, the Chicago Board of Trade report includes backstory on why a board of trade was needed in the first place. Many of these reports are available at *archive.org*.

Early Chicago

This site is organized like an encyclopedia and is published by the authors of *A Compendium of the Early History of Chicago to the Year 1835, when the Indians left*, Ulrich Danckers and Jane Meredith, with the help of the contributing editor John F. Swenson. The topics are extensively researched, and site includes a massive bibliography. Early Chicago is a great resource for authoritative information on Jean Baptise de Sable (and why it's *de* Sable and not *du* Sable). *earlychicago.com*

Find A Grave

Find A Grave is a helpful site for finding birth and death dates and, of course, where people are buried. Portions of the family tree are often listed, as well as brief biographical information. Because it's built by user-generated content, it's a good idea to confirm accuracy. *findagrave.com*

HathiTrust Digital Library

Don't get me started on this incredible resource, because I may not stop talking about it. This is a researcher's mother lode. And it's free! HathiTrust is a "not-for-profit collaborative of academic and research libraries preserving 17+ million digitized items." This is where I found Louis Sullivan's autobiography, an Official Street Guide to Chicago from 1890, an 1856 Chicago city directory, and the catalogue of the collection Samuel and Matilda Nickerson donated to the Art Institute, among many, many others. *hathitrust.org*

Hidden Truths

I bow down to the research skills and dedication of Pamela Bannos. Her project details the story of the Chicago City Cemetery and Lincoln Park, and it is an extensive and exhaustive look at a specific piece of the city's past. She used the same tenacity to research the Museum of Contemporary Art and its location, and her efforts provided insights into notorious scallywag Cap Streeter (see the Drake Hotel chapter). *hiddentruths.northwestern.edu* and *shifting-grounds.net*

Illinois Secretary of State Document Teaching Packages

This site provides historical documents intended for educators from the Illinois State Archives. The Early Chicago, 1833 - 1871 section includes a Census Report from August 9, 1852; a July 12, 1849, *Petition for Frederick Douglass' Use of City Hall*, signed by several prominent Chicagoans; and a *Petition Relating to Geese Running at Large* from August 29, 1845. There's also Suggestions for Further Reading. Because this site is a teaching guide, there are suggested questions and an instructor's manual. Educators can request physical copies of these documents. *cyberdriveillinois.com*

Library of Congress

The Library of Congress is the largest library in the world, and it has an enormous digital collection. Of particular interest for this book were maps of Chicago, as well as historic photos that helped provide context.

National Register of Historic Places Nomination Forms

Several of the landmarks are listed on the National Register of Historic Places. Information on the nomination forms is similar to what's on the Chicago Landmarks Designation Reports. Many of these are available at *archive.org*.

Newspapers.com

Two words: Rabbit Hole. Newspapers.com publishes scans of newspapers dating to the 1700s. The database is searchable by keywords, dates, location, and specific paper. There's a version available through my local library, but I subscribed to gain access to Chicago Tribune's archives. This resource not only provided information current to the construction and early years of many landmarks, but also the context of what was happening in Chicago and the world. *newspapers.com*

Preservation Chicago

This passionate organization "protects and revitalizes Chicago's irreplaceable architecture, neighborhoods and urban green spaces." Each year they select seven historic sites that are in danger of being lost. Landmarks in this book that have been protected include Union Station, the New York Life Insurance Building (Kimpton Gray), the Federal Life Insurance Building (Hotel Julian), and Carbide and Carbon Building (Pendry Chicago - the win is attributed to the St. Jane renovation). *preservationchicago.org*

Wikipedia

Wikipedia can be a good resource, if used with caution. The reason I find it useful is the References section. This can sometimes provide resources, including articles, books, links to authoritative sites, and academic papers. I would *never* pull information from Wikipedia without verifying it elsewhere, and I do mean never, but it's a decent starting place. *wikipedia.com*

Additional resources:
livinglandmarksofchicago.com/resources

Image Citations

1804: **Origin Story**: Map of Chicago, Incorporated as a Town August 5, 1833., Conley & Stelzer, 1933

1836: **Clarke House**: Historic American Buildings Survey, Creator. Henry Clarke House, South Wabash Avenue moved from Michigan Avenue, Chicago, Cook County, IL. Cook County Illinois Chicago, 1933. Documentation Compiled After. Photograph.

1836: **Grant Park (Lake Park)**: Detroit Publishing Co., Publisher. Lake front from Illinois Central station, Chicago, Ill. Superior Chicago Lake Illinois United States Superior, Lake, None. [Between 1890 and 1901] Photograph.

1856: **Jane Addams Hull-House Museum (Charles Hull House)**: Hull-House (Chicago, I. (1907). Hull-house year book. [Chicago]: Hull House.

1864: **Lincoln Park (Lake Park)**: World's Columbian Exposition (1893: Chicago, I., Campbell, J. B. (James Bartlett). (1892). The World's Columbian Exposition illustrated. Chicago, Ill.: J.B. Campbell.

1869: **Water Tower**: Rand, M. & co. [from old catalog]. (1916). One hundred and twenty-five photographic views of Chicago: a collection of reproductions from photographs of the most prominent streets, buildings, statues, park scenes, and other features of interest in the city. Chicago and New York: Rand, McNally & company.

1872: **Page Brothers Building**: The Land Owner. An Illustrated Newspaper 1873.

1873: **Palmer House**: (1884). Picturesque Chicago. Chicago: Chicago engraving company.

1873: **Delaware Building (Bryant Block)**: Andreas, A. T. (Alfred Theodore). (1884-86). History of Chicago. Chicago: A. T. Andreas.

1883: **Driehaus Museum (Nickerson Mansion)**: Historic American Buildings Survey, Creator, Edward Burling, Francis Merideth Whitehouse, and George Maher. Samuel M. Nickerson House, 40 East Erie Street, Chicago, Cook County, IL. Cook County Illinois Chicago, 1933. Documentation Compiled After. Photograph.

1885: **Fine Arts Building (Studebaker Brothers' Lake Front Carriage Repository)**: Detroit Publishing Co., Publisher. Fine Arts Building, Chicago, Ill. United States Illinois Chicago, ca. 1900. Photograph.

1887: **Glessner House**: Historic American Buildings Survey, Creator, Narcross Brothers, John J Glessner, Henry Hobson Richardson, David T Van Zanten, Osmund R Overby, Janis J Erins, et al., Borchers, Perry E, and Cervin Robinson, photographer. John J. Glessner House, South Prairie Avenue, Chicago, Cook County, IL. Cook County Illinois Chicago, 1933. Documentation Compiled After. Photograph.

1888: **Rookery Building**: Historic American Buildings Survey, Creator, George A Fuller, Edward C Waller, Burnham & Root, Frank Lloyd Wright, George A. Fuller Company, Illinois Terra Cotta Lumber Company, et al., Robinson, Cervin, Philip Turner, and Perry E Borchers, photographer. Rookery Building, 209 South LaSalle Street, Chicago, Cook County, IL. Cook County Illinois Chicago, 1933. Documentation Compiled After. Photograph.

1888: **Auditorium Building**: Historic American Buildings Survey, Creator, et al., photographers by Robinson, Cervin, et al. Auditorium Building, 430 South Michigan Avenue, Chicago, Cook County, IL. Documentation Compiled After. Photograph. Retrieved from the Library of Congress.

1891: **Monadnock Block**: Rand McNally and Company. (1913). One hundred and twenty-five photographic views of Chicago: a collection of reproductions from photographs of the most prominent streets, buildings, statues, park scenes, and other features of interest in the city. Chicago and New York: Rand, McNally & company.

1892: **Charnley-Persky House (James Charnley)**: Historic American Buildings Survey, Creator, James Charnley, Adler & Sullivan, Frank Lloyd Wright, George Grant Elmslie, Larry J Homolka, J William Rudd, et al., Allen, Harold, and Cervin Robinson, photographer. James Charnley House, North Astor Street, Chicago, Cook County, IL. Cook County Illinois Chicago, 1933. translateds by Young, Kellymitter Documentation Compiled After. Photograph.

1892: **Macy's (Marshall Field and Company Building)**: Detroit Publishing Co., Publisher. Marshall Field's Marshall Field & Co. store, Chicago, Ill. United States Illinois Chicago, None. [Between 1907 and 1910] Photograph.

1893: **Museum of Science & Industry (Palace of Fine Arts)**: World's Columbian Exposition (1893 : Chicago, I., Higinbotham, H. D., Arnold, C. D. (1893). Official views of the World's Columbian exposition issued. [Chicago]: Press Chicago photo-gravure co.

346

1893: **Art Institute of Chicago**: Detroit Publishing Co., Publisher. Art Institute, Chicago, Ill. United States Illinois Chicago, 1900. [Oct. 3] Photograph.

1893: **Newberry Library**: Newberry Library. Report of the Trustees of The Newberry Library. 1903 Chicago.

1894: **Kimpton Gray (New York Life Insurance Building)**: Detroit Publishing Co., Publisher. New York Life Building, Chicago. United States Illinois Chicago, 1900. [Sept. 11] Photograph.

1894: **Tree Studios**: (1922). Architectural record. New York City: The Record and Guide.

1895: **Harry Caray's (Chicago Varnish Company Building)**: Chicago Architectural Club. 1897. Yearbook of the Chicago Annual Exhibition League, and catalog of the ... annual exhibition. Chicago, Ill.

1897: **Chicago Cultural Center (Chicago Public Library)**: Chicago Public Library. The Chicago Public Library, 1873-1923. [Chicago]: The Board of directors, 1923.

1899: **Sullivan Center (Schlesinger & Mayer)**: Architectural Record Vol. XVI. New York City: The Record and Guide, 1904.

1904: **Symphony Center (Orchestra Hall)**: Otis, P. Adams. (1924). The Chicago Symphony orchestra: its organization, growth, and development, 1891-1924. Chicago: Clayton F. Summy.

1906: **CIBC Theatre (Majestic Building and Theater)**: Northwestern Terra Cotta Company. (190). The Northwestern Terra Cotta Company, Chicago. [Chicago: The Company.

1910: **The Blackstone Hotel**: Architects' and Builders' Magazine, Vol. XLIII No. 1. October 1910. [New York, N.Y.: W.T. Comstock Co.].

1911: **Arlo Chicago (Federal Life Building)**: Federal Life Insurance Company. The federal: devoted to the interests of the policyholders and agency force of the Federal Life Insurance Company. (March 12, 1912) Chicago, Ill.: The Company.

1912: **Hotel Monaco (D.B. Fisk & Company)**: The Illustrated Milliner. (1913) New York, N.Y.: The Illustrated Milliner Co.

1916: **Navy Pier (Municipal Pier #2)**: Rand, M. & company. [from old catalog]. (1921). 125 photographic views of Chicago in the order in which they may be seen most conveniently during a tour about the city. Chicago: Rand, McNally & company.

1920: **DuSable Bridge (Michigan Avenue Bridge)**: Rand, M. & company. [from old catalog]. (1921). 125 photographic views of Chicago in the order in which they may be seen most conveniently during a tour about the city. Chicago: Rand, McNally & company.

1920: **The Drake Hotel**: Chicago Architectural Club. Yearbook of the Chicago Annual Exhibition League, and catalog of the 1922 annual exhibition. Chicago, Ill.

1921: **Wrigley Building**: Rand, M. & company. [from old catalog]. (1921). 125 photographic views of Chicago in the order in which they may be seen most conveniently during a tour about the city. Chicago: Rand, McNally & company.

1921: **Field Museum of Natural History**: Field Museum of Natural History. (1933). Handbook. 4th ed. Chicago.

1921: **The Chicago Theatre**: Motion picture news. Nov. 1921. New York: Motion Picture News.

1923: **LondonHouse Hotel (London Guarantee Building)**: Hamilton, H. Raymond. (1932). The epic of Chicago. Chicago: Willett, Clark & Company.

1924: **The Chicago Temple**: Architecture. (1924) [New York]: C. Scribner's Sons.

1925: **Union Station**: Railway age. v. 79 no. 1 (July 4, 1925) Bristol, Conn.: Simmons-Boardman.

1925: **Tribune Tower**: Tribune tower building, looking northeast, Chicago, Illinois. Illinois Chicago, ca. 1931. Photograph.

1926: **Hotel Allegro (Bismarck Hotel)**: Building age. Vol. XLIX No. 6 June 1927. New York: David Willaims company [etc.].

1926: **James M. Nederlander Theatre (Oriental Theatre)**: Architecture and building. Vol. LIX No. 5 May 1927. [New York, N.Y.: W.T. Comstock Co.].

1927: **Hilton Chicago (Stevens Hotel)**: The Architectural forum. Vol. XLVII No. 2. August 1927. New York [etc.]: Whitney Publications [etc.].

1929: **InterContinental Chicago (Medinah Athletic Cub)**: The Western architect. Vol. XXXIX No. 1, January 1930. Minneapolis: The Western Architect.

1929: **Carbide and Carbon Building (Pendry Chicago)**: Carnegie Steel Company. (1929). The skyline of America. Pittsburgh, Pa.: Carnegie Steel Company.

1929: **Civic Opera House**: The Western architect. Vol. XXXVIII No. 11, November 1929. Minneapolis: The Western Architect.

1930: **Adler Planetarium**: Drury, J. (1933). A century of progress authorized guide to Chicago. Chicago: Consolidated book publishers, inc.

1930: **Shedd Aquarium**: Chute, W. Harris. (1933). *Guide to the John G. Shedd aquarium.* [Chicago: John G. Shedd aquarium.

1930: **Chicago Board of Trade Building**: Carnegie Steel Company. (1929). The skyline of America. Pittsburgh, Pa.: Carnegie Steel Company.

1931: **The Merchandise Mart**: The Western architect. Vol. XXXIX No. 11, November 1930. Minneapolis: The Western Architect.

1932: **Chicago History Museum (Chicago Historical Society)**: Chicago Historical Society. (1935). Illustrated handbook. Chicago.

Acknowledgments

After writing more than ninety-thousand words, these last are probably the hardest. I may have spent the last year in isolation, with only my husband and my cat to keep me company and a few weeks of vital visits from my parents, but I most certainly have not been alone. I've been able to get through simultaneously conquering cancer and writing a book because of the hundreds of cheerleaders who have urged me to keep going. The "you've got this!" "you're amazing!" "you're so strong!" atta-girls drove me, lifted my spirits, told me that yes, yes indeed, I could do this.

As I mentioned in the Preface, this book saved me, and it's in large part because of the constant support I received as I publicly shared my struggles, both with cancer and with completing a project that was supposed to be easy.

Deep breath...

Thank you, Jim, my husband, my rock, my sanity, my love. I won't go into everything you've done—that's for a different tome—but I will shout to the world how grateful I am for your endurance and patience through the madness of writing another book, during a pandemic, while undergoing chemo. You're my person. (But please, don't suggest any more "easy" projects for awhile, okay?)

Mom and Dad—you dropped everything to help, staying with us for weeks, putting off your own health concerns—everything. I needed you and there you were. Then you put your gentle parenting aside to be the critical editors this book deserves. It's better, I'm better, because of you.

Mom and Dad Goodrich—I'm kind of at a loss. How do I thank the couple that made my person? But more than that, how do I thank you for the love you bring to the world and to me? I'm lucky to be a Goodrich.

Tatiana—editor extraordinaire. You said this one didn't need much editing. That's because I could hear your voice in my head. Beautiful soul, you have profoundly helped me be a better, clearer, more consistent writer. I owe you twelve thousand bottles of bubbly.

Bull—Can you just write every foreward for every book I ever write ever? Seriously, friend. You make me blush.

To the medical team at Sherman Cancer Center: you have made this most difficult of experiences much easier than I could have imagined. Thank you.

Thank you to everyone who has emailed, called, texted, prayed, commented, liked, loved, hoped, encouraged, and commiserated. Thank you for the many and unexpected gifts; I'm surrounded by warrior amulets.

To the people and places that aided my research:

Thank you, Grant DePorter, CEO of Harry Caray's and all-around awesome guy, for not only the in-depth tour of your historic building, but also for showing both Jim and me the titles and documents related to Jim's third cousin, four times removed, Grant Goodrich. Holy Cow! that was cool.

Thank you, Hillary Marzec, for the fun and entertaining tour of InterContinental Chicago. You have so much passion for this city, and such a great way of describing architectural styles. Your pastry case analogy is the most descriptive I've heard. Readers, if you want to see these landmarks in person and learn more well-researched and entertaining stories, book a tour with Hillary's company, Inside Chicago Walking Tours.

Thank you to Palmer House, Kimpton Hotels, Blackstone Hotel, Hotel Julian, LondonHouse, Hilton Chicago, and InterContinental Chicago for hosting me and for providing inside information about your landmarks. I began writing these chapters in the rooms where it happened, and that atmosphere gave me insight into the buildings' pasts.

Thank you to you, the reader, who loves Chicago and wants to know more about this passionate, mercurial place. And finally, thank you to the dreamers, malcontents, philanthropists, and grifters who made Chicago what it is today.

ABOUT THE AUTHOR

Theresa is an Emmy-winning author and content creator with a penchant for storytelling and a keen eye. She's the founder of The Local Tourist, author and publisher of multiple books. Under Theresa L. Carter, she's also published novels. Theresa has appeared in several Chicago media and has spoken across the country on travel, road trips, publishing, marketing, motivation, entrepreneurship, and storytelling. Since 2019, she's taught the Midwest Travel  Network's Writing Workshop and her writing and self-publishing courses are available online. When Theresa's not writing, speaking, or on the road, she's cooking and planning her next adventure.

You can follow Theresa at thelocaltourist.com and theresalgoodrich.com.

Made in the USA
Las Vegas, NV
20 October 2024

10134383R00215